THE
PROJECT
BOOK

THE PROJECT BOOK

THE COMPLETE GUIDE TO CONSISTENTLY DELIVERING GREAT PROJECTS

COLIN D ELLIS

WILEY

First published in 2019 by John Wiley & Sons Australia, Ltd
42 McDougall St, Milton Qld 4064

Office also in Melbourne

Typeset in 12pt/14.5pt Adobe Caslon Pro

ISBN: 9780730371410

© John Wiley & Sons Australia, Ltd 2019

The moral rights of the author have been asserted

A catalogue record for this book is available from the National Library of Australia

Cover design by Wiley

10 9 8 7 6 5 4 3 2 1

Disclaimer
The material in this publication is of the nature of general comment only, and does not represent professional advice. It is not intended to provide specific guidance for particular circumstances and it should not be relied on as the basis for any decision to take action or not take action on any matter which it covers. Readers should obtain professional advice where appropriate, before making any such decision. To the maximum extent permitted by law, the author and publisher disclaim all responsibility and liability to any person, arising directly or indirectly from any person taking or not taking action based on the information in this publication.

CONTENTS

ABOUT THE AUTHOR

The important thing for you to know about me, before you start reading, is that for the past 20 of my 30 years of permanent employment, my entire world was projects. I moved through the ranks from project manager to program manager to PMO manager to heading up large project departments and sponsoring projects. I did this in three countries—the UK, New Zealand and Australia—in both public and private sectors.

I had my fair share of successes and failures and was part of some fantastic teams along the way. I never had any desire to work for myself and yet, after attending a conference in 2015 where I felt like I was hearing the same messages about projects I'd heard 15 years earlier, I decided that someone had to inject a bit of life, energy and honesty into a profession that had stagnated for far too long.

So here we are.

I now speak at conferences and work with forward-thinking organisations around the world to help them evolve their cultures and create a motivated and energised environment where great work flourishes and targets are met.

Liverpool in the UK was home originally. The eldest of three boys, I wasn't particularly good at school. I just wanted to leave as soon as I could, to earn money to buy records. From the second I started work I loved it. I wanted to be in and around people and be part of something that was consistently new and exciting. So maybe it's surprising it took me 10 years to find my way into the project world.

I emigrated with my family to New Zealand in 2007 and had six great years in Wellington before settling in Melbourne, Australia, which is very definitely home now. When not flying to different parts of the globe or researching how to improve individuals and working cultures, I can often be found at home watching my football team, Everton, play in the English Premier League or hanging with family watching our latest comedy obsession.

I sincerely believe that when done well projects can change the world. I wrote this book because I felt like someone had to provide the real (not theoretical) information on how to do this. I hope you find it useful.

Colin
Melbourne, 2019

PREFACE

Projects are the lifeblood of organisations. They are used to fix things that are broken, to add to things we already have or build things we don't, to keep organisations relevant, or simply to improve the bottom line. However you look at it, they are absolutely critical. We talk about them all the time and assume, before we even start, that they'll surely be successful. So a quick reality check before we get cracking: usually they won't be. Here are a few recent statistics:

- On average 34 per cent of projects around the world are considered successful, a rise of only 5 per cent in the past 20 years.

- Of the 84 per cent of organisations that said transformation projects were crucial, only 3 per cent said they had completed any successfully.

- Only one in five organisations say they are effective at scaling agile methods for project delivery, with a further 30 per cent indicating they are only 'slightly effective'.

- Only 34 per cent of organisations deliver projects that are likely to achieve customer satisfaction.

These figures don't make great reading (in fact some of them are plain appalling), but in my experience, they do accurately represent the daily experience in most organisations when it comes to discipline and maturity around the way they deliver projects.

Many reasons get wheeled out in reports on why projects fail, yet in reality there are only two: poor project sponsorship and poor project management. This book addresses both of these problems. It gives project managers the information they need to inspire and motivate their people to do great things, and it provides senior managers with a blueprint for what it means to role model public accountability and decision making.

Consulting organisation The Standish Group, in its 2016 *Chaos Report*, identified the three key success factors for projects as (1) executive sponsorship, (2) emotional maturity and (3) user involvement. In my experience, all play an important part, and all are within the control of the project sponsor and project manager.

Organisations around the world have been throwing money at project management for years now and they still haven't seen a return on this investment. In its 2016 *Pulse of the Profession* report, the Project Management Institute (PMI) noted declines in many of the success factors they track. 'Even more concerning, the percentage of projects meeting their goals—which had been flat for the past four years—took a significant dip.' To check this trend, 'organisations [need] to shift their thinking and embrace project management as a strategic competency for success'.

For me this is a chicken-or-egg problem. When organisations witness great project sponsorship and project management in action they can recognise it as a strategic competency for success. However, only by putting time and money into developing this competency can it produce truly great results.

What's it going to take for senior managers to take projects seriously?

We need to invest in lifting the skill sets of people to help organisations evolve and be better at getting things delivered.

It's time for senior managers to put time, effort and real money into developing a delivery capability that is both fit for purpose and capable of evolving as the organisation grows. A capability that recognises what it means to deliver projects successfully every time. And at the heart of that are project sponsors and managers who do the right things at the right time and in the right way.

Without strong leadership from the top, projects are like cheap Post-it notes. Sure, they'll stick at first, but all too soon they'll come unstuck and be found in the bathroom on someone's shoe.

Organisations know all the reports tell them the same things. There's been no shortage of front-page headlines and even, in a few (rare) cases, public accountability for failure. And reading them it's hard to avoid getting a flash of déjà vu.

A government inquiry into the failed Novopay Education Payroll project in New Zealand found that most of the errors were identical to those revealed in a failed police project (INCIS) 13 years earlier. At the time of writing, the incomplete Crossrail project in London is £500 million over budget and nine months late because of poor risk management. The US Department of Veterans Affairs wasted more than US$1 billion over six years on IT projects alone.

When did it become okay to continually fail and waste money in this way?

The response to such failures, unfortunately, has become all too predictable. Post–year 2000 (Y2K) projects continually ran over budget, because the management of budgets hadn't been a priority for those of us who were project managers at the time when all IT systems around the world needed to be changed. Our focus was to get systems delivered, systems that worked, by 31 December, 1999.

The UK government's response to this budget overspend was to introduce a project management method, PRINCE2. If you're not familiar with PRINCE2, it's a set of principles and processes for capturing information and setting up the structures necessary for projects to be successful. To be honest, it works fine if it's used in the right way... and there's the rub: organisations often don't use these methods in the right way.

'Waterfall' or 'agile' methods (the latter being the latest quick-fix solution many organisations are turning to) are only as good as the people who use them and the teams created to develop the products.

The best projects are made possible by the person who leads them or the environment they create—in short, by leadership and culture. To be consistently successful at delivering projects, this is where you need to start. You then use the methods to create the right approach and capture the information you need to stay on track. In this way a project sponsor and project manager can jointly ensure that projects meet stakeholder expectations around time, cost and scope.

Yet it's easier for organisations to send everyone on a certification course so they can tick a 'We've spent money on improving the way we deliver projects' box than it is to set a new standard for behaviour and to ensure those who don't have the discipline are coached or managed out.

Leadership is not a program, though. It's making a series of choices that demonstrate the courage to do things differently. To challenge the status quo. To invest in people and team building, and to have the discipline to get things done.

The world is full of project managers who collect method badges by demonstrating their 'experience'. And yet, as the statistics show, there are very few leaders who are role modelling what the profession needs in order to build and retain its credibility.

The first section of this book sets out the skills and behaviours project managers need to become project leaders. It's an important distinction. Only through committed leadership can projects be successfully completed in line with stakeholder satisfaction.

The second section sets out what it means for senior managers to do their bit, because simply achieving a particular position in the hierarchy doesn't automatically qualify them to sponsor projects.

Having worked in the project management world for 20 years in a variety of roles, I know what works well and what doesn't, and my aim in this book is to pass this knowledge on to you.

Intent is good. Action is better.

HOW TO USE THIS BOOK

If I'm being honest, I'd say I've tried to write the book I would want to read. Too many business books are dry and boring. Either they're too theoretical to ever be used in your working day or they don't contain a call to action to hold you accountable. They drone on and on, labouring their points yet leaving you confused over what the chapter was all about to begin with.

I've not done that. Instead, I've written lots of short chapters that contain some context, a case study or an activity where I feel they are needed.

The book should be read in its entirety first, before targeting specific actions. You can choose to focus on one topic a week or a month, or you can work collectively as a team or organisation to evolve the way you do things. A number of my clients already do this. You can pick it up at any time and read the whole thing again or simply refer to a chapter where you believe you need more work.

The two most popular methods of delivering projects are *waterfall* and *agile*, and both are covered by this book. Agile is the current darling for delivering projects, but when applied inconsistently or incorrectly it has the same outcomes as waterfall projects delivered in the same way.

Each chapter ends with a set of 'actions'—things to do, read or watch—and if you want to hold yourself publicly accountable, things you can post on social media too. Remember to add the #ProjectBook hashtag and name check me @colindellis and I'll make sure it's retweeted or reposted.

I read a lot of great books while I was writing this one, and you can find a list of those at the back, along with a list of music I was listening to at the time.

If you're a project manager, the first section is where you'll want to start, although the second will give you insights into what to expect from your sponsor. If you're a senior manager looking to improve the way your project or organisation delivers, then you might choose to start with the second section, though in the first I cover what your project managers should be doing to support this evolution.

I hope you'll not only learn from *The Project Book* but find a few laughs here too. If you enjoy it, please provide a recommendation (written or verbal) so others can benefit from it too.

PROJECT MANAGEMENT

The best projects are made possible by the people who lead them and the environment they create for good people to do great work. These projects are led by project *leaders*, not managers.

Yet for the past 20 years organisations have focused on method implementation as a means of achieving consistent success. Great leadership, we're told by the management books, is the cornerstone of success, so why has this truth been missing from project management for so long? The world is full of qualified project managers with endless certificates and letters after their names, yet time and time again they're letting project stakeholders down.

PROJECT MANAGEMENT HAS TO CHANGE

Organisations simply cannot continue to see more than 60 per cent of what they do fail every year. They should be angry and embarrassed. They should be looking for every way possible to improve on this record, rather than continuing with the same tired old quick-fix approaches they have used for 20 years.

What's worse is that there are no statistics to prove that these old approaches even work, except for those produced by the companies that sell them. I've read many public- and private-sector project management capability reviews, all of which say the same things:

- Projects lack leadership.
- Project managers lack emotional maturity.
- Project sponsors aren't interested enough.
- The cultures that projects exist within aren't conducive to success.

- Organisations are doing too many projects.
- The methods used by project managers aren't used consistently.

When they receive such a report, most organisations will skip over points one to five and head straight to six, insisting on more process to generate greater consistency of delivery.

They're wrong, of course. The only way to get consistently good delivery is to ensure that the people responsible and accountable for project delivery know how to lead and create cultures that others want to be a part of, then have the discipline to get it done.

PROJECTS ARE ABOUT PEOPLE

My view is that there are only two reasons for project failure: poor project management and poor project sponsorship. Every factor that contributes to project failure will come back to one of these root causes.

Part of the problem is that lots of organisations still don't really understand project management, despite having shelves full of textbooks. They think of project management as the triple constraints triangle.

The triple constraints diagram (or iron triangle) depicts the three elements that projects are bound by and that project managers need to be mindful of when planning and delivering projects.

Project managers used to say that two of these elements must remain fixed at any one time, but that was in the days when IT 'dictated' projects. Nowadays if a customer wants to change the scope and has the time and money to do so, then frankly they can do whatever they want and the role of project management is to make it happen.

It's also worth saying here that time, cost and scope are characteristics of a project, not of project management, and project managers should not be measured on these variables.

The next figure illustrates the characteristics of project management, whose job it is to deliver the outputs (not the benefits) required by the customer within the constraints that have been set.

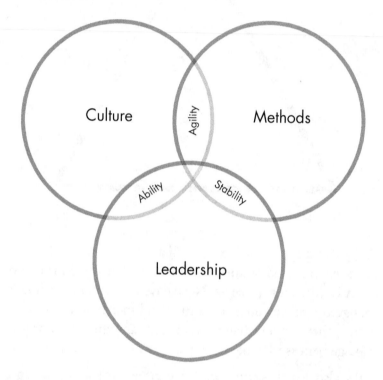

Remember, it's who you are as a person and the environment you create for others to do great work that will make you successful as a project manager.

You need to understand the difference between leadership and management and be able to switch between the two as required throughout the lifecycle of your project. Great leadership provides the foundation for successful project management.

You also need the ability to build and maintain team cultures and be flexible about how you do things in order to reflect the nature of your project. This is the agility we now yearn for, an agility that existed before the technology boom in the late 1990s and early 2000s, and that can be used just as easily today, although not on all projects. More on that later.

Finally, there are the methods, the process and techniques that support project managers in building and implementing the plan. Applying these approaches alongside the behaviours expected of leaders will provide the stability and consistency of success that organisations seek from their project management.

Today there are many methodologies and associated techniques that you can draw on, and I have tried not to dwell on these in this book. My emphasis, as you will see, is on ensuring that you understand the leadership and culture aspects of project management, because these are the things you rarely read about and practise, yet they are certainly the most important factors for success.

Remember, the best projects are made possible by the people who lead them and the environment they create for good people to do great work. In comparison to project managers, these project leaders are few and far between. Read this book, then set yourself on a course to becoming one of them. The world needs you.

PART I
LEADERSHIP

There are about a million (really, I've counted them) blogs and articles that articulate what leadership is. Many great business figures and authors have added their own thoughts on this. From the business world, Peter Drucker proposes, 'Leadership is lifting a person's vision to high sights, the raising of a person's performance to a higher standard, the building of a personality beyond its normal limitations'. For Ken Blanchard, 'The key to successful leadership today is influence, not authority'. Bill Gates predicts, 'As we look ahead into the next century, leaders will be those who empower others'.

'It is better to lead from behind and to put others in front,' wrote the inspirational leader Nelson Mandela, 'especially when you celebrate victory when nice things occur. You take the front line when there is danger. Then people will appreciate your leadership'.

My favourite definition of leadership was offered by Maya Angelou: 'I've learned that people will forget what you said, people will forget what you did, but people will never forget how you made them feel'. If you aspire to becoming a project leader, this empathetic approach to people will be the foundation for success in everything you do.

To become a leader, you don't need an MBA or PhD or project management qualification or Nobel Prize. Nor do you automatically become one when you have 'manager' or 'director' in your job title. To become a leader you need to make a decision. You need to decide whether you want to serve others and be the kind of person they aspire to be. Or not.

If you don't want to serve others and be a role model, that's totally fine. Being a project leader isn't for everyone; after all, if everyone in the world was a leader, we'd get nothing done!

If you're still determined, then you're on the wrong side of a lot of hard, but ultimately rewarding, work on the journey to becoming a more emotionally intelligent version of yourself, starting with changing the way you behave, talk, listen, laugh, deal with poor performance and innovate. It's possible you'll have to completely reinvent who you are. You'll have to identify and learn about the stuff you're not so great at and spend your weekends cramming, reading books, blogs and magazines, and mapping out new routines to change old habits.

For far too long the corporate world has downplayed the importance of emotional intelligence, dismissing it as one of the 'soft' skills, which are among the hardest things to change.

In his ground-breaking book *Emotional Intelligence*, published in 1995, Daniel Goleman identified emotional intelligence (EQ) as the key differentiator for leaders. 'What makes the difference between stars and others is not their intelligent IQ, but their emotional EQ.'

This is every bit as true today as it was 24 years ago, and it will remain so into the future, not just for us but for our children too.

A 2017 *Harvard Business Review* article predicted, 'Skills like persuasion, social understanding and empathy are going to become differentiators as AI and machine learning take over other tasks'. Not only is it good for continued relevance, but another study found that 'people who have a high EQ have been proved to be happier in their lives, and more productive in their work, than those with low EQ'.

Emotional intelligence is a learnt skill. And like any worthwhile accomplishment, it isn't always easy. However, developing yourself and inspiring people who put their reputations on the line for you are among the greatest rewards you can get in the corporate world.

You will have to unlearn some things and work hard to learn others. You will have to challenge your assumptions and beliefs, and to listen when you'd rather be talking. Mostly, though, you will have to make time for all this and to make becoming the best version of yourself a priority.

You need to make the time to understand and work through what it means to be emotionally intelligent, to know how to recognise when you've got it right and to celebrate the win!

When the projects and programs you have managed are held in high regard, when people want to work with you again, when you're held up as a role model for others, then you'll know what it means to be emotionally intelligent and you'll be halfway to becoming a great project leader.

CHAPTER 1

KNOW YOURSELF

'All you can change is yourself,' Gary W. Goldstein argues, 'but sometimes that changes everything!' Self-awareness is perhaps the biggest challenge to developing as a person. The ability to look ourselves in the mirror, admit our flaws, celebrate what we're good at and actively seek feedback isn't something we're all blessed with.

And this self-knowledge isn't enough in itself. You have to use it to analyse what you do before committing to change, and change you must if you are to achieve the goals you've set yourself. Sometimes you'll need to change the way you communicate, while at others you'll need to reset a habit or behaviour. Abraham Maslow said, 'Self-knowledge and self-improvement are very difficult for most people. It usually needs great courage and long struggle'. But don't let this stop you!

All too often in the project management world, people forget to look at themselves while insisting that others are to blame for the problems they are encountering.

A few years back a friend of mine introduced me to the Dunning–Kruger Effect. For those of you who are unfamiliar with it, Cornell University students David Dunning and Justin Kruger found, through a series of experiments, that unskilled employees weren't as good as they thought they were — or, as the *Harvard Business Review* titled their article 'Those Who Can't, Don't Know It'.

The Dunning–Kruger Effect may come as something of a surprise to you, unless of course it speaks to you personally, in which case you probably already knew it all too well. The researchers found that incompetent people (their words) didn't recognise their own lack of skills or the extent of it. Worse, they couldn't recognise the skills that others had either. Results from a follow-up study suggested that with 'minimal tutoring' on the skills they were previously deficient in, people were better able to understand their skill level. Or, if you prefer, they were more aware of their own shortcomings.

The resulting paper, 'Unskilled and unaware of It: How difficulties in recognizing one's own incompetence lead to inflated self-assessments', is definitely worth reading, and perhaps passing on to others you feel might benefit from it (*cough*).

The easiest way to become more self-aware is to ask others for their honest opinions of your behaviour and performance. Choose people who know you well and have seen you in action. It might be a project sponsor, a team member, a fellow project manager or a line manager familiar with your work. It's important that you ask them about your *behaviour*, as this is something we can often miss in the heat of the moment.

You have to welcome and be prepared for frank and critical feedback. You should also repeat this regularly and show your gratitude for their time and effort (see chapter 13).

Something I like to do is document how certain situations made me feel and how I responded to them. This is particularly important if you seek to change a behaviour, but it's also useful if you want to become more aware of how you react emotionally in different contexts. Write it down as soon as possible after the event. It will be invaluable to your development as a leader.

It's also important to acknowledge the things you're good at, as self-awareness isn't just about the bad stuff. While you won't be cartwheeling down the corridor screaming 'I can plan, I can plan, I can plan', these positive affirmations should give you the confidence that your skills and behaviours have been recognised and provide an emotional springboard to improvement in other areas.

There are many benefits to being more self-aware, including:

- greater personal contentment
- improved relationship building
- improved collaboration
- enhanced respect from peers
- reduced stress and anxiety.

In his book *Emotional Capitalists*, Martyn Newman rates self-awareness as the number one component to becoming more emotionally intelligent. Once you've received feedback on something you weren't aware of, and have taken action to change it, you'll recognise why it's so important.

ACTIONS

DO: Ask for regular feedback on your performance and behaviours.

DON'T: Think the Dunning–Kruger Effect only happens to other people.

WATCH: Rosalinde Torres's TED talk, 'What it takes to be a great leader' ('Knowing what I'm good at, and not so good at, makes me a better leader').

CHAPTER 2

PRACTISE EMPATHY

Empathy is about seeing something from someone else's perspective and 'feeling' it as they do. To be able to do this you need to know who they are, how they view the world and the cultural traditions that are important to them.

There's a good chance that others will see things completely differently from you. If you don't respond empathetically to them, then there's a good chance that any relationship you thought you had will be lost.

To be more empathetic to others, you first need to understand your own emotions, to be self-aware (see chapter 1). In *Emotional Intelligence*, Daniel Goleman said of empathy, 'the more open we are to our emotions, the more skilled we will be in reading feelings'. Opening yourself up is critical to getting others to open up.

Every Monday morning I would take my team for breakfast between nine and ten. No one wants to sit down at their desk at 9 am on a Monday, having had a great weekend, and start firing off emails and making calls. I saw it as a great time to find out what they had done over the weekend and get to know them better. We'd share stories about days out, days in, sports events, family, weather, hospital visits, beach visits and plans for the future.

After each breakfast session I would make lots of notes about children's names, sports affiliations, upcoming birthdays and holidays, and a wealth of other personal information we shared with each other. Not being blessed with the greatest recall, this was an important means for me in understanding (and remembering) what was important to them so as to become a more empathetic leader.

I would pay for these breakfasts, and that $60 was the best money I spent all week. It enhanced our relationships and enabled me to develop empathetic responses based on other people's emotions, rather than my own. It also meant that as members of a team we could put our colleagues' interests before our own, and nothing says 'I care' better than that. Seeing how we treated each other also had a positive effect on other teams.

Project leaders spend the first two weeks of any assignment building relationships, because they recognise that relationships are the foundation for success. They identify and meet with key stakeholders and hold conversations that provide them with information about each person's personality and their drivers. These initial sessions are informal and don't focus on the project. Questions may cover family, career and experience (previous projects). They ask direct questions around communications and availability. They listen intently and say very little.

These meetings lay the relationship groundwork for the months ahead. We've watched great leaders set aside their own concerns in order to better relate to those of their peers and teams.

Strong relationships are key to the success of your project, and shared empathy is the bedrock for those bonds.

ACTIONS

DO: Think of how others might be feeling, not just how you feel.

READ: *Emotional Intelligence* by Daniel Goleman.

POST: I'm making an effort to be more empathetic towards my team. #ProjectBook

CHAPTER 3

BE YOURSELF

At a retirement function for Steve (not his real name—his real name was Brian!), a project manager in my team at the time, I got the chance to speak with his wife.

She seemed genuinely shocked about the things people were saying about her husband. 'Grumpy', 'negative' and even 'curmudgeonly' were thrown out there, all of which Steve took in his stride. 'But that's not who he is at home,' she insisted. 'He's a fun granddad. He sings silly songs and never stops cracking jokes.' It was my turn to be shocked, and when he walked over I said to him, 'Steve, what's this I hear about you being a really fun guy outside the office?' He said, 'Yeah, but I can't bring that to work, can I?'

YES YOU CAN! Bring it every day. Bring it to every meeting, every workshop, every coffee break. To the performance evaluation when I ask, 'is there anything more I can do to create an environment in which you feel you can do your best work—and enjoy it?' But what could I say then? So instead I smiled and said, 'I'm really sorry you didn't feel able to do that'.

Putting on a different face should *never* be necessary— unless you're Arnold Schwarzenegger in *Total Recall*. You don't have to pretend to be someone else. You don't have to suppress your feelings, to conform to what you see around you.

That's not to say, though, that you use authenticity as an excuse for staying in your comfort zone and expecting everyone simply to accept you as you are. It's about acting and behaving in line with your values in order to do the best job you possibly can.

To be content with who you are, you need to put yourself in challenging positions so you can develop a style and approach that you're comfortable with and that gets the job done in a range of situations.

Being clear about your values is a start. The challenge for you then is to stay aligned with them while accepting that in order to get better at what you do, your skill set must constantly evolve. For example, you may value peace and quiet, but if you're leading a team, they'll expect you to be energetic. You don't lose the value you have; rather, you respond to the needs of the team. It might not feel natural, but it's part of your project leadership journey.

In my experience you can overthink being your authentic self, until it starts to get in the way of your progress. This is a point that Herminia Ibarra makes in her book *Act Like a Leader, Think Like a Leader*. In a survey she conducted, 50 per cent of managers reported that their leadership style got in the way of their success. 'People get caught up with self-analysis because to be a healthy, happy person, you need to practice some form of introspection,' she commented in a related interview. 'The problem is, if you're constantly analysing your emotional and mental processes—especially when you're moving into a new professional position or an unfamiliar role—introspection becomes a bad thing.'

Being the real you is about 'playing' with different ways of doing things while not losing sight of the things that got you there.

When I asked Steve why he felt unable to bring his fun side to the office, he put it down both to his generation and to how he felt he would be perceived or judged. Had he opened himself more and brought some of that fun to work, he would almost certainly have developed stronger relationships, and the perception of him by stakeholders would have been a lot more positive than it was.

ACTIONS

DO: Hold fast to your values, but continue to develop as a leader.

READ: *Act Like a Leader, Think Like a Leader* by Herminia Ibarra.

POST: I'm going to bring the real me to my role and continue to grow as a leader. #ProjectBook

CHAPTER 4

STAND FOR SOMETHING

In *Conscious Capitalism*, John Mackey and Raj Sisodia write, 'The best conscious leaders are merchants of hope and entrepreneurs of meaning. They continually engage their colleagues around questions of identity and purpose'. I love this quote because it sums up the difference between leadership and management. Of course, standing for something (or being 'passionate' about something, as you'll sometimes hear it expressed) is only one part of leadership, but for me it's a really important part.

When I was an employee, it was what I looked for in my leaders, what I bought into and what motivated me. I wanted to be part of something better (not necessarily bigger), something that delivered what it promised, that I could look back on and say 'that mattered'.

As a project manager I had to learn how to do this by watching others. Through observing the good and the bad, I was able to determine what it was that *I* stood for, and I brought that to my role every day of the week.

Like others, I have been inspired by the stories of those who didn't accept the status quo when they believed that the lives of others could be improved.

Emmeline Pankhurst believed that married women should have a vote in the British elections. She led the suffragette movement and went on hunger strikes to draw attention to it.

She showed reactionary and inefficient political institutions little respect, which astonished them. She died in 1928, shortly before women were granted equal voting rights with men (at age 21).

Rosa Parks refused to give up her seat on a segregated Alabama bus to a white person in 1955. She was not ill or old (she was 42), just tired of giving in. She became an international icon for racial equality, despite losing her job and receiving numerous death threats. Alabama repealed its segregation policy on the Montgomery buses in 1956, ruling that it was unconstitutional. She remained active in the civil rights movement until her death in 2005.

In 1844 Florence Nightingale decided to become a nurse, then considered 'lowly work' for someone of her social standing. In 1854, she took a team of nursing volunteers and cleaned up a hospital treating war victims in the Crimea in an era when the roles of infection and hygiene were still little understood. Her dedication to sanitation and cleanliness was recognised by Queen Victoria, who set up a royal commission to help her analyse the state of army hospitals. Her work with the Sanitary Commission reduced fatalities in hospitals by 99 per cent in a single year and gradually introduced reforms in the British healthcare system. By her death in 1880 the nursing profession had gained significant respectability. She became the first woman to be awarded the Order of Merit.

Mikhail Gorbachev became General Secretary of the Soviet Communist Party in 1985. He was seen as someone who could modernise and rehabilitate the ailing Communist Party. In a few short years he radically changed the culture of the party, introducing the policies of *glasnost* (government transparency) and *perestroika* (political and economic reform). He developed strong ties with the west, and by refusing to keep pace with US military spending he played a major part in ending the cold war. His actions also led to the tearing down of the Berlin Wall and the disbandment of the Soviet bloc, resulting in the independence of the Eastern European satellite countries. He was awarded the Nobel Peace Prize in 1990.

The reason their stories are quoted so often by leadership writers is that these are individuals who believed wholeheartedly in what they were doing and who refused to compromise when others said they should. It takes courage to be different and to stand out in this way.

When leading people in projects, you'll find the right way to behave, communicate and serve your team, and without doubt you'll come up against those who steadfastly refuse to do things this way. They will cite company culture, the need for certification, historical precedent or just the 'nature of projects'. They'll never admit they simply lack the courage to be different, to stand up for what they believe in and face down the nay-sayers.

This is what you must do if you want a team to believe in you, follow your lead and stand by you when things aren't going so well.

A 2014 Harvard Business School survey of 330 000 people rated the ability to inspire and motivate as the number one requirement of leaders, yet all too often in projects I see people who do neither. It's part of the reason that our profession polarises people so much. Organisations look for ways to remove the project management layer, not because it's not important, but because the people in those roles do little to prove they are willing to stick their neck out and lead with purpose.

We all believe in something and we should use that passion to inform our values, stir our emotions and impel positive action. This is the foundation of your leadership ability, but standing for something doesn't mean standing still, and you need to work hard to constantly develop it. As Jason Fried and David Heinemeier Hansson write in their book *ReWork*, 'Standing for something isn't just about writing it down. It's about believing it and living it'.

ACTIONS

DO: Spend some time thinking about the things that are important to you and how you can use them to inspire the work you do and the project team you lead.

READ: *ReWork* by Jason Fried and David Heinemeier Hansson.

POST: Standing up for my beliefs is the right and courageous thing to do. #ProjectBook

CHAPTER 5

DETERMINE YOUR VALUES

Maitland, a financial PR company in the UK, found three words, *integrity*, *respect* and *innovation*, crop up continually in the values of FTSE100 companies. I won't argue that these are the wrong words (although I'm amazed that *agile* wasn't in there!). It's just that if people are *told* that these are their values, rather than being engaged in a process to uncover them, it's very easy for them to disengage. One sure sign of this disengagement is seeing these values pinned up next to their desk as a reminder.

Values shouldn't be pinned up on a wall; they should be lived, no matter what situation we're in. They define our leadership style, our approach to problem solving and what we become known for.

So what do you stand for?

Quite often, this feels like too big a question to answer and we don't really know where to start. So let me help you. List the things you don't like or you think are wrong. These should be single words: confusing documents might be 'complexity'; aversion to change could be 'resistance'. Now, next to these words, write their opposite or antonym. For example, complexity = simplicity, resistance = resilience, and so on. Keep the antonyms.

Next, list the things that are important to you (for example, family, timeliness or involvement). Now compare the two lists and strike through the duplicates. Once you have done that, list the five most important things to you. These are your core values. If they don't feel right—and you'll know this immediately—go back to your lists and do the exercise again until you have a top five you're happy with.

Always one to practise what I preach, I ran this exercise again before writing this chapter and here, in order, are my top five:

1. Family
2. Equality
3. Simplicity
4. Democracy
5. Education.

I live all five of these principles at home and in my work—for me, there's no distinction between the two settings. Equality at home is just as important as equality in the workplace. The same with simplicity! Yet it's fair to say that these values are different from those I would have chosen 10 years ago.

Over that time my life has changed and I've grown as a person. I've become more compassionate, humble and generous. I've learned lots of new things and met lots of great people. I've had money and been flat broke. I got married, became a father (twice), emigrated (twice) and worked for and with over 20 organisations in many different sectors.

In 2019 I know the right way to do things, and it's not the way we were doing them in 2010. I also know that by 2020 that will have changed again. That's the thing with values. They're part of our evolution and our drive to be better versions of ourselves.

Project leaders take the time to work with their teams to understand what their values are. They understand that this allows them to create the kinds of cultures in which they do their best work and lays the foundation for people to be the best version of themselves in the office.

ACTIONS

DO: List your values to better understand what's important to you.

DO: Get your team to do likewise and to share their lists with the group.

POST: Knowing the values of my project team helps us to build something we can all be proud of. #ProjectBook

CHAPTER 6

SAFEGUARD THE FUTURE

In 1995, long before the global financial crisis (GFC), one man — Nick Leeson — managed to bankrupt the UK's oldest merchant bank, Barings.

Leeson had been sent to Singapore as a market trader aged 25, and almost immediately he made a bad trade. Rather than come clean and admit his error, he created a dummy account and 'hid' the debt generated by the trade in there. For the next two years, he made similarly poor short-term decisions, until he had accrued a debt in the dummy account to the value of US$400 million. This was the end of 1997, when the bank was worth around US$500 million. Leeson had another opportunity to admit his failings, but once again he chose to gamble. He lost.

On 23 February 1998 he sent a fax to his boss announcing his resignation as a result of poor health. He then holed himself up in a hotel room in Malaysia. By that stage the debt stood at an incredible US$1.3 billion.

Barings never recovered. The bank collapsed, investors lost their money and many of Leeson's co-workers lost their jobs. Leeson was eventually arrested in Frankfurt and sentenced to six and a half years in a Singaporean prison.

The same short-term thinking lay behind the GFC in 2008, and it's seen in organisations every year.

When money is tight at financial year-end, the first affected are usually employees, who face reduced training budgets, travel bans and hiring freezes, all three of which are critical to morale, productivity and delivery of key projects. A better idea would be to kill more 'pet projects' early in their life, but organisations are still not very good at doing this.

Timely decision making that takes account of the long-term future of the project and organisation is a key skill to develop. There is a long line of evidence to show that decisions made without due thought will only cause further problems later on. Or, as Nick Leeson's lawyer Stephen Pollard put it, 'when you are in a hole, you need to remember to stop digging'.

Here are some short-term decisions to avoid:

- **Don't plan, just get on and do it.** Without a plan your project will fail. No question. If you don't spend enough time on the plan, you'll likely create something not founded in reality.

- **Fail to build relationships with stakeholders at the start.** You will need these relationships at various stages throughout your project, so putting the effort into building them at the start is critical.

- **Say 'yes' every time you're asked to add scope.** At various stages of the project you'll be asked to increase the scope by adding new stuff. As long as this can be controlled and doesn't impact existing work, then it's fine to do so. If it does affect current plans and productivity, then you need agreement to extend time and cost; otherwise expect the worst.

- **Avoid investing in the right tools at the start.** You need your team to start working collaboratively from day one. Waiting until day 97 to invest in a tool to make their life easier will lead to pain that could have been avoided.

Inevitably there will be trade-off decisions to make throughout the life of your project. However, as Stephen Covey says in his book *The 7 Habits of Highly Effective People*, you should always 'begin with the end in mind' and base your decisions on that.

Of course, facing up to conflicting demands requires courage and discipline. Too many project professionals cave in to demands on their projects and risk long-term reputational damage. Don't be that sort of leader.

Your integrity as a project manager will depend as much on the things you say 'no' to as on the things you say 'yes' to. Every addition to your project will have a knock-on effect. Similarly, some projects veer away from the expected outcomes very early on and need to be challenged.

Ultimately it is the project sponsor who decides whether or not to continue, but it's still your responsibility to ensure that everything is done in the best interests of the organisation's long-term future.

Don't let short-term decision making bring your project to its knees.

ACTIONS

DO: Keep the end in mind when making decisions.

READ: *Rogue Trader* by Nick Leeson — a great lesson in what not to do.

POST: Knowing what we're working towards guides my project decision making. #ProjectBook

CHAPTER 7

BEHAVE IN THE RIGHT WAY

The biggest challenges you'll have in becoming a project leader are in dropping poor behaviours, adopting those expected of you and helping others to do likewise.

Your emotional intelligence (EQ) affects the way you behave. Project managers with low EQ don't understand the consequence of the way they behave, while those with high EQ are aware of how their behaviours affect individuals and situations, and adjust them accordingly.

Behaviours and *skills* are often used interchangeably, which is confusing and a mistake. A behaviour is something you 'are'. It's the way you respond to a situation or the way you function under stress (for example, Jenny dealt with that issue *calmly*, or Jenny *supported* our approach on this). A skill is something you 'have'. It's your ability to do something well (for example, Jenny *builds great teams*, or Jenny is an *excellent speaker*). The former affects the latter, not the other way around. Skills will always be enhanced by behaviours (for example, *Jenny is funny, which aids the planning process*, rather than *Jenny is a great planner and that's what makes her funny*).

Your behaviours are the things about you (both positive and negative) that make you memorable. When you're being the best version of yourself, you encourage others to do likewise. Sadly, the opposite is also true.

Think about the best person you've ever worked for. It's likely they were memorable for one or more of the following qualities: caring, empathetic, supportive, considerate, decisive, confident, charismatic, thoughtful, kind, honourable, proactive, productive, courageous. These characteristics enhanced their skills in creating an environment or culture in which you enjoyed working.

Conversely, think about your least favourite person. It's likely they were one or more of the following: aggressive, bossy, selfish, controlling, deceitful, moody, rude, thoughtless, angry, anxious, erratic, inconsiderate. They may have had all the skills necessary to do the job, but their behaviours are what you will remember and how you will describe them to others.

The balance between behaviours and skills helps us distinguish between leadership and management. Leaders and managers generally have much the same skill set; it's how they behave that sets them apart. Leaders understand you. Managers understand the tasks you need to do. Leaders put you before the task. Managers put the task before you. Leaders want you to complete the task to the best of your ability. Managers want the task completed.

Importantly, leaders know when to manage and when to lead. Managers aren't able to do this. The ability to change the way you behave is challenging, but very rewarding.

Most of our behaviours are habits formed throughout our lives. Charles Duhigg, in his book *The Power of Habit: Why we do what we do, and how to change*, describes habit forming as a three-stage process: cue, routine and reward. For project managers this may play out as follows:

Cue: Frustration with a project sponsor

Routine: Talk to team member about the project sponsor

Reward: The positive feeling of allaying your frustration

The problem with this is that they haven't actually resolved the issue they face. Also, by talking about the sponsor behind their back, they are undermining their own credibility and building a culture where this kind of behaviour is seen as acceptable.

To change our habits, we need to recognise the cue, fight the old routine (habit) and replace it with a new one. Recognising the cue is made easier by a higher level of emotional intelligence or by others providing direct feedback, as habits are based—for the most part—on unconscious ways of thinking. Once you understand the behaviour, you can develop a new routine to replace or enhance it. In the following example, you not only resolve the issue, but also create a culture of honest feedback, which is a much stronger foundation for project success:

Cue: Frustration with a project sponsor

Routine: Schedule time to speak with the project sponsor to explain the frustration

Reward: Resolution of the issue

To become a project leader, you will need to change the way you behave—and never stop looking for ways to improve on that.

ACTIONS

DO: Draw up a list of behaviours that are expected of you, then pick three to work on.

READ: *The Power of Habit* by Charles Duhigg.

POST: I'm spending time with people who make me a better version of myself. #ProjectBook

CHAPTER 8

GIVE YOUR MIND A BREAK

Okay, a quick admission. I'm not a brain specialist. Never have been, never will be. Which means when I start reading about the complexities of the brain—all the neo-cortex and hippocampus stuff—my brain, knowing me as it does, replaces the words with the theme song from *Sesame Street*, and within seconds I'm lost. I know I have a brain and that it's really important, and I know I have to feed it periodically so it doesn't get bored and leave for pastures new. I also know that every now and then it needs a rest and that playing FIFA on PlayStation is a great way to provide it.

'Mindfulness' continues to be one of the most searched words on Google. Jon Kabat-Zinn is credited with developing the idea in the west, although it is a form of meditation that has existed in Buddhist cultures for 2000 years. Despite what you may have read, it's not 'the latest corporate fad'; it is widely and successfully practised around the world. Neither can it be dismissed as new-agey, which men of my age are prone to do whenever they fear their fixed ideas or even their masculinity may be undermined. Note to all men: living longer and being happier and more productive is an incredibly masculine thing to do.

When we emigrated from New Zealand to Australia in 2013, we knew no one here, had no jobs to come to and very little money, and had to find schools for the children. Unsurprisingly, it was a tiring and stressful experience, and given that our priority was settling the children, there was a lot of tension between my wife and me. We decided to resolve it by spending time together relaxing, doing yoga and meditating 15 minutes each day.

Meditation was quite new to me and to begin with I was sceptical. We found a good app (Headspace) for our smartphones and got into the routine of running through a guided session every day. Some days we'd fall asleep, some days we'd be more restless, but we stuck to it. The outcome was it brought us closer together at a time when we could easily have drifted apart, and it kept our minds fresh for the challenges ahead.

In his book *Emotional Intelligence 2.0*, Travis Bradberry suggests five simple ways to become more mindful:

1. **Focus on your breathing.** Sit in a quiet space and concentrate on each breath in through the nose and out through the mouth. What helped me here was removing all technology from the room and turning off notifications so I couldn't hear them pinging or vibrating in the background!

2. **Go for a walk and notice your environment.** Leave your phone behind and take in the sights and smells around you. Try to discover one thing you've never seen before. Invest in a pedometer if you'd like to record your steps. Take deep breaths as you go and try to clear your mind of anything work related.

3. **Feel your body.** Feel the weight of your legs on the chair and your hands in your lap before mentally scanning down your body, identifying areas that feel tense. This is a great exercise for spotting where tension is in your body and helping you to relax and 'feel' your body.

4. **Repeat one positive about yourself over and over.** Everyone has something they've done well or they're good at. When your confidence is low, find one thing

and focus on it. Alternatively, I'll create an email folder into which I place my positive feedback. Every now and then, in moments of self-doubt, I'll open this folder to read some of the nice things people have said about me.

5. **Interrupt the stress cycle.** Stand up, move, do something different. Be aware of the feelings you have when you're stressed and interrupt them with something different. Knowing my stress triggers has been life-changing for me. I can now very quickly spot stress and anxiety and deal with it by changing my environment or what I'm working on.

Each of these five strategies can help you improve as a project leader and as a person in the following ways:

- **It's a stress buster.** Cortisol is a hormone that our bodies produce in the adrenal glands (puffy things behind our kidneys). When we get stressed, our adrenal glands produce more cortisol, which in turn increases our blood sugar and suppresses our immune system. Ten minutes of mindfulness reduces the levels of cortisol in your body and makes you happier and healthier.

- **It makes you smarter.** A recent study by the Association for Psychological Science (APS) showed that by introducing a regular mindfulness session into your day, your capacity for learning increases by 15 per cent. There's also a better chance that you'll retain that information.

- **It makes you more productive.** A regular mindfulness session will increase your concentration power. Not only that, but you'll find you don't get distracted in the way you may do now. Better concentration means getting more done, which benefits both you and your team.

- **It makes you a nicer person.** The same APS study found that people who attended regular mindfulness sessions were 35 per cent more likely to come to the aid of someone in pain or distress than those who hadn't attended. That means that currently four out of every five members of your team would ignore your crying. Well, not your team obviously, but that team over there! No, really.

- **It improves your active listening.** With practice, you can train your body not to check your phone a thousand times a minute and can instead sit and listen to someone talk without your mind wandering elsewhere. You will earn trust, respect and probably more money (not scientifically proven) when you take the time to listen to others in a way that values what they have to say.

Reasons not to practise mindfulness:

- You think you'll look stupid.
- You don't have time.

You won't look stupid, honest. Anyway, who cares what you look like when you're a calmer, healthier, more relaxed, more productive version of you? Oh, and the time thing is all down to priorities. Everyone is busy. Don't kid yourself into thinking you're the only one or that you're busier than everyone else. It's how you prioritise your time that's important. A relaxed mind leads to a more contented, ordered and relaxed you. Who doesn't want to feel like that every day?

ACTIONS

DO: Take the time to get some exercise, leave your smartphone on your desk and notice the things around you.

READ: *Emotional Intelligence 2.0* by Travis Bradberry.

POST: I just got my 15 minutes of peace — when do you get yours? #ProjectBook

CHAPTER 9

ADAPT YOUR STYLE TO FIT THE PROJECT

My very first interview for a project management role wasn't about my attention to detail around planning and controlling a project—thankfully! I don't recall talking at all about the 'technical' side of the job. The bulk of the conversation revolved around my personality and how I would use and change it to suit the situation.

This concept was quite new to me, and something I'd never thought of before. However, I would be leading major transformation projects while also managing a team of software developers, and the two, I was told, would need different approaches.

Fast forward 20 years and this is something that rarely, if ever, makes it into the project management textbooks, let alone interviews. It doesn't often make it into blogs either, as we don't appear to understand or admit that the project manager is the key determinant of whether or not a project succeeds.

The research tells us otherwise.

In 2007, Purcell and Hutchinson found a direct correlation between an individual's personality and a successfully delivered project. A report in the *Journal of Industrial Engineering and Management* in 2014 confirmed that to be successful, project managers need to demonstrate extravert and perceiving personality traits (more about that soon).

Noted project management researcher Lynn Crawford argues that once a project manager has achieved an entry level of project management knowledge (yep, entry level), then more knowledge doesn't make them more competent: 'It's their personality and leadership style that does'.

Conversely, every leadership and management blog or book you read will tell you that a strong personality and leadership are critical to organisational success. Barely a week goes by that we don't happen on quotes from luminaries such as Drucker, Godin or Peters on just how vital it is.

So why the disparity between the two? Asked by the Project Management Institute in 2005 to research this, Turner and Muller couldn't find a reason, concluding unsatisfactorily that 'the question can only be answered if it's directly measured'.

Thankfully, tools to perform this measurement now exist. Whether organisations consider measuring the leadership ability of project managers important, however, is another matter given how much easier it is to use the project metrics of time, cost and scope. Consultants will be hired to tell you the problem is your framework or templates, and will create months of work for themselves, only for nothing to change.

Of course, no one personality can successfully deliver all projects. What the research tells us is that different projects require different personalities and few organisations match these up well. Typically, whoever isn't massively overworked at that time is given a project and (despite people like me delivering governance training that recommends otherwise) few project sponsors pick their project managers.

All research, blogs and personality 'measurement' tools link back to the work that Carl Jung did on personality back in the 1920s. Jung identified four functions of consciousness (*sensing, intuition, thinking* and *feeling*) and two attitudes (*extroversion* and *introversion*). These functions and attitudes combine to create four types of personality.

It's important here to point out that any kind of personality profiling or testing can never be definitive, despite how it may be 'sold' to you. We are complex human beings and encounter different combinations of emotions and situations every day. So our personality will be made up of each of the four types in a mix that may change from day to day. Having said that, our DNA is hardwired towards a particular personality type, which makes us recognisable to others. It's what others talk about (over our skills) when they speak of us.

This is how the four personality types fit in the project management world. They're presented in circles because no one can put you into a box!

Detail PM

Thinking

Working alone
Paperwork
Method-adherence
Detailed emails
Stand ups
Quality checks
Thinking then acting
Punctuality
Facts

Action PM

Getting things done
Meetings
Being direct
Challenging the status quo
Acting then thinking
Creativity
Authority
Logic
Taking risks

Introversion

Sensing/Intuition

Extraversion

Harmony
Coaching others
Coffee shop chats
Building lasting relationships
Familiarity
Sticking to the rules
Loyalty
Ensuring things are done
for the right reason

Thinking on their feet
Social activities
Drawing pictures
Storytelling
Having fun
Workshops
Presenting
New ideas
Flexibility

Feeling

People PM

Social PM

- **Detail project managers** like to work alone or in quieter environments. They take the time to think before speaking, focus on quality and require facts and data before making decisions. They are reserved and speak softly.

- **People project managers** put time and effort into building relationships. They are fiercely loyal and take the time to understand 'why?' so they can explain it to others. They're warm and friendly, like harmony and do empathy really well.

- **Action project managers** just want to get things done and will get frustrated if things get in the way of that. They like logic, take risks and approach everything they do with an air of formality. Their language and communication are direct!

- **Social project managers** like to be in front of the room! They are flexible and creative, like to have fun and are always looking for better ways to do things. They are positive in outlook and will draw pictures with their hands or with pens!

Different personalities are best suited to different projects. For larger projects (in terms of both team size and organisational scope), an extravert may be best suited to the role, someone who can build key stakeholder relationships early and take the necessary steps to build a culture that will evolve and grow as the project progresses.

These people will be comfortable speaking to large groups of people, radiating their passion for the project. They know when to consult and when to direct, and ensure that senior management actions and behaviours are in line with the required outcomes. The author Beatrix Potter once said, 'I hold that a strongly marked personality can influence descendants for generations'.

Introverts may be more suited to smaller, more localised projects. Relationship building is still key, along with the evolution of the project culture, but the groups will likely be more specialised and the stakeholder group smaller.

These people will have a greater subject matter knowledge, will focus on more collaborative activities and will favour faster delivery with less organisational impact. As Susan Cain says in her book *Quiet: The Power of Introverts in a World That Can't Stop Talking*, 'Introverts prefer to work independently and solitude can be a catalyst for innovation'.

That said, there are no hard and fast rules as to which personality type is 'better' or more effective. Both introverted and extroverted project leaders will need to adapt their behaviour and personality to the situation.

And there's the rub. Project leaders have to know how to do all of the personality types and to adapt their style based on the situation they're in. (This is easily the most popular part of my project leadership academy and also the most challenging thing for people to change.) Because whatever your predominant style, at various stages of your project you'll need to be empathetic, kind and considerate and to role model leadership behaviour. You'll need to put time and effort into maintaining plans, managing risks, dealing with issues and reporting on progress, and should always be able to answer the question 'what's left to do?'

Being a project leader is a never-ending personal development journey, and to grow and be successful you need to draw on all personality types.

ACTIONS

DO: Take the time to understand your personality type and how you need to change depending on who you're talking or working with.

DO: Take the time to understand the personalities in the project team.

POST: Understanding the personalities of the people I'm working with is critical to the relationships we need to build. #ProjectBook

CHAPTER 10

EMBRACE THE NEXT GENERATION

Midway through last year I met with a project manager in his late fifties. I'd been introduced to him following a speech I gave at a conference, and he proceeded to tell me everything that was wrong with project management and 'young people' today. I reached for my tablet and battered him over the head with it while tweeting 'This. Is. How. We. Do. Things. Now'. My Instagram of him lying in the gutter got 3476 likes.

Of course none of that is true. Instead, I politely disagreed with most of what he said and provided facts to support my points. Two weeks later I ran into him again and he said he'd given my response a lot of thought and asked me to mentor him. He admitted to feeling out of touch. Ironically such self-awareness is a value keenly sought after in today's emotionally intelligent marketplace and demonstrated that he was open to learning.

Most of the points raised in this chapter were covered in those mentoring sessions because although project management hasn't changed that much in the past couple of decades (barring the introduction of new methods discussed in later chapters), the world most definitely has.

In 1987 I was at an early crossroads in my life. I was a fairly bright, hard-working student, but I didn't warm to the school system so hadn't done particularly well (actually I did really badly). So I did what many school leavers did and asked my dad to help me write letters to potential employers. Six weeks later I landed a full-time position with a national bank. That was 30 years ago, and something I just can't imagine happening in our world today.

Baby boomers, Generation X, Millennials or Gen Y — every generation has different expectations and faces different challenges. New ways to communicate, a new language to learn ('whatevs', I hear you say), new tools to use and new ideas to embrace. The old movies are remade, only with better special effects.

Social media entered my life in 2007 when we immigrated to New Zealand and we needed to stay in touch with family and friends and share photos of our new life, mainly to rub in the better summers we had there. That's the kind of thing Facebook is for and we embraced it enthusiastically. Twitter soon followed, and within three years I'd opened myself up to ways of communicating, educating myself and sharing ideas that hadn't previously been possible.

I rejected some social media platforms that weren't of interest or use to me, though I gave them a try first. Social media as a way of communicating is here to stay. Ignoring it, and hoping the world will go back to the way it used to be, is not an option.

By 2030 Millennials are expected to make up 75 per cent of the workforce. It's kind of an obvious statistic, I know — it's not like baby boomers are going to be making a comeback, is it? What's important, though, is to recognise that the next-generation workforce is among us already and it's time to embrace the things that are important to them. A great place to start is *When Millennials Take Over* by Jamie Notter and Maddie Grant. This book aims to prepare people and organisations for the way we work today, not in the future, through introducing four organisational capacities:

- **Digital**. It's about the tools of our digital world, and the psychology of Millennials. Project leaders recognise Millennials have a digital-first mindset. It means finding the right tools to get the job done.

- **Clear**. It's about the access we have to endless amounts of information. Millennials are said to be our most educated generation yet, and given their access to almost infinite sources of information it's easy to see why. However, it's how and when this information is used that is important to project leaders.

- **Fluid**. It's about how we are thinking, acting and learning at all levels. Time was that project managers simply directed their teams, using their 'positional power' over them. That approach isn't acceptable to Millennials. They're looking for flatter structures, more autonomy and decision making at lower levels. For project leaders this means focusing less on 'control' and more on empowerment.

- **Fast**. It's about taking action only when it's needed. Millennials just want to get things done. They don't have time for endless bureaucracy and vacillation (who does?). They want to make a decision, move on, make another decision, move on. Project leaders need to harness this eagerness to get things done quickly.

For project managers, these organisational capacities help provide an understanding of the expectations of the new generation. Our world today is dominated by technology that has made our lives immeasurably better in many ways. Sure, we're talking less than we used to, but we can still control that, and reports of the death of direct verbal interaction have been wildly exaggerated.

Project leaders don't do things the way they've always been done and expect the next generation to follow. They find new ways to leverage technology, information, ideas and a willingness to get things done in a timely manner to ensure they not only stay relevant but can motivate their next-gen project team.

ACTIONS

DO: Explore social media and other productivity tools — you never know, they may transform your life.

READ: *When Millennials Take Over: Preparing for the Ridiculously Optimistic Future of Business* by Jamie Notter and Maddie Grant.

POST: Anything! It's what the new generation does now :-) (and remember to add the hashtag #ProjectBook).

CHAPTER 11

BE PREPARED

The Standish Group's 2014 *Chaos Report* asserts, 'All success is rooted in either luck or failure. If you begin with luck, you learn nothing but arrogance. Failure begets knowledge. Out of knowledge you gain wisdom, and it is with wisdom that you can become truly successful'. Any project failure should take this into account.

'When people believe that their basic qualities can be developed,' writes Carol Dweck in *Mindset*, 'failures may still hurt but failure doesn't define them'. In *The New Rules of Management*, Peter Cook advises, 'Give yourself permission to fail. Keep choosing whether to fail the project or complete it. But it has to be one or the other—either fail it with no regrets, or give it 100 per cent'.

Most. Negative. Start. To. A. Book. Chapter. Ever.

Or is it?

Great leaders speak from a position of possibility and look at what can be gained when things go wrong. When it comes to projects, lots of things will go wrong. For some reason, though, we still tend to start projects with the misplaced conviction that this time—this time!—everything will be different and we'll hit time and budget targets, no problem.

That's not to say we should start every project knowing it will fail. Absolutely not. We should, however, be prepared for the high likelihood that things won't go to plan—that's the nature of projects—so we can extract the learnings quickly and move on.

When I work with project sponsors, one of the things I talk about is the need to resist overanalysing things that have gone wrong in order to focus on what's important: finding a solution and getting back on the job. However, I do recommend that they run a pre-mortem before starting the planning process to ensure they've done as much as they can to understand what could kill the project at the very start (see chapter 69).

Post-mortems and kangaroo courts have no place in projects — or in organisations, for that matter — if you're to get on with the business of transformation. Your experience and that of others will go a long way to preparing you mentally for the things that can go wrong, and I'm not just talking about project risks here. Our self-belief can take a hammering when things don't go as planned, but if we react quickly we can uncover the positive lessons to be shared and carried forward.

Inaction or paralysis in the face of failure of any project component will fracture the culture you've worked so hard to create and undermine your leadership ability. So be prepared for failure — and learn from it.

ACTIONS

DO: Keep notes, or a project diary, on your (personal) learnings, and carry them forward to each new project.

READ: *Mindset* by Carol Dweck.

POST: I'm mentally prepared for the things that could go wrong in my project. #ProjectBook

CHAPTER 12
BRING THE HUMOUR

I haven't got the greatest memory when it comes to my childhood, but I can remember laughing—a lot. It has a lot to do with where I'm from. Liverpool has a worldwide reputation for its comedy and has produced many famous comic performers. Actually, almost every person on the street is a comedian.

When I was a child, every week we'd go and visit a relative. Dad came from a family of eight, so there was always someone to drop in on. And unlike other kids who dreaded being packed into the back of a car for a family visit, we couldn't wait. It wasn't like we were calling on rich aunties and uncles; more often than not the walls were yellow from cigarette smoke, there was a pervading smell of damp and you were served tea you could stand a spoon in. But we knew that at some stage in our visit my two younger brothers and I would be in absolute pieces laughing at something.

I'll never forget their self-deprecating stories of hardship and endeavour and the fact that they could find laughs in just about any situation. I'd love to rewind the clock to those days and do it all over again.

My parents played their part too, and we got to watch shows on TV when we were children that continue to be a source of inspiration for me: *Monty Python, Dave Allen, The Two Ronnies, Fawlty Towers* and, as we got older, *Not the*

*Nine O'clock News, The Young Ones, Blackadder, A Bit of Fry
and Laurie, The Mary Whitehouse Experience, The Fast Show,
The Office, The Royle Family* and so on. This humour became
part of who I am and greatly affected my leadership style.

Not all humour works in the office, though. First off, you
have to drop the tasteless stuff. Humour has to be measured,
used at the right time, delivered in the right context, and
should never be offensive or personal. Get it right and it
works brilliantly; get it wrong and you could be out of a job.
It's important to remember that work is not, and never will
be, a stand-up show, unless you're Jerry Seinfeld. If you're
delivering jokes endlessly, either verbally or in the things you
write, then firstly there's a good chance you won't be taken
seriously, and secondly you're wasting time and energy.

So why is humour important to project leaders? Here are
five reasons I've learned:

1. It reduces stress. This is proven. And not just your stress
   but your team's stress as well. People feel more relaxed
   knowing that the environment in which they work
   supports laughter and the odd joke here and there. They
   also know that if they're having a rubbish day, someone
   will be on hand to lighten the mood and put their
   problems into context. As a leader you'll also be easier
   to live with, and work will be left in the office and never
   taken home at night.

2. All the best teams use it. Think of all the great teams
   you've been a part of. Why were they great? You were
   put under pressure, you got the work done, you got
   the rewards — and you enjoyed doing it. You need all
   of those elements to make it great. You spend more
   time with people at work than with your family, so

why should it be anything other than enjoyable? Forget Oliver Twist, think Bugsy Malone.

3. It bridges the gap between leaders and the people doing the real work, creating warmth, trust and interest. It shows the human side of leaders that is itself motivational, and let's face it, for teams to perform at a high level, they need to be motivated. Humour singles you out as a positive contributor, someone who isn't beaten down by life or the organisation's approach to, well, everything.

4. It increases social interaction. Self-deprecation, good-natured banter and stories all enhance the relationships we have. They can be written or spoken and can work on many different levels, although I'd advise against sending jokes by email. We did that 15 years ago, but best leave those to Facebook now.

5. It breeds creativity. The more relaxed the workplace, the more likely that people will speak up and share their ideas. If your working environment is tense and stuffy, then those ideas will remain in people's heads and you'll move forward in baby steps. If you want someone to participate, give them a safe and encouraging arena in which to do so, and humour can be at the heart of this.

Of course, there are way more examples of how humour can help, nurture and support successful leadership, but this isn't an exhaustive academic study, nor does it cover the fact that success can be achieved without humour. I'm sure it can, I've just not seen it. And anyway, my daughter is begging me to watch *La La Land* for the 92nd time, so I'm really going to have to wrap this chapter up.

At a morning tea to mark my leaving one role (I think they just wanted to make sure), the CEO very kindly said, 'Colin is one of the funniest people I've ever worked with'. Which begged the riposte, 'So, not the most hard-working and dedicated then?' But inside I was thinking, 'ONE of the funniest? Must. Try. Harder'.

ACTIONS

DO: Ensure you use humour as a way of motivating the project team.

WATCH: Anything at all that makes you laugh. Your stress levels will thank you for it.

POST: I take my work seriously, but not myself. #ProjectBook

CHAPTER 13

MAKE GRATITUDE YOUR ATTITUDE

A 2017 Gallup survey found that just 3 in 10 workers in the US feel appreciated by their employers, indicating widespread disengagement. People spend as much time at work as they do at home with the people they love (sometimes more). To spend it in an environment where you don't feel appreciated for what you do is appalling. Apparently we need a day—the first Friday in March, Employee Appreciation Day—to remind us to do it! It's like Valentine's Day but with cheaper flowers.

Gallup estimated that these disengaged employees cost US business between US$483 billion and $605 billion every year. In short, where staff aren't given opportunities to share their ideas, or their work isn't consistently acknowledged and appreciated, a significant impact on the bottom line can be expected.

The same is true of projects. Poor project management almost inevitably leads to the team either losing interest or working around the project manager to get things done. In both cases, schedules will slip and costs will rise.

One very simple way to help avoid this is by saying thank you, *merci, gracias, danke, dank u, grazie, dōmo arigatō, kamsahamnida, obrigada, dhanyawādāh* or *dankie*. One or two simple words that make a world of difference. Parents teach their children early to say please and thank you, but this simple courtesy is sometimes lost by the time they start their working life.

Project leaders don't do any of the real work, of course. It's your job (for the most part) to ensure you build a team of people with the right skills and behaviours. So your principal form of communication should be the one that shows gratitude for the work done, even if you're not too happy with the outcome ('Thanks for the effort you've put into this, but this isn't the approach we agreed on').

Project leaders take the time to show gratitude in a range of different ways—some personal, others for the whole team or for individuals who have gone above and beyond what was expected of them. Ways you can show gratitude include the following:

- **Verbal.** Simply look them in the eye and say thank you. How hard can that be? If it's in a group situation, take care you don't embarrass them. Whole Foods in the US has an 'Appreciations' agenda item in meetings to reinforce the importance of gratitude.

- **Email.** Send an email to the team calling out the work of one or more individuals, taking care not to alienate others.

- **Note.** Write a brief thank you on a sticky note or similar and stick it on their screen.

- **Card.** You don't have to wait until someone's birthday or Christmas to send them a card saying thanks.

- **Coffee/lunch.** Consider this an extension of the verbal thank you, but also a 'reward', to be paid for out of your own pocket, to show your appreciation.

- **Something more personal.** Once you get to know your team members you can buy them a gift you know they'll like. Movie or shop vouchers are lazy, unless of course films or shopping are what your team particularly enjoy!

In his excellent book *Emotional Capitalists*, Martyn Newman says, 'Leaders who treat people in a way that supports their self-confidence make it possible for people to achieve things they initially thought impossible'. Make gratitude your attitude today and watch the confidence of your project team grow.

ACTIONS

DO: Say thank you in lots of different ways.

READ: *Emotional Capitalists* by Martyn Newman.

WATCH: Drew Dudley's TED talk 'Everyday leadership', TEDxToronto, 2010.

POST: I'm grateful for the work my project team does and I'm going to tell them so more often. #ProjectBook

CHAPTER 14
BOUNCEBACKABILITY

As a kid I didn't much care for playing football in the freezing cold, and Liverpool could get *very* cold in the winter. Worst of all was when the ball hit you full on the thigh, as it would sting like only a leather missile striking cold flesh can. You would wince in agony, at which point you'd be harangued from the touchline: 'Don't stop, keep running, keep running! It'll feel better in a minute'. The last thing you want to do when your leg is screaming in agony is keep running, yet you know there's truth in those words, and sure enough a minute or so later there's only a perfect imprint of the ball on your leg to remind you of the blow.

As a child these were the adversities I learned to bounce back (or forward) from. Whether it was catching a well-struck football on the leg, falling off my bike, getting bitten by a dog when delivering newspapers or failing my final-year school exams, I learned to get over it fast, find some kind of positive in it (the dog bite was a hard one!) and move on.

Today we call it resilience. Back then, my dad called it 'the bulldog spirit'.

The bulldog spirit actually had nothing to do with dogs; rather, it referred to the courage and resoluteness shown by the British people whose homes and livelihoods had been destroyed during Second World War bombing.

In his book *The Resilience Breakthrough*, Christian Moore writes, 'Becoming resilient starts with the realisation that the adversity you experience—any pain, discrimination or challenge—can be converted into powerful fuel that can actually bring opportunity'. As a project leader, you'll face many challenges that will test your confidence in what you're trying to achieve. If you're to turn the challenges you face into energy for activity and success, resilience is an important skill to develop.

Like almost every other quality or skill discussed in this section, resilience can be learned. Here are some steps you can take to build your own bulldog spirit:

- **Maintain healthy relationships.** Building relationships is at the heart of everything that will be great about your leadership, but don't assume that once you've built them they'll look after themselves. You have to put time and effort into ensuring they remain effective and honest, so when challenges arise you don't have to rebuild them in an environment of stress.

- **Be more optimistic.** No one can tell you to be more positive. It just doesn't work like that...

  'Colin, be more positive!'

  'Thanks so much. I've waited 30 years for someone to tell me that, and now I feel great. Silly me for being negative so long.'

  That said, you can (and must) learn to become more optimistic in your thought processes. People are rarely deliberately incompetent. We all make mistakes; recognising them and keeping a focus on solutions is a step towards becoming more positive.

- **Surround yourself with people who can help you.** In their research on resilience, Reeves and Allison found that the 'more resilient leaders always made time for coaching, while the less resilient leaders were always too busy'. Calling on help when you need it most from those you trust helps you learn how to deal with different situations and gain perspective. A good coach or mentor will remind you of the actions you need to take to stay on top of your project and your emotions.

- **Look after yourself.** If you don't take care of your body, it won't take care of you. With good management you can avoid those afternoon tiredness slumps. Project leaders look after their body and mind, giving them priority over everything else.

- **Look for opportunities to grow.** You can also improve your resilience by taking responsibility for things outside your comfort zone. Someone told me early in my career that if there was something I liked the sound of, but I didn't feel I had the skills for, then I should just 'feel the fear, then do it anyway'. By taking on tasks that stretch your current skills you start to think that anything is possible, which plays a key role in enhancing resilience.

In her book *Lean In*, Sheryl Sandberg writes, 'Being confident and believing in your own self-worth is necessary to achieving your potential'. Being resilient will ensure that as a project leader you will never doubt your self-worth and will unlock your potential to deliver projects successfully every time.

ACTIONS

DO: Develop your resilience skills.

DON'T: Reach out to pet dogs that are trying to rip newspapers from your hand.

READ: *The Resilience Breakthrough: 27 Tools for Turning Adversity into Action* by Christian Moore.

POST: Being more resilient means I'm better able to deal with the demands of my project. #ProjectBook

CHAPTER 15

LEAD A REMOTE TEAM

Some of us used to dream of managing a geographically dispersed project team. Our job title would begin with 'Global'; we'd get to fly business class, have a big expense account and return home with a camera full of culture.

Of course the reality is different.

I managed a geographically diverse team in my first three years as a project manager. I flew economy, got a slap on the wrist for spending too much on a team meal in Belfast and returned home with a longing for baked beans on toast and a liver detox.

Leading a team remotely is a skill everyone should have these days, because working nine to five in an office is becoming a thing of the past. Flexible hours are now a need, not a want, for people with hard-to-find skill sets. And as populations grow, office space becomes more expensive and technology improves, it makes sense to find smarter ways to work.

The move away from the office is happening now. According to Forrester Research's US Telecommuting Forecast, 43 per cent of the American workforce are already working remotely and the number will only increase. Almost 90 per cent of Cisco's employees telecommute once a week, saving them more than three million hours of commuting, providing them with US$378 million more productive time, which in turn will free up valuable and costly real estate. The numbers for remote working certainly stack up.

The days are gone when everyone would file into a meeting room at a set time and file out again an hour and 20 minutes later (they always overran — see chapter 40). This is a welcome change. As Jason Fried and David Heinemeier Hansson comment in their book *Remote*, 'It's incredibly hard to get meaningful work done when your workday has been shredded into work moments'.

We've already started dialling people in to stand-up meetings on the phone or from designated video rooms. Forward-thinking organisations also use collaboration tools to create a virtual rather than physical workplace. Building and maintaining a vibrant team needs more than tools and video conferencing, though. You need to be able to motivate someone who may be 10 000 kilometres away rather than in the next cubicle.

Business excellence consultant Tom Peters, author of *The Project 50*, believes that projects with a widely dispersed team should still set aside a large travel budget for the project manager to call on when required, and I tend to agree, though with the tools available to us today it's perhaps not entirely necessary.

Project leaders build and maintain vibrant cultures by involving all team members (regardless of where they're located) in the activities listed in part II of this book. In particular, they need to be involved in:

- building the vision
- agreeing on the behaviours

- embracing the collaboration tools
- simplifying the language used
- celebrating success
- making the project fun.

If you do have a travel budget, use it early to establish the relationships and to ensure that everyone understands who you are and the way you intend to do things. And use this opportunity to find out about the team members and what makes them tick.

If you can't travel, you're going to have to build all of these relationships over the phone or by video conference (*not* by email). If you're getting to know your 'local' team members by taking them out for coffee, then take your calls and videos in a coffee shop or similar too. Go to extraordinary lengths to demonstrate that just because a team member isn't physically there beside you, they're still a vital part of the team. If you're in a different time zone, then schedule calls for late night or early morning. Send out questions to get specific inputs into meetings that may happen when your team are in bed, or allow them to message in real time.

The culture of your remote team should also be taken into consideration. For example, in one project I ran I had a development team based in India. We celebrated Diwali with them via video, despite being separated by 8000 kilometres.

The leaders you appoint remotely should lead in just the way you do. There should be no loss of service to stakeholders or blame apportioned as a result of using a remote team. Too often I've heard it used as an excuse for not getting work done. That reflects directly on the project manager, who has failed to do enough to create a vibrant working culture that includes remote team members.

Project leaders build and maintain a vibrant culture regardless of where they or their team are in the world. They recognise that the organisational world is mobile now. They embrace the challenges this brings and turn them into opportunities for innovation and enhanced collaboration.

ACTIONS

DO: Ensure you seek the opinions of remote team members when building your culture.

READ: *Remote: Office Not Required* by Jason Fried and David Heinemeier Hansson.

POST: We're a team, no matter where in the world we are based. #ProjectBook

CHAPTER 16

BE AN INTREPRENEUR

Startup CEO Jeremy Bell told *Business Insider* magazine, 'I suppose our failure can be summed up quite easily: an inability to show traction'. Entrepreneur Amit Goel recalled to the same publication, 'Everything was going good. But we always had one issue. We never had enough money... and this became the cause of our death. We ran out of money'. Over at *Medium*, entrepreneur Martin Erlic admitted, 'It turns out that we underestimated the complexity of the project and overestimated our ability to complete it on a limited budget'.

Sound familiar? Most project managers with a few projects under their belt will recognise one or more of these scenarios. Each, however, is related not by a project manager per se, but by an entrepreneur. Someone who had the guts to stake everything they had on an idea, even if the idea ultimately failed.

What does it teach us? They had the courage to pursue their dream. They invested time and their own money (or funds they could raise from investors who bought their dream). In the end, it didn't work out so they had to shut it down.

Many people believe that project managers need to develop an entrepreneurial mindset. Although I recognise the value of this mindset (more on that in a minute), I'm not sure I fully agree with the proposition. After all, they are two very different beasts. Statistically, start-ups have a much higher failure rate than corporate projects. Indeed, according to an article in *Fortune* magazine as many as 90 per cent of startups fail, which makes the record for IT projects look great!

Some assertions you'll hear often:

- 'Project managers should treat the money as if it were their own.'
- 'We need to take more risks.'
- 'We need to get faster at failing.'
- 'We need to get better at pivoting.'

All easy enough to say, but as Eric Ries (an early pioneer for entrepreneurship) said, 'A startup is a human institution designed to create a new product and service under conditions of extreme uncertainty'.

Most of our projects unfold in a very uncertain context, so I might answer those assertions like this:

- 'Give them complete autonomy and let them do with it what they will.'
- 'Then don't expect the same outcomes.'
- 'How about we just don't start most of our projects?'
- 'Wait, what?'

What is true is that project managers need to be less rigid in their thinking and actions and better able to take calculated risks should the time and budget allow. There is most definitely a lack of courage out there, which is a result of project managers being measured on things over which they have little control (time, cost, scope).

In his book *The Art of the Start*, Silicon Valley venture capitalist Guy Kawasaki makes 12 recommendations for intrapreneurs (a word coined by Gifford Pinchot), most of which I believe are relevant in the right context to project leaders.

Here are Kawasaki's 12 recommendations, with my suggested actions:

1. **Put the company first.** Ensure that all decisions balance the potential impact with the benefits expected by the sponsor.

2. **Kill the cash cows.** Projects that don't deliver a good immediate return on investment, mitigate risk or provide a foundation for future growth should be stopped or better still never started.

3. **Stay under the radar.** Ensure you create the right environment to make your project successful without seeking recognition for it or, worse, making a 'noise' about what it needs.

4. **Find a godfather.** Ensure you have a committed sponsor from the very start.

5. **Get a separate building.** If you're not able to find an existing space to bring your team together, then look at what is available externally.

6. **Give hope to the hopeful.** Develop a vision and encourage your people to be the best they can be in pursuit of it.

7. **Anticipate then jump on tectonic shifts.** Keep your eye on potential changes (organisational, political or technological) and have plans to respond should they eventuate.

8. **Build on what exists.** Don't chase the shiny objects if you have something that works well already.

9. **Collect and share data** — particularly around what supports the successful delivery of a project.

10. **Let the VPs come to you.** Don't insist on presenting your project at the top table; let them come and see what your team is doing based on the great things they hear.

11. **Dismantle when done.** Don't try to keep the team together after achieving your goal. Accept that it was a fantastic thing you created, then move on and make your next project just as special.

12. **Reboot your brain.** Take some time to recharge, refresh and retrain—then you're good to go again.

ACTIONS

DO: Apply the 12 recommendations to each new project.

READ: *The Lean Startup* by Eric Ries.

POST: By thinking like an entrepreneur I make sure we do the right things at the right time and in the right way. #ProjectBook

CHAPTER 17

SWITCH ON YOUR EARS

When I was young, my parents told me I had two ears and one mouth for a reason. Well yes, it would look weird the other way around, but one mouth is enough for anyone. The funny thing is that listening is not something we're taught to do, it's something we learn, usually from others who aren't very good at it either. Think about all the people you interact with in your working life. How many of them are great listeners? The friends we retain tend to be those who listen to us and take an interest in our lives. So while it's not something we're taught, we know it's really important.

Recently I was talking with a client about whether conversational skills were in decline. I offered up that talking isn't a problem in organisations, but listening most certainly is, especially in the people business of project management.

A recent research paper published by Baldwin Wallace University listed 'Listening respectfully and attentively to others' as a key behaviour necessary for success. Few things irk me more than someone talking over the top of me. Among other things, it demonstrates a lack of courtesy and respect. By talking over me, they're implying at least one of three things:

- What you're saying isn't of interest to me.
- What I'm thinking is more important than what you're saying.
- You're not making your point quickly enough.

One of the best techniques I've found on how to listen better is in Tanya Drollinger and Lucette Comer's work on active empathetic listening, which remains as relevant today as it was when first published in 2005.

Listening combined with empathy has three stages:

- **Sensing.** What is the person saying, what emotions and expressions are they using, and what are they implying but not saying?

- **Processing.** Take the time to write down and think about what they're saying, the emotions they show, how they might normally react, and the themes or messages conveyed.

- **Responding.** Acknowledge what they've said in your own summary of it, give an appropriate response, ask more questions or provide reassurance.

Throughout these stages, maintain eye contact and use head nods or other body language to demonstrate that you are following them. Set aside your phone, tablet or laptop to give the person your full attention. (If it's not a suitable time to talk, then say so at the start and arrange a better one.)

Working with organisations to help build their project cultures, when I ask what they'd like to see change, 'more listening' almost always comes up. Better listening in projects starts with project leaders. Make active empathetic listening part of your culture and you'll be amazed at what it does for collaboration and innovation.

It's no coincidence that listen and silent share the same letters. Both should be used in equal measure.

ACTIONS

DO: Sense, process then respond.

DO: Take your eyes away from your screen when listening to others.

POST: I'm taking the time to listen to what others have to say before responding. #ProjectBook

CHAPTER 18

CREATE MORE LEADERS

As a fan of many sports, the biggest problem I have with the stars we watch on TV is that they're not role models for the next generation of athletes. We cheer them on in stadiums and living rooms around the world, but we rarely hold them up as examples off the field.

The few exemplars that do stand out have often had to work hard to overcome extreme adversity in their personal lives before becoming masters at their sport. Their followers see them as models not only for their sporting ability, but for their approach to life. They are leaders who are creating more leaders, not just followers.

Both Ralph Nader and Tom Peters have said it: true leaders don't create followers, they create more leaders. First you need followers, though. I know, it's so confusing!

In his book *Turn the Ship Around!* L. David Marquet offers some valuable insights into how to do this. As the captain of the submarine USS *Santa Fe*, he was charged with reinvigorating the team he was leading, 250 metres under the sea. What he discovered was a culture of order takers who hung on the words of the captain, not a team of leaders prepared to make autonomous decisions. So he decided to stop giving orders. It's a great lesson for project managers. 'Don't preach and hope for ownership,' Marquet writes, 'implement mechanisms that actually give ownership'.

Move the language of your team away from 'Can we?' and 'Do you think we should?' to 'I will' and 'I intend to'. Words can make a big difference to empowerment, and as a leader you need to encourage this awareness.

Derek Sivers's 2010 TED talk 'How to start a movement' takes this a step further by showing how a leader can create followers, who in turn become leaders of the new movement. The catalyst for the movement isn't the leader, he explains, but the first person to follow them. Once others see it's the right thing to do, they'll do likewise.

At one organisation I got it right. I put time and effort into creating a team of leaders. Finding ways to develop them. Encouraging them to use the right language. Showing them how to behave and communicate with different personalities. When I left the role, one of the team stepped up and is still there now.

At another organisation I got it wrong. With hindsight I understand that I put most of my time and effort into building a culture, rather than looking for opportunities to put my management team into different scenarios where they would learn what it would take to lead. Consequently, when I left the job, there was no clear candidate to step into my role and the culture slipped back into its old ways. This remains one of my biggest disappointments. I didn't do enough to turn followers into leaders.

As leaders today, we have to work harder than we did 15 years ago. Not only do we need to behave impeccably and demonstrate the technical skills to those who follow us, but we also have to be technically savvy and embrace new and smarter ways of working.

Encouraging the team to think for themselves and outside of what they're used to is one of the biggest challenges leaders face when converting followers. As L. David Marquet says, 'Those who take orders usually run at half speed, underutilising their imagination and initiative, and that's no good for anyone or the performance of your project when you're not around'.

ACTIONS

DO: Set the right example for others to follow, then look for opportunities to grow their leadership potential.

WATCH: Derek Sivers' 'How to start a movement', TED talk, 2010.

READ: *Turn the Ship Around!* by L. David Marquet.

POST: I'm looking for opportunities to grow the potential of the team. #ProjectBook

CHAPTER 19

BE GENEROUS

One project director I worked for back in the UK always bought the first round of drinks. Whether it was coffee or alcohol there was no question, the first round was his. Yet that wasn't what I liked about him the most. The thing that I liked most is that he would happily give up his time for any of the team at any time of day. Breakfast, lunch, dinner—none was sacrosanct when any of us had an issue.

Time is the most precious commodity we have, so for a leader to give up theirs to share their wisdom or to give you a shot of inspiration when you need it most is taking generosity to a different level, and I've never forgotten it. What he got back was loyalty, respect and a willingness to model this behaviour with others.

In their book *Conscious Capitalism*, Raj Sisodia and John Mackey write, 'The virtue of generosity does not merely apply to giving money, but primarily to the gift of ourselves—our time and our service to others. True generosity should not be thought of as some kind of self-sacrifice where what we give to others comes at our own expense. Rather it is an extension of love from our own hearts, which takes genuine delight in the flourishing of other people'.

Our new world culture, post-GFC, is much more focused on community spirit and generosity of time. In one survey Deloitte found that 92 per cent of Gen Ys want to see organisational measures for social purpose rather than just profit. The B Corp movement is changing the way people think about the organisations they do business with. B Corps (as they're known) are focused on 'social and environmental performance, public transparency, and legal accountability, and aspire to use the power of markets to solve social and environmental problems'.

But you don't have to be a B Corp to show you care; there are any number of ways you can do this through random acts of kindness:

- Give up some time to coach or mentor others.

- Buy a book you enjoyed for someone else.

- Buy a coffee for the person behind you in the queue, or suspend a coffee for a member of the community in need.

- Along with the team, use your volunteer day to help out in a soup kitchen or other charitable organisation.

Just as B Corps are a force for corporate good, so your generosity is a force for human and project team good. By giving up your time you're sending a message that you value them as human beings and that you're focused on giving, not receiving.

ACTIONS

DO: Seek out ways to perform random acts of kindness.

WATCH: TED Playlist on Generosity.

POST: I'm finding ways to be generous with my time and my knowledge. #ProjectBook

CHAPTER 20

SAY SORRY

'The refusal to express regret and to apologise,' writes Marshall Goldsmith in his book *What Got You Here Won't Get You There*, 'is one of the top 20 transactional flaws performed by one person to another'. A preparedness to say sorry is critical to maintaining the respect of the project team and the stakeholders. It's your way of admitting that you got something wrong, that you recognise its implications and are prepared to own it. It also demonstrates your humanity.

There is a lot of arrogance in project management today, as evidenced by the fact that most projects still fail to deliver what's expected of them. And it's exhibited mainly by the people who sponsor and manage projects, convinced they're doing a good job and that others are to blame when things go wrong.

Bad projects are hotbeds of finger-pointing, and more often than not the project manager is the recipient of it. I've found that in some 85 per cent of cases where I'm asked to investigate why a project is off-track, the project manager hasn't accepted responsibility for their actions. They haven't done enough planning, haven't built the relationships with the team. They're slavishly following a method that no one cares about but them, and they're not monitoring or controlling delivery. As a result, the team are working around them to get the job done.

In these cases, the project manager should of course hold up their hand and admit their mistakes in order to win the team back and set about regaining their confidence. This doesn't happen nearly as much as it should.

Author Brené Brown says, 'We pretend that what we're doing doesn't have an impact on other people. Just be real and say that you're sorry'. Apologising makes you a better person and the recipients healthier. A study done by researchers from Hope College and Virginia Commonwealth University found that heart rate, blood pressure, sweat levels and facial tension decreased in victims when they imagined receiving an apology.

So how can you be honest with conviction? Well, you can always use the five As:

- **Apologise.** If you've made a mistake or said something you shouldn't have, say sorry as soon as you can.

- **Articulate.** Explain what happened, taking care to ensure no blame is placed on the other person.

- **Acknowledge.** Admit you understand how your actions or words could have made them feel.

- **Apologise again.** Repeat your apology and promise you won't make the same mistake again.

- **Advance.** Now find a solution and move on. (If you keep apologising you'll only make things worse.)

A good example:

> 'Peter, I'm terribly sorry. I had assumed you'd been fully briefed on this project given that your area will be most affected and that none of what I had to say would be new to you. I can imagine how upset you feel finding out in this way. I'd never have spoken about this had I known and I can't apologise enough. I'll speak with your line manager to explain what's happened and will be happy to answer any questions you may have.'

A bad example:

> 'Peter, why didn't you tell me you hadn't been briefed? You could have stopped me at any stage to let me know this was all new to you and I'd have talked to you separately. I'll mention it to your manager that you found out this way, but we need to move on as we have a lot to do.'

In my experience this #sorrynotsorry approach is all too prevalent in projects that are failing to achieve their objectives. In these situations it's easy for people to forget how to be the best version of themselves and to drag others down around them with blame and counter-blame.

This is where a more self-aware version of you needs to recognise the emotion you are feeling and resist the urge to do this. Apologising and showing humility is the first step to moving forwards.

In *ReWork* Jason Fried and David Heinemeier Hansson write, 'The number one principle to keep in mind when you apologise, is how would you feel about the apology if you were on the other end? If someone said those words to you would you believe them? Keep in mind that you can't apologise your way out of being an ass'.

ACTIONS

DO: Follow the five As when you've got something wrong.

READ: *The Power of Vulnerability: Teachings on Authenticity, Connection and Courage* by Brené Brown.

POST: I'm making sorry the easiest word to say. #ProjectBook

CHAPTER 21

SET AND MANAGE EXPECTATIONS

At the heart of most misunderstandings with my team when I was a project manager was my inability to set expectations in the right way. I was too vague, too trusting. Or worse, I just assumed the person knew what I was thinking! It sounds ridiculous, yet most people in management roles will have found themselves in a similar situation at some stage of their career.

In a 2016 Globis survey, 90 per cent of respondents admitted they hadn't set expectations clearly enough at the start, which had led to the need for a difficult conversation. In this scenario, the conversation you have should start with an apology, before you set expectations properly.

Setting expectations correctly is another thing we're generally not taught to do. What's served me well is a process I devised called ACDC.

- **Articulate**. Ensure that what you plan to ask someone to do is absolutely clear in your own head. You have to be able to articulate it and understand it yourself before you communicate it.

- **Communicate**. First think about the person you're going to be communicating with. If you've taken the time to build relationships and get to know the team, you'll understand their personality and will be able to tailor your message appropriately.

If they're a detail person, the message might be delivered as a series of bullet points. If they're a people person, you might meet informally over coffee, where you'll take the time to talk to the value of the task in relation to the project. If they're an action person, you're going to keep the message short and sharp, avoiding unnecessary waffle. If they're a social person, you'll communicate in a positive, enthusiastic way and (where possible) allow time for creative feedback.

At the communicate stage it's all too easy to send an email to everyone. But it's the worst thing you can do.

- **Discuss.** Once you've talked through what you need, you provide the other person with the opportunity to ask questions. It now becomes a discussion, with your aim being to ensure they fully understand what needs to be done and by when. At this stage you are looking to take as much uncertainty out of the request as possible before moving to the next phase.

- **Confirm.** Here you want to ensure the other party fully understands what's being asked of them. After you've finished the conversation, you should send an email confirmation. Confirming your expectations in writing provides assurance that your verbal expectations have been understood.

This may seem like a laborious process to follow. In reality (like most things in life), once you practise it and have run through it a few times, it becomes second nature.

Of course, setting expectations is the easy part. You then have to manage them, which requires regular dialogue and checking in for some and a complete hands-off approach for others. Again, this comes down to the personal relationships you have built and how well you understand how they work.

If you check in with them too much it can be seen as micro-managing; too little and they may become distracted from the task at hand. You need to be disciplined and to ensure that the person feels empowered and motivated to meet your expectations without constant input from you. Given the amount of work required to deliver projects successfully, it's critical that expectations are clear and fully understood. Using the ACDC process may just mean you avoid the Highway to Hell.

ACTIONS

DO: Use the ACDC process to set clear expectations.

LISTEN: To ACDC's *Greatest Hits*!

POST: Setting expectations in the right way will mean we get the outputs we need. #ProjectBook

CHAPTER 22

MANAGE DIFFICULT CONVERSATIONS

Possibly the worst part of being a leader is that from time to time you have to manage a poorly performing team member or deal with a behavioural issue. In an ideal world, everyone will turn up for work, buoyed by the culture you've co-created, and will perform as agreed. They'll get the work done, you'll all get the recognition you deserve and you'll sail away under clear skies, contentedly watching the sun go down over the horizon. Every now and then, though, an iceberg looms and if you don't react quickly and appropriately, there's the risk that your ship could be sunk. No more Leo, no more Kate, no more boat. Just a lot of people out in the cold.

Before getting to those difficult conversations, you first need to ensure that you yourself are not the problem and that you have set expectations in the right way (see previous chapter).

Once you've confirmed the source of the problem, you need to prepare for the conversation. Ask yourself the following questions:

- What is the issue?
- What will the other person see as the issue?
- What is the aim of your conversation?
- What is the risk to the project if the issue isn't resolved?

It's a good idea to ask the other person to prepare too, so they understand what the meeting will be about and won't feel 'hijacked'.

When preparing for a difficult conversation, it's important not to rehearse a 'speech'. I understand that this kind of preparation provides a level of confidence for some people, but active listening is key during the conversation, and this will be impossible if you're standing at a metaphorical lectern.

In her book *Fixing Feedback*, Georgia Murch suggests the conversation should contain the following elements (and it's important to include all of them, although the order may change slightly depending on your style):

- **State the issue.** Ensure you don't dress it up to be something other than it is.

- **Provide examples.** Relate them to the expectations you've set.

- **Share your opinions and feelings.** Use words like 'surprised' and 'disappointed' in the early conversations so you're not seen to be overreacting.

- **Clarify what's at stake.** Make it about the project, not you.

- **Identify your contribution.** Talk about the expectations you've set.

- **Propose a resolution.** This is the olive branch moment. Ask for their perspective.

It may play out something like this:

> 'Jeff, last week we agreed that you would have the report to me by Friday. It's now Tuesday and I've yet to receive it. I told you last Monday when I set the task how important it was to meet the deadline, and in the three conversations we had during the week you assured me it was on track.

'I'm really disappointed to be having this conversation with you, as you agreed that timeliness was a key principle of the culture we've set. When I don't receive the report on time, I'm unable to include any commentary on the work you're doing, even though it's key to what we're trying to achieve.

'If it's a question of capacity, I'm happy to see if there's any way we can free up more of your time. But getting that report in on time is a key expectation of your role and I can't accept another delay like this one. I'm interested in your perspective on this and what we can do to ensure it doesn't happen again.'

It's vital that during the conversation you never lose sight of the goal, which in this instance is to ensure that the report is never late again. It's also important that it doesn't turn into an argument or become personal.

Having agreed on a course of action (see chapter 24 on negotiation), you need to summarise it and repeat it back, then document it so you set a new level of expectation to hold them to.

What you can't afford to do in this scenario is to agree to disagree. I see this a lot and it gets in the way of productive work. Managers take this line in order to avoid conflict. We're not taught how to manage healthy conflict, yet it's absolutely vital to ensure you keep your project running and to consistently get better at what you do.

We all do our best work on the edge of uncomfortable. This means being prepared to stand your ground and explain articulately why you feel the way you do about an issue. It also means having the courage to speak up when you'd rather be quiet.

Patty McCord, former Head of Talent at Netflix, believes healthy conflict was critical to the ongoing success of the streaming service. In her book *Powerful*, she recalls, 'Our Netflix executive team was fierce. We were combative in that beautiful, intellectual way where you argue to tease out someone's viewpoint because although you don't agree, you think the other person is really smart so you want to understand why they think what they think'.

Take the time to prepare for the questions you may be asked and practise your answers, which should focus on the value the project needs to deliver and their role in that.

During the conversation you'll need to do the following:

1. Keep your emotions in check. Demonstrating emotional intelligence throughout a conflict is critical, as you need to be good at identifying the triggers that may lead you away from being the best version of yourself. When you feel anger or annoyance, manage those emotions and stay focused on the solution. Everyone looks to you, as the project manager, to role model the behaviours you expect of others.

2. Practise active empathetic listening. By actively listening to the views of another and understanding their emotions, you get a much better idea of their intentions. Throughout this process, ask questions to ensure you fully understand their viewpoint before offering an alternate view. You may also uncover the root cause of their poor performance or behaviour.

3. Present your viewpoint and look for areas of common ground. Stay focused on the issue and the value your solution offers, don't waffle, and be respectful of others' views. Don't create right/wrong divisions and don't allow yourself to be interrupted.

4. Continue the debate until a solution is found that both parties can support, then get behind it. Don't ever 'agree to disagree'.

Allowing any member of the team to perform or behave below expectations will undermine the culture of the project and cause people to doubt your leadership ability, so it's important to deal with it quickly. It's not a skill you'll want to exercise regularly, but when you do, you'll need to get right.

ACTIONS

DO: Prepare well before having a difficult conversation.

WATCH: Fred Kofman's Lean In video 'How to Have Difficult Conversations and Stay True to Yourself'.

POST: When it comes to difficult conversations I get straight to the point and look for solutions. #ProjectBook

CHAPTER 23

GET HELP

With my first project management job I got lucky. I got to work for someone who was prepared to show me the right way to do things. I had no idea what project management was and had been hired on my ability to build relationships, so to say I needed help was an understatement.

At that time, 1997, it had not yet become fashionable to read about all this stuff in a book and assume you could do it. And the internet wasn't really a thing you could turn to; instead, you looked to the people who'd delivered things before.

I had questions. Lots of them. Particularly around where to start, how to win over difficult people, what techniques to employ to build a plan and how to manage risk. We were on a tight schedule to complete a number of geographically diverse projects in the two and a half years to 31 December 1999, and I was mildly panicking about my role in that.

Not only did my mentor (as I now recognise him to have been, although it wasn't a formal arrangement) teach me how to do the things I needed to do, but he encouraged me to read about other things—in the library (remember those?) over the weekends. He would demonstrate the right way to talk to people, build my confidence by accentuating the positives of my work and provide honest feedback on the mistakes I made. He was never judgemental and never lost his cool, and at the end of our time together I was not only a good project manager but also a better version of myself.

To become a project leader you need a mentor. We have a lot to do to improve the image of our profession, to move it from one that reeked of arrogance and blame to one based on humility, humanity and success. Good mentors can help us do this.

Mentoring can't be learned from books. The wisdom you tap into can only be found in the hearts and minds of leaders and passed on anecdotally. It's someone else's experience, with all its enjoyment, frustration, success and failure, the sum of the personalities and situations they have dealt with and the challenges they have overcome.

Not everyone can be a mentor, and it's very important to find the right match for you. In her book *Think Great, Be Great!* Lailah Gifty Akita breaks down the mentor's role as follows:

M = Motivator

E = Empowers

N = Nurture

T = Teacher

O = Originator

R = Role model

What I love about this model are the final two elements. Most people think of mentors just as people who've 'been there and done that', but the true value of a good mentor is in what they're continuing to do *now*, rather than what they did in the past. They are more than the sum of their experience. They're pushing you to try new things and adopt new ways of behaving, and they lead by example, so they are in every way someone you look up to and aspire to be. They understand the new generation, the new methods and the things that are important in our world today, and they build this knowledge into their feedback and counsel.

Mentoring is now valued by senior leadership, who generally see it as a better use of training budgets than the traditional 'send them on a course' approach. Good mentoring is an investment (of time and money), which is why you should choose yours carefully.

More and more organisations are building project management communities of practice to share ideas and introduce new concepts or ways of operating. In his article 'What's Keeping Project Managers from the C-Suite', Bruce Harpham talks about IBM's approach to mentoring: 'IBM did not rely on knowledge management software alone to share project management wisdom. The company actively encouraged project management classes and mentoring'.

I'm currently running monthly project management mentoring clinics for three organisations around specific topics, providing advice, encouragement, techniques and information to collaboratively help build capability around getting things done.

There are many independent mentors out there in the marketplace. A good way to find one is to ask others in your networks for recommendations, or you can approach people whose work you admire. Remember, though, experience alone doesn't make someone a good role model with original ideas. Talk to them before you start, taking the time to run through Lailah's model, asking them questions such as 'How do you motivate your mentees?', 'What original ideas do you have that may help me?' and 'How will you help make me the best person I can be?'

Good mentoring is priceless and never forgotten. In Steven Spielberg's view, 'The delicate balance of mentoring someone is not creating them in your own image, but giving them the opportunity to create themselves'.

ACTIONS

DO: Find yourself a potential mentor and be relentless in the questions you ask.

READ: Voraciously to open yourself up to new ways of behaving and working.

POST: Because I don't have all the answers I welcome the knowledge a mentor can bring. #ProjectBook

CHAPTER 24

NEGOTIATE EFFECTIVELY

I recently rewatched the excellent movie *Bridge of Spies*, in which New York insurance lawyer James Donovan (played by Tom Hanks) negotiated the release of both U2 pilot Francis Gary Powers and an American student in East Berlin, Frederic Pryor. Reading up on the true story behind the film, I was in awe of the negotiating skills that Donovan deployed.

Projects are one long negotiation. According to the Corporate Executive Board's *Australia Key Imperatives* report, if you want to succeed as a leader, then you need to be proficient in negotiation management. From getting the people you need to complete the planning process to resolving conflicts between stakeholders to securing meeting rooms for workshops, your ability to strike mutually acceptable compromises will be key to ensuring you have what you need to be successful. On the very day of the project closure meeting, you're likely to have to persuade decision makers that this meeting is more important than others they may have scheduled. It's a never-ending process.

But we're not all wired to be negotiators. Most of us are uncomfortable with confrontation, which is why we avoid it. With some basic skills, however, you can change the way you do business and greatly improve your chances of success.

Negotiation is a four-stage process:

1. **Prepare.** Assemble the facts, figures, parameters (time and cost) and options (for mutual gain). Understand your best alternative to a negotiated agreement (BATNA), the worst-case scenario should the other party refuse to negotiate.

   Most important is to prepare your emotions. In *The Handbook of Negotiation and Culture*, Michele Gelfand and Jeanne Brett observe that a 'positive mood helps negotiators create value and reduces contentious behaviour, whereas other-directed anger, and more generally negative [attitude], has the opposite effect'. They recommend that 'prejudice-free thoughts, emotion and bias-free behaviours are helpful'. Essentially, you need to be the best, most positive version of yourself without any preconceived ideas or closed judgements that might undermine the process.

2. **Negotiate.** Duly prepared, you can now start negotiations in earnest. Avoid any outward expression of your emotions that may communicate your intentions and feelings. If you show anger, it will almost certainly trigger negative feelings in the person you're negotiating with, leading to a reduction in their willingness to deal with you. The same applies if they get angry with you. Research shows that in such a situation the 'opponent'—when not emotionally stable—is quick to back down and cede ground, and that's something you'll definitely want to avoid.

   Don't give too much ground too early, and use empathy to better understand the other person's position. If you've factored this into your preparation, then you'll be able to offer responses or options that will allay their fears or concerns.

In my experience, the person who prepares best, has a good level of understanding of the issues faced by the other person, and doesn't give in at the first sign of behaviour change, is most likely to get the outcome they seek.

Take notes throughout the negotiation. If you're getting nowhere, throw your BATNA on the table as a last resort.

3. **Agree.** Once you've concluded negotiations, summarise and play back the agreements reached to ensure the commitments are clearly understood by both (or all) parties. Too often I've seen project managers leave the room with an assumption of what's been agreed, rather than an actual shared agreement, which means they can't move to the next stage without going through the negotiation process all over again!

4. **Action.** Once you've confirmed what has been agreed, don't wait to action it—confirm it in writing then get on with it.

Without the right preparation, negotiation can cause anxiety and stress. If you don't feel you have the skills, seek out a mentor who can help you get there.

ACTIONS

DO: Follow the four-stage negotiation process.

READ: *Getting to Yes: Negotiating an Agreement Without Giving In* by Roger Fisher and William Ury.

POST: When I'm negotiating I know why it's important to keep a cool head. #ProjectBook

CHAPTER 25
TELL STORIES

As a new manager of a project management office back in the early 2000s, I decided that what was required was more consistency, and by that I meant more paperwork. I'd been on a course, grabbed myself some new knowledge and decided to implement the method I'd learned.

I spent the best part of four weeks rewriting a 450-page manual into a format that would be suitable for my organisation to use. It was like rewriting *The Lord of the Rings*, but with less adventure and no kind of enjoyment for either author or reader. I didn't talk to my stakeholders, as I was convinced that this was what the organisation needed and that its implementation would be welcomed. I simply had the work approved by my line manager.

Oddly, it wasn't welcomed at all. It was met with stony silence. No one responded to the emails I sent out. No documents were received on the due dates, and the dramatic organisational progress I'd promised never happened.

I'd forgotten to do all of the things that had made me successful as a project manager: to ensure the sponsor was engaged and understood the organisational need; to build relationships with the users to find out what would work best for them; to produce a plan to implement the new approach in the right way.

Luckily I was given the chance to rectify my mistake, and I discovered, ironically, that taking much of the method out and providing a tool for them to capture their information was much more effective and laid the groundwork for future success.

This is a story I like to tell in my talks to corporates who are stuck in the bureaucracy trap. I throw in a lot of arm gestures and humorous asides and it always gets a laugh, which reinforces the message.

Personally, I've always responded to storytelling. Learning from others' experiences is vital if you're to reach your full potential. Rather than have someone theorise at me all day, I want to hear how they did it. More importantly, I want to know what it taught them. And neuroscience tells us that information presented as a story is 20 per cent more memorable than dry data.

When we're immersed in a story our brain releases a hormone called oxytocin (known to us non-specialists as the 'cuddle hormone'), which accounts for those warm feelings we get. It's a response that doesn't switch off until the end of the story and is the mechanism for building trust. I have a couple of people in my network who I could sit and listen to for hours. A former boss of mine in New Zealand had some incredible stories of when he first went to work for a bank in the UK that I could listen to all day. They were informative and funny and always had a point.

Stories are a great way for project leaders to demonstrate their fallibility and vulnerability as they build trust around subject matter. It helps them to create unity and build respect, while making subtle points about how to do things differently.

Everyone has stories. Unfortunately not everyone is good at telling them. It's another one of those leadership skills that doesn't come naturally, but there are a couple of strategies out there to make it easier.

Paul Smith, whose excellent book *Lead with a Story* gives more than 100 examples of leaders' stories and how they use them, articulates the seven elements required to create a good story:

1. **Start with context.** Set the scene so your audience understands 'the point' of your story.

2. **Use metaphors and analogies.** We all respond differently to information. Metaphors and analogies help make stories understandable and engaging.

3. **Appeal to emotions.** Recognise what the team (or individual) may be feeling and use a story that they can relate to.

4. **Keep it tangible and concrete.** The story must add value for the listener, and it should be factual, not fictional. It's not a stand-up comedy routine.

5. **Include a surprise.** The best stories have an element of surprise, something that you didn't see coming, that keeps you interested.

6. **Use a narrative style appropriate to business.** Remember, you're not talking to your friends. You need to use a style that's interesting and relevant to your audience, particularly in the language you choose.

7. **Create a scene or event for your audience to participate in.** Bringing your audience in, either by asking them a question or by placing them rather than you in the event, will keep the conversation and participation going.

Many organisations are now training their leadership team to use storytelling as a tool for upskilling their staff. Nike is probably the most famous of these, although to be fair they're replicating a model that 3M has been using for years. Kimberly-Clark sends its teams on two-day seminars specifically on storytelling.

Stories are not only great motivators for the team, but they're good for you too, providing you with the opportunity to discuss issues or problems you've encountered or continue to face. I often joke to my audience that my stories are merely a therapy session and they are all my psychiatrists.

ACTIONS

DO: Use Paul Smith's seven elements to create a story of your own.

READ: *Lead with a Story* by Paul Smith.

POST: Stories are good for my team and for me too — I'm going to use more of them. #ProjectBook

CHAPTER 26

MANAGE UPWARDS

Almost every week I hear of senior management facing criticism for their lack of availability or interest, indifferent decision making or disengagement from a project or initiative. Indeed, according to the Standish Group's *Chaos Report*, lack of executive sponsorship is still the number one reason for project failure. However, if I'm told you're not getting the time or decisions you need from a sponsor, my response is always to ask what you're doing about it. After all, why should it all be down to the senior manager? Why should you be right and they be wrong?

Don't get me wrong. There are certainly cases where project managers exhaust every avenue and every trick to get airtime, using up all their powers of persuasion to get what they need—to find it still isn't forthcoming. Sometimes, though, they need to do more than they've ever had to do before to secure the backing they need.

To get what you need from a sponsor, here are four things you must do:

1. KNOW WHO YOU'RE DEALING WITH

Conversations are so much easier when you know what kind of person you're talking to. You have to fully understand the senior manager's position and responsibilities, as well as their personality (detail, people, action or social?), their availability and the way they operate. Knowing the senior manager or project sponsor's buttons will help you anticipate their moods, sensitivities and likely responses to your direct questions. Without knowing who you are dealing with, you're unlikely to gain the trust required to get the job done.

All this groundwork is key to building a relationship and it should be done as early as possible. You can start immediately. I recommend walking and talking, even if it's just to exchange greetings. It can be hard, so take baby steps, but don't be shy—just get in there.

2. BE DIRECT

Don't dance around the subject. Be explicit, unambiguous. If you don't go in and ask for something plainly, you'll come out without it. That's obvious, right? If you crave an ice cream with a chocolate bar in it right now, you're not going to ask for a milk-based product with a cocoa insertion to be delivered when the vendor has time, are you? Or worse still, take two weeks skirting around the request, by which time summer has ended (the British summer at least) and you've moved on to craving a cocoa-based powder mixed with hot milk by the fire.

When you need a decision, say so. 'I need your decision on …' tends to works well. If you need time off, say, 'I'd like to take a day off on Monday please'. Want to be left alone to do your thing and not be micro-managed? Say, 'I really respect your input but trust me, I can deliver this'.

3. BRING SOLUTIONS, NOT JUST PROBLEMS

When I first started out in project management I was excellent at being direct with my sponsor. The downside was that once I had their attention all I delivered were problems and not solutions. The conversation would go something like this:

> Me: 'We've lost our test leads in the week we need them most.'
>
> Sponsor: 'Okay, what do you need me to do?'
>
> Me: 'Er, I just thought I'd tell you, because, you know, a problem shared is a problem halved, right?'
>
> Sponsor: [*Reaches for trap door button*]

You have to be able to demonstrate that you have given the problem some thought, rather than presented them with an ultimatum. Better is to propose a number of possible solutions to fix it. Then of course you're going to be direct and ask them to choose one.

4. FIBBING IS NOT AN OPTION

As your parents always told you (or the police, depending on your level of offending), if you lie, you will eventually get found out. If something goes awry, confess as soon as possible. Don't point the finger or do anything other than support the person involved (if it's not all down to you) and start thinking of ways to sort it out.

Explain how it happened and what you intend to do to put things right. If you try to fabricate a story, you'll end up digging yourself a deeper hole and making your position untenable. Always be honest. You'll have far fewer sleepless nights that way.

Project leaders apply these four rules to break through seemingly unbreachable brick walls. There are no secrets or Jedi mind tricks involved, just sensible strategies and an appreciation of the sponsor's role. The rest is down to them.

ACTIONS

DO: Take the time to build relationships with senior managers when you *don't* need anything from them.

READ: The following chapters to fully understand the role of the sponsor.

POST: Getting what I need from a sponsor starts with me, my behaviours and my approach. #ProjectBook

PART II
CULTURE

In my 20 years in the profession, the best projects I've worked on and seen have had the best cultures. It's something you can feel, sense and hear the moment you walk into a room. It's electric. You know something special is happening, and you want to be part of it.

If there's anything I miss about day-to-day office life it's that. I love the energy that great cultures generate. I've been involved in rubbish cultures too, some of my own making!

Cultures exist at every level of an organisation, and the strength of an organisation's overall culture is created by its subcultures. The four types of cultures illustrated overleaf depend on two things: the emotional intelligence of the team and how interested or engaged they are in the work they're doing.

As discussed in the previous chapter, emotional intelligence, along with the ability to be the best version of yourself (and for others to do likewise), is critical if you're to be consistently productive and to challenge each other to get the project delivered in line with stakeholder expectations. If you are unable to understand and control your emotions, you run the risk of creating a toxic culture that people don't want to be part of.

Being interested not only in the project but also in your role in it and in what the organisation is looking to achieve overall, is a key motivator for individuals regardless of their role. Without engagement, a crucial source of energy is lost, which can lead to procrastination and in rare cases a 'don't care' attitude that undermines work quality and productivity.

Project leaders need to be role models for both of these qualities. This means talking passionately about what the project is to deliver and how it lines up with organisational goals, while being the best version of themselves and creating a team environment in which others can do likewise.

Cultures can be situated in one of four quadrants:

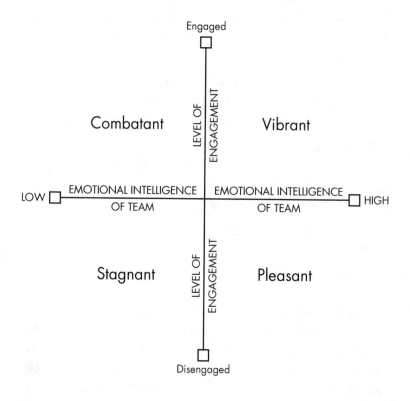

- **Stagnant** cultures are a bit 'meh'. No one really cares about the project, there's no sense of team spirit and no one seems to know what's happening.

- **Pleasant** cultures are too nice. Everyone is pretending that everything is good, but they're not so sure. Meetings are inefficient: they spend lots of time talking about anything but work.

Project cultures that are stagnant or pleasant consistently fail to deliver.

- **Combatant** cultures are prevalent where time and cost are especially constrained. Unconstructive arguments proliferate and the team just doesn't gel. Yet people are engaged in their work, so things do get done, despite the conflict.

- **Vibrant** cultures are memorable. The team have each other's backs and come together in times of crisis. They look forward to work and celebrate every success together.

The ultimate goal for project leaders is to create a vibrant culture *before* any work is started.

Some projects suffer from 'personality disorders', meaning they may spend time in each of the four quadrants. As leader, it's important that you recognise where your team are on this chart and ensure that you quickly move them back towards vibrant.

Culture, and advice on how to create one, is largely missing from project management textbooks, apart from some very formal advice in the Project Management Body of Knowledge (PMBoK).

Your job as a project leader is to create social harmony and a safe workplace where honesty is valued and people can be the best versions of themselves every day of the working week. Together you can create something to be proud of, something that will be talked about for years to come. None of this happens by chance.

Remember, you are the catalyst for culture. The ideas explored in the chapters that follow build on the strategies you've implemented from the previous chapters on leadership.

CHAPTER 27

BUILD AND CARE FOR THE TEAM

I've mentioned that I got my first project management role because I loved to build relationships and bring people together. I seldom worked alone and I firmly believed in the power of 'we' over 'I'. Knowing no better, I maintained this approach in my new role, hoping it would keep working, and it did. Indeed, it turned out that working together was key to our success.

The best part of project management isn't completing the project, it's knowing you brought a team of people together and collectively created something special. Teamwork is often taken for granted in project management. Organisations believe they can throw together a bunch of people in a project team and that magic will happen.

Sometimes it does, but only if the person leading the team invests the time and effort in understanding each personality and uses techniques and skills to create an environment that supports different ways of working. Such project managers don't think of *their* needs when doing this, they think of the collective.

There must be a shared vision, collective ownership and responsibility for progress, and a willingness to challenge each other to be better. The team will then think and talk in terms of 'we'. In this they'll be led by you. If you think and talk in terms of 'you', you are distancing yourself from the collective and passing responsibility across to the person you're addressing, who may feel they will be blamed if the task doesn't go as planned.

When you think and speak in terms of 'I', you are shouldering a lot of the responsibility yourself and there's a danger that you'll focus on the detail of the project rather than the job of managing it. The team may also be left with the impression that you'll also take credit for the collective success of all they achieve.

When you think and talk in terms of 'they', you are distancing yourself from the team and risk becoming alienated from the very thing you need to get the job done successfully. It can create a barrier, and while the team may get the work done they'll be doing it in spite of you. As Dwight D. Eisenhower said, 'It's better to have one person working with you than three people working for you'.

Project leaders think and talk in terms of 'we'. They create a team with a shared purpose and responsibility for success and failure. A team that accepts all personalities, skills, knowledge and circumstances. A team committed to being the difference they want to see in others and to creating an experience like no other. A team that is happier and therefore (according to a study by the University of Warwick in the UK) up to 12 per cent more productive.

In his book *The Five Dysfunctions of a Team*, Patrick Lencioni argues, 'Not finance. Not strategy. Not technology. It is teamwork that remains the ultimate competitive advantage, both because it is so powerful and so rare'. Never is this more apparent than in your projects, and those that have it succeed. Every time.

It's not enough to build the team, though—you have to care for them too.

A study by the Centre for Creative Leadership recently found that leadership failure is primarily caused by different kinds of emotional incompetence. The three key ones are poor interpersonal skills, difficulty in handling change and inability to work well in a team. The impact of these traits in our workplaces and projects continues to baffle and frustrate me. In my experience, the number one reason people leave their job is because of their boss. For me, though, leaving is better than moaning about it endlessly. Being English, I'll admit that moaning is our national sport, so it's always hard to resist it. My dad, though, is a quadruple gold medallist.

Most people don't get up in the morning determined to do a rubbish job — in fact I'll go out on a limb here and say no one does. Sure, there may be the odd personality clash or grievance, or the Dunning–Kruger effect (see chapter 1) might be in full flow, but we still have a sense of pride in what we do.

It's the project manager's job to ensure that the team feel cared for and involved, or, as HR like to call it these days, 'engaged'. There. Done. Simple, right?

Apparently not. Some US$11 billion is lost every year as a result of employee turnover, and the impacts that can have on projects can be huge. If you don't start finding different ways to engage your project team, it's likely that this statistic will get worse.

According to a 2015 survey from Deloitte, Millennials entering the workforce place far greater emphasis on employee wellbeing and employee growth and development, compared with present-day priorities of personal income/reward and short-term financial goals. They want to be mentored, coached and developed. They want to be opened up to new opportunities and to be able to grow into a role. This is what excites employees and enhances their loyalty to you, the project and the organisation.

Successful organisations build cultures that foster friendship and caring within their teams. Ever worked in a team where you felt you could share your opinions without judgement?

The kind of team where people cared for each other? Now, I get that some people are uncomfortable with the use of terms like *caring* and *love* in the office, so find different ways to say it, but make sure it's practised.

And remember that introverts and extroverts need different approaches. In general, introverts prefer:

- private conversations to public ones
- time to think
- few interruptions
- privacy

while extroverts prefer:

- compliments
- options
- encouragement
- talking things over publicly.

To build a great team you first need to learn how to care for them individually and collectively. Only then will you have their permission to create something unique.

ACTIONS

DO: Take the time to show the team that you care about the work they're doing and their wellbeing.

DO: Think about ways you can develop them throughout the life of the project.

POST: If I care about my project team, they'll care about the project. #ProjectBook

CHAPTER 28

DEVELOP A VISION

In the early 2000s I joined an organisation that was looking to become the biggest online retailer in the UK. At that time, it had little if any online presence and while as a team we were excited by the prospect, it didn't feel real. The company's market share was being slowly reeled in by newer online retailers, so action had to be taken.

A month later we were invited to join the rest of the senior management team of the organisation at an event at a local hotel to talk through the transformation plans. Here the Managing Director stood up and introduced the vision. It was 'To inspire every household to shop with us for life'. For an organisation that had previously sold its wares through a catalogue, this was confronting for some, but for those of us who were in tune with the move to online shopping it was a beacon.

Here was a statement that was bold and exciting and gave our day-to-day work purpose. It was at the heart of every investment decision we made ('How does this line up with our vision?') and enabled us to make priority calls on less important work. In short, everything we did lined up with the vision and everyone knew that.

A great project vision sits between your skills as a leader and your ability to build the culture. It gives your project an identity, inspires you in your work, and joins the dots between effort and organisational success. It's not a statement of the desired outcomes or benefits of a project ('To save $30 000 on our photocopying costs' or 'For HR to become more productive'). Rather, it's a statement of possibility. 'A vision,' write Ben and Rosamund Stone Zander in *The Art of Possibility*, 'helps to inspire and capture aspiration and assist people in overcoming the inherent incohesion associated with moving away from the familiar'. What's important is to create a statement that describes the future, and to motivate the team to do the work required to get there.

So how do you create a vision? Well, like everything in projects, you collaborate. You bring the team together at the planning stage and work with them to agree what it is, remembering that it has to link to the organisation's overall vision if one exists. Start by asking the team some simple questions:

- What does the organisation look like when this project has been completed?

- What can it do that it's never been able to do before?

- What can the customer see or do that they've never been able to see or do before?

Split the team into small groups and ask them to write down on Post-it notes words that describe the future state. From those words ask them to construct one sentence to describe that post-project future. Returning to our examples of photocopying and HR projects, their vision statements might be something along the lines of, respectively, 'To leverage technology to reduce wastage' and 'To provide HR with the tools to support the transformation of the organisation'.

Memorability is important, something you want everyone to know and learn. To achieve this, go small. The shorter the vision statement, the better. That's not to say you compromise on the quality of the vision to get it into one brief sentence. It does mean that as soon as it becomes wordy, it ceases to be memorable. Here are some easy-to-remember vision statements:

- 'A just world without poverty' (Oxfam)
- 'To create a better everyday life for the many people' (IKEA)
- 'To be the best retailer in the hearts and minds of consumers and employees' (Walmart)
- 'Whole Foods, Whole People and Whole Planet' (Whole Foods call this their 'motto').

Interestingly, The Walt Disney Company's former vision 'To make people happy' has been succeeded by 'To be one of the world's leading producers and providers of entertainment and information'.

I know which one inspires me more.

ACTIONS

DO: Create a short but memorable vision for your project.

WATCH: John Kotter, 'How to create a powerful vision for change' (*Forbes*, 7 June 2011).

POST: Our vision creates energy and inspiration. #ProjectBook

CHAPTER 29

GET YOUR COMMUNICATION RIGHT

One of the biggest mistakes that project managers make is treating every person the same when it comes to communication. That's not to say you don't need to be consistent with your behaviours, but the language and medium you use should always be tailored to the individual(s).

One project manager asked me, 'So does that mean I have to write four versions of the same report?' My answer was, 'No, you write one report but ensure there's something in there to suit every personality within your audience'.

For example, there's a myth circulating that all senior managers want to see is pictures. That may be true for some, but there are others out there who need to see the data behind that picture so they can be confident that the course of action being taken is the right one. Similarly, some senior managers will be primarily concerned with people. They will want you to demonstrate that you understand the nature of being human and the fears that change brings.

This is not about changing who you are, though. It's about changing how you communicate to ensure your message is received and understood.

Mark Murphy, author of *Hundred Percenters*, suggests there are four communication styles we need to adopt in order to appeal to the different personality types and also to suit the situation we find ourselves in. For example, a senior manager usually predisposed to a more social conversation may require more data should an issue arise that they have no knowledge or experience with.

Mark's four styles, along with my assessment of what project leaders need to do to tailor their approach to each, are:

- **analytical**—unemotional presentation of facts and figures. Have the data to back up the data you have, don't um and ah or interrupt; use graphs and charts.

- **intuitive**—passionate, big-picture explanations. Draw diagrams, use demonstrative body language, talk about vision and goals, use stories.

- **functional**—direct, step-by-step and ordered. Be on time, focus on the process and give definitive answers to any questions.

- **personal**—diplomatic, emotional language, listening. Use their name (a lot) and demonstrate an understanding of their concerns.

Which of these communication styles are you most comfortable with? Your default will likely be the one most suited to your personality. Regardless of your approach, you should maintain eye contact at all times during face-to-face interactions, but don't expect to get it back from everyone.

My default is the intuitive approach. I like to get passionate about the subject matter, and to articulate visions and goals. I tell stories to reinforce a point and like to write on whiteboards!

At different stages in my career I've led very different teams. In one organisation I led a team of largely analytical software developers, while my stakeholder group was made up of more functional, intuitive and personal line managers. After gathering feedback from them over the course of three months, I tailored my weekly update to ensure there was something for everyone. My executive summary allowed me to get passionate about our progress towards the goals. I then listed the top five tasks we had completed, followed by the five things we needed to complete next.

I spoke about team and stakeholder morale and about some of the team-building exercises we had done in that period. I finished off with some statistics around money spent, days to go, change requests in progress and issues resolved. In short, there was something in that update to keep everyone happy.

To build and maintain relationships with your team and stakeholders, it's critical to use different communication approaches for each. If you don't know how they like to receive their information, ask! If they're not replying to your emails, you know you have work to do.

ACTIONS

DO: Take the time to think about the personality of the person you're dealing with and the communication style that would work best for them.

READ: *Hundred Percenters* by Mark Murphy.

POST: Choosing the right communication style is critical to great stakeholder engagement. #ProjectBook

CHAPTER 30

COLLABORATE FOR SUCCESS

The way we work has changed significantly over the past 10 years. In 2005, email use was prevalent and texting was yet to be accepted as a means of communicating important messages. It was another three years before people stopped phoning in sick, putting on their sick voice, and started texting in the details instead. 'Got flu. CU tmrw.' Right.

Fast forward to today and texting has been supplanted by a multitude of social media tools and apps that we use on our smartphones and tablets. One survey found that tablet usage has increased 1721 per cent and smartphone usage has increased 394 per cent since 2010.

Email is still king, though, with McKinsey reporting that office workers spend an average of 28 hours a week writing emails, searching for information and collaborating internally. As a collaboration tool, email is poor, however, and too often it is misused. Endless people are copied in to 'ensure there's an audit trail', or staff members put Tolstoy to shame with an epic diatribe that no one will read.

In 2012 the UK retail giant Debenhams was storing 13.8 million new emails a month, a figure that was then predicted to increase by 20 per cent year on year.

The role of email in projects is important for confirming conversations or ensuring the right people have the right information at the right time. It can't compete, though, with face-to-face conversations or the huge number of social and collaboration tools we have access to.

These apps and tools aren't fads or only 'for young people'. They are the way we communicate with our friends and family as well as the way we do business now. It's almost inconceivable to think of our world without Facebook, Twitter, Instagram and LinkedIn. Similarly, those running projects can use a range of collaboration tools that can make the delegating and tracking of work so much easier than it used to be. Indeed, according to the Pew Internet Project, 75 per cent of all internet users now use social media and collaboration tools to share content and stay informed.

These tools are also critical for maintaining connections with those working off-site or in different parts of the world.

Project leaders are tech-savvy and have embraced these new tools; they are curious and open to looking for better ways to collaborate with their project teams. Large project management information systems are fast becoming a thing of the past as we turn to simpler, more cost-effective ways of doing business. And mobility is key. If it's not available on your phone or tablet, then it likely won't get a second look.

I used collaboration tools in my projects and project departments for years. Having never been a fan of being copied into an email, I implemented Evernote in a number of organisations to ensure that notes from meetings could be read (by me and other team members) if we felt they were of interest. More recently, I used Yammer and Sharepoint to establish project areas in which ideas could be shared and suggestions made.

Within my own small practice team we communicate, collaborate, plan and share ideas using a combination of Trello, Slack and Google Drive. Implementing tools such as these requires change and agreement on how to do it. You can't just expect everyone suddenly to play ball.

In organisations that don't already have collaboration tools, the assessment and implementation of tools that could benefit project teams is a great exercise to undertake. More often than not, you can trial them for free.

Before selecting a tool you need to answer the following questions:

- What works well in the way you collaborate now?
- How could this be enhanced by using collaboration tools?
- What does the organisation currently use that could be leveraged?
- What changes to the current culture are required in order to embrace them?
- How will you ensure that everyone uses them consistently?

The benefits of these tools will be realised only if everyone uses them in the right way, so agreeing this up front (rather than simply telling the team) is key.

All of 150 years ago Charles Darwin wrote, 'In the long history of humankind, those who learned to collaborate and improvise most effectively have prevailed'. Communicating and collaborating face to face will always be the best way to get things done, but that's just not the world we live in anymore. As a project leader you must learn to collaborate for the age you live in.

ACTIONS

DO: Assess the need for a collaboration tool, then work with the project team to select the one that best suits your needs.

READ: 'The 15 Best Project Management Tools for Business', *CIO*, 10 March 2018.

POST: Collaboration tools make our job easier — we're going to pick one then use it! #ProjectBook

CHAPTER 31

MAKE TIME FOR INNOVATION

No word is more overused or misunderstood in business than *innovation* (although *agile* is currently giving it a run for its money). Despite that, one of the greatest innovations has been propping up project management techniques for years.

Founded at the turn of the 20th century, the company 3M struggled for years over how to run a sandpaper factory they'd bought. New money was required to keep the company going while they toyed with new ideas and ways to use the minerals they had access to. In 1925, one of their employees, Richard Drew, created a low-tack tape to help reduce the amount of touch-up work auto-body workers had to do once they'd removed the protective butcher paper. His invention of cellulose tape (now known as Scotch tape) in 1930 completely turned 3M's fortunes around.

After the Second World War, the owners of the company recognised that if they wanted to continue to make money and not return to the struggles of their early existence, they needed *lots* of new ideas. So they introduced a staff perk like no other: '15% time', or six hours a week to work on the things they didn't get time to pursue during normal working hours. That's right, almost a day on 'pet projects'. In those days, 3M called this 'Permitted Bootlegging', which I much prefer.

'What are you doing this afternoon, Colin?'

'Oh I'm off to do a bit of permitted bootlegging.'

See, much better than 'working on some new ideas'.

A pet project Richard Silver was working on was a super-strong adhesive for use in the aerospace industry. The problem was it was just too weak and was roundly rejected by the 3M management team. Silver tried to think of a way of marketing his adhesive but couldn't come up with one, so he gave a number of seminars to ask others for ideas through a 'Tech Club'. The 15% time had fallen into disuse under the previous CEO (who had instead introduced cost-cutting six-sigma management techniques), so the Tech Clubs were used to reintroduce it.

In 1974, 3M scientist Art Fry came up with a marketable use for the adhesive at one of the Tech Clubs. He found that the notes he used to mark his place in his hymn book on a Sunday kept falling out. He asked Silver to send him some of the adhesive and over the next few weeks they worked together to get the adhesive and notes to work as they wanted.

They created some of these new 'sticky pads' and circulated them to 3M employees to test. They weren't as popular as they had hoped, but Fry then had another idea. He handwrote some questions on a sticky and stuck it on a report. He then shifted the note from one report to another and passed it to a colleague—and a whole new way of communicating was born.

There were numerous obstacles before the invention was commercially viable. It required new machinery to coat the notes, and given that nothing like it had ever been done before it was still deemed to be too risky. So using his own time (remember, he was still doing his day job), he developed a prototype machine in his garage to demonstrate that it wouldn't be as hard as the engineers thought! It was so big they had to remove the doors of his garage to get it out.

On 6 April 1980, the world was introduced to the Post-it note, and today 3M has revenue of over $8 billion.

The moral of that story is that if you truly want innovation in your projects or business, you need to give the people with the ideas the time and opportunity to be creative with them, and to accept that they may fail. You can't hold them to immovable deadlines or push them to work 60-hour weeks and expect magic. Worse still would be to force them into a process for being creative, then admonishing them for not delivering. As comedy legend and motivational speaker John Cleese said, 'Nothing will stop you from being creative so effectively as the fear of making a mistake'.

You need to ensure that time for innovation is built into your schedule to allow the creative minds in the team to try out different ideas to address the problems you face. You also need to ensure that having committed to innovation, everyone—senior management in particular—adopts the same mindset, and that failure is seen as nothing more than finding out what doesn't work.

Mindset is very important, as often the biggest barrier to innovation is the simple fact that people don't want to (or don't know how to) think differently. You need to create a different dynamic, something that doesn't feel like business as usual, that feels more creative than normal. As a project manager, I had a box of tools to encourage this—pens, Post-it notes, games, Lego, stress balls, anything I could get my hands on that might help people change their energy or way of thinking.

Projects consistently require this kind of stimulation not only to ensure the final product delivered is fit for purpose, but also when resolving issues. All too often an individual tries to solve a problem on their own at their desk, when a group of people thinking and working differently could have solved it in half the time.

'For good ideas and true innovation,' said American entrepreneur Margaret Heffernan, 'you need human interaction, conflict, argument, debate'. And she's right, but what you need more than anything else is time. Give your people the time to be creative and great things will follow.

ACTIONS

DO: Build in time for your people to be creative around the problems you face.

READ: *Ten Types of Innovation: The Discipline of Building Breakthroughs* by Larry Keeley.

POST: Innovation is a mindset, not a process. We're giving our people time to be creative. #ProjectBook

CHAPTER 32

FIND THE RIGHT SPACE FOR WORK

In an informal survey I conducted on a Sydney street this morning, I found that by any measure *everyone* is different. This was confirmed even by the twins I questioned, which was a relief for my statistical analysis. Some were listening to music, some talking on their phones, some were talking with friends and colleagues, others just scurrying briskly to work. Some seemed to be doing their best to get killed crossing the road.

Any culture is a mix of introverts and extroverts. Great leaders know you need environments in which each may flourish. So why is it that most organisations create only two kinds of environment and then expect employees to produce their best work?

Most project and line managers continue to assume that meetings and workshops are the most effective mechanisms for collaboration. While this may be true for some people and some activities, it's certainly not true of everyone and every activity.

The open-plan office layout now in vogue is linked to a more 'agile' way of working. While on the face of it, it might seem like a good idea to remove barriers and walls in order to improve face-to-face interaction and cut down on email, there is no proof whatsoever that it actually does so. In fact, quite the opposite seems to be true, with one Harvard review finding that people in open-plan offices spent 73 per cent less time in face-to-face interactions while email and messaging use shot up by over 67 per cent!

Different personalities need different environments in which to do their best work, and this needs to be taken into account at the start of the project planning process.

On a practical level, by making the assumption that everything is done best face to face in a meeting room, we create a secondary problem of taking up a space that others might use more productively. Cushman and Wakefield (2013) found that meeting rooms were generally occupied by just one or two people, and that these people used up the larger meeting spaces on almost 40 per cent of occasions.

As a general rule, four types of working environment are needed:

- **Quiet environments** suit people who do their best work when there is silence and a lack of distraction. They like to close themselves off from what's happening around them and focus on the task at hand. These environments can also be used for one-on-one meetings that don't require confidentiality.

  Conventional: workstation, pod, hot desk

  Less conventional: chat or communicator conversations, virtual working, 'library' space

- **Private environments** suit those times when a designated space is required to contain a conversation, discussion or task. This might sometimes include taking a conversation outside. Projects generally use private environments to hold team meetings.

  Conventional: small meeting room, café, conference call

  Less conventional: walking meeting

- **Group environments** are suited to those exercises that require a number of people to come together to work through a problem or issue. Projects use group environments to build plans, identify risks and workshop new ideas.

  Conventional: larger meeting room with whiteboards and flipcharts, boardroom (if applicable), conference call

  Less conventional: external space (including outdoors), virtual meeting room, video call, webinar, message board or collaboration tools

- **Social environments** can be used by teams to share ideas, to break the monotony of tasks, to interact in a different way or simply as an opportunity to build relationships.

  Conventional: kitchen, café, bar

  Less conventional: large open space, table tennis table, external space.

Once you've selected the right kind of environment for your activity, you need to ensure that you make each personality type feel comfortable within it. If you're holding a workshop, for example, a more introverted person might not feel comfortable about speaking up in the way an extroverted person would. This is why it's really important that you get to know each person's personality.

In a workshop I ran to identify risks, I would approach all of those who didn't generally speak up in large workshops and ask for their input via a simple template by email. I received more than 15 suggestions, which I was able to use to produce a consolidated register. This was then circulated to the group before the session.

Project leaders don't turn everything into a meeting. They take the time to think about the most appropriate approach for each situation. They recognise that different people require different spaces to do their best work and they work hard to create these spaces.

Organisations have more than enough meeting rooms; they just don't have enough people who know how to use them appropriately.

ACTIONS

DO: Think about the kind of environment you need in the situation you face.

DO: Ensure you tailor your approach to meet the needs of the personalities in the room.

POST: Not every meeting needs a meeting room. #ProjectBook

CHAPTER 33

HIRE FOR CULTURAL FIT

'Hiring for cultural fit' is something I often hear, yet very few projects (or organisations) do it well. You need to know and be able to describe your culture, and you need to understand the people in the project team and the skills they bring. This means not just their subject matter skills, but their values, personality type and potential.

Slack CEO Stewart Butterfield looks for humility and an acknowledgement that luck has played some part in their success and places great emphasis on diversity: 'If you don't have people who come from different backgrounds and experiences, you'll miss out on meeting the needs of groups of customers'.

The key to hiring the right people is understanding the personalities you already have in your team. Once you know your team, and you have collectively developed the culture you need to get the project delivered, you can look for the personalities and skills to fill the gaps. Quite often the best-qualified person isn't the right person for the culture you have created.

I always prided myself on working with my teams to develop a culture that people wanted to join because of a vibrancy they could feel or see or had heard about. This was no accident; it was well planned, and it took time and courage. When I was hiring, the culture was never compromised, no matter how urgent our need. At each interview I would take the time to explain the culture using simple statements and examples of how we worked together. Netflix took this a step further by developing a 'Culture Deck', a set of presentation slides that neatly and succinctly describes their culture. I love this idea and now work with lots of organisations to help them do likewise.

Once, during a large program of work, I appointed an executive assistant to the position of project manager. It wasn't a popular decision at the time and many questioned my judgement, despite my track record. I did it because her personality type wasn't represented in the team at that time. She had the ability to communicate well with difficult stakeholders. She could challenge the status quo around the way we currently worked and brought an energy and passion for her work that our culture then needed.

She was a positive force internally and externally and lifted those around her to a different level. They could see the relationships she built with the sponsor and steering committee and were keen to learn from her. All this despite never having (formally) managed a project before. Because she wasn't wedded to poor practices of the past, she took the way we delivered to new levels. I spent a great deal of time mentoring her in those early days. She was a hire I'm still proud of today.

Of course, there have been times I've got it wrong too. In the early days it was because I hadn't taken enough time to understand the potential of those already in the team. Nothing undermines a person's confidence in their leader more than being passed over for something they passionately believed they could achieve. There was also the time I forgot to ask a candidate which football team they supported... (Note for non-Brits, this is usually a key hiring criterion.)

One of the biggest challenges for project leaders is mixing introverts and extroverts, which is often like bringing the Montagues and Capulets together to form a bowling team.

Carl Jung first introduced the concepts of introversion and extroversion as extremes of a person's personality. Put simply, introverts direct their thoughts and feelings inward, whereas extroverts direct their energy outward, seeking to engage with others. Project teams need a mix of both. Too many introverts and the project will lack energy and the outward communication necessary to succeed. Too many extroverts and the project will lack the attention to detail and hands-on effort required to get the job done.

Getting the culture right is seen as so important that as many as 70 per cent of organisations in the US are now reportedly including personality testing in their hiring process; the personality testing business is worth $500 million a year and growing. Happiness at work breeds productivity and productivity breeds positive project results and experiences.

The 1985 film *The Breakfast Club* charted the interactions between the differing personalities and upbringings of a brain, an athlete, a princess, an outcast and a criminal. While your project can probably do without the latter, it absolutely needs all of the others. Oh, and the project leader will usually be the princess, regardless of gender!

ACTIONS

DO: Get to know the project team personally and collectively in order to be able to add the right people in the future.

WATCH: *The Breakfast Club* (d. John Hughes, 1985), because it's a classic!

POST: Getting the right mix of people is critical to the success of the project. #ProjectBook

CHAPTER 34

START AS YOU MEAN TO GO ON

One role I took involved three interviews. The first was with the recruiting agent to assess my suitability for the organisation in terms of skill set. Next came a first interview with the hiring manager and one of his peers to assess my cultural fit and my attitude towards team building, project management excellence and the like. A third interview, over coffee with the hiring manager and one of the team, focused on some of the specific challenges they were facing and how I would deal with them.

I enjoy interviews, and these were no different. At the end of the third I was confident I would get the work, and I received a positive result the next day. On starting the assignment two weeks later, the hiring manager (my new line manager) wasn't available owing to meeting commitments. In fact he wasn't even on site. It took 20 minutes for someone to pick me up from reception. When I got to my desk, nothing had been set up and no instructions had been left for me.

Being full of initiative I worked my way around the office, introducing myself to people, and started making a list based on the conversations we'd had at the interview. After lunch I received a call from my line manager, who told me to read the intranet and complete the compliance 'exams', of which there were five, each taking between 30 minutes and an hour. I was also sent the acronym dictionary so I could familiarise myself with the corporate terminology.

What was unusual about this scenario was ... well, nothing. It happens time and time again in organisations (and projects) and does nothing to inspire confidence in the new employee, who has been extensively and expensively (in time at least) hired. It's an immediate demonstration that people aren't considered as that important, despite everything said at the interview. Excuses will be made ('I have a governance meeting every Monday that I just can't get out of') and pretty soon—within 30 days according to one survey—we've decided whether or not it's an organisation we want to be a part of.

As a project leader it's your job to make new team members feel part of the team from the very first minute, and this means blocking out (at least) two days to do just that. Talya N. Bauer recommends what she calls the four Cs to successfully integrate new people:

- **Compliance**. Ensure new hires understand the organisation's policies and regulations, from health and safety to acceptable internet usage.

- **Clarification**. Ensure new hires understand their responsibilities and what you expect of them in the next week, month, three months and so on.

- **Culture**. Give them an overview of the way you do things, what's acceptable and what's not. Also use this opportunity to encourage them to add their own ideas through the regular team catch-ups you'll have.

- **Connection**. Introduce them to the team and stakeholders, and ensure they know where to go to get information.

At the very minimum you need to set their goals. According to the aforementioned survey, 60 per cent of companies interviewed don't do this at all. People take project roles to advance their career, to challenge themselves or to be part of something unique. Having taken the time to hire the right person, it's critical to your culture and continued success that you induct them in the right way. If you don't, don't be surprised if they underperform or leave within the first 30 days.

ACTIONS

DO: Clarify a new hire's role and goals, introduce the team and explain the culture.

READ: 'Onboarding New Employees: Maximizing Success' by Talya N. Bauer.

POST: Onboarding my new team member is the most important thing I'm doing this week. #ProjectBook

CHAPTER 35

SOUNDTRACK TO YOUR SUCCESS

My first job after leaving school was in a bank, and one of my early roles was in the counting house. This was a small, dark room where a group of about eight people counted the money that came in over the counter or via armoured trucks and bagged it up ready for redistribution.

There was no natural light in the room and no air conditioning and money is, well, dirty. Yet people really enjoyed working in there, mainly because it was one of the only places in the office where you could play music and sing. So we did.

We learned the words to ridiculous songs ('Didn't We Almost Have It All' by Whitney Houston is a particularly vivid memory) and goaded each other on our respective musical tastes. It did wonders for the culture. We got the work done, we were never anxious or angry, and people frequently came down to visit us in the hope of joining in one of our impromptu karaoke sessions. Particularly at Christmas when every day conjured up Nat King Cole, Bing Crosby, Slade and, of course, Band Aid.

Having always been a music lover, I made sure to incorporate it into my own project cultures, buoyed by the knowledge that the research supported my own early experiences. A University of Sheffield research study found that 79 per cent of people would benefit from listening to music at work. 'When music listening in the work environment is encouraged by project directors and the workers are amenable to music listening,' reported researcher Teresa Lesiuk, 'then certainly music listening has a positive effect'.

Note: I'm not advocating that you get your guitar out — no one wants to hear your rendition of 'Space Oddity'. Except your mum of course. She's still super proud and wonders why you gave it up to work in an office... Also, you do have to be a good multi-tasker, as your reading comprehension and memorisation will both be affected, particularly if the music is fast and loud.

Background music can be a challenge in open-plan offices, so in these situations headphones should be considered. When it's piped directly into your ears, though, it ceases to enhance the culture.

And wearing headphones isn't something I'd recommend for project managers as it reduces their approachability. One option is to designate a particular day to update your project controls (Friday always worked best for me), in which case let your team know.

Like everything in office culture, playing music in the background isn't for everyone, so it's something that needs to be talked about and agreed within the team early on in project planning. You could create a weekly music rota or select a different radio station each week.

But I do recommend that music be included in your project culture. It has a positive calming effect, it's a mood changer and a talking point, and it may even serve as a springboard to an appearance on *The Voice*! Once the project has been completed, of course.

ACTIONS

DO: Have a music rota! It's a great topic of conversation and means everyone gets their turn.

LISTEN: To anything! Although check first that it's safe for work.

POST: I'm looking at ways to introduce music into our workplace. #ProjectBook

CHAPTER 36

KEEP STAKEHOLDERS SATISFIED

Recently I was engaged by the head of an IT department who had a problem with 'the business going around us for their project delivery' (their words). The first question I asked was, 'Why are they so dissatisfied with the service you provide that they would do this?' The answer, disconcertingly, was, 'They don't get the way we do projects'.

I spent some time reviewing their project portfolio, to find that 11 of their 12 projects were considered to be off-track. Their measures were based on a percentage variation (at a point in time) on the traditional triple constraints of time, cost and scope that I first mentioned in the preface of this book.

When heading up project departments I always ensured that we had in place metrics to capture our statistics around on-time and on-budget delivery. CEOs, CIOs and CFOs have insisted that hitting budget and time targets are the benchmarks for successful project delivery. That's a dated view now, because ultimately if the stakeholders are dissatisfied, then *everything* should be flagged as off-track. Stakeholder satisfaction, however, isn't a metric that's captured or reported on at all, except when it's too late.

All projects start out with the best of intentions, of course. Their initiation is driven by the stakeholders, who are involved at the start when their requirements are determined. They should be included in the planning and delivery teams in order to set the project up for success. Then, for some reason, project managers neglect to check the health of this relationship as the project progresses.

The concept of customer service or advocacy is studied long and hard in product- and service-oriented industries. IT departments survey customers when they're asked to resolve issues with hardware or software. In the billion-dollar project management industry, however, we shrug our shoulders and look to the triangle.

In 1997, Richard L. Oliver defined customer satisfaction as 'pleasurable fulfilment...where the confirmation or disconfirmation of pre-consumption expectations is the essential determinant of satisfaction. This means that customers have a certain predicted product performance in mind prior to consumption'. Which means it is measurable from the start. We should use face-to-face meetings, customised surveys (given the project layers) or whatever it takes to capture the 'pulse of the stakeholder' with regard to the delivery of their project.

Project leaders do this consistently. They speak with their sponsors and ask direct questions: 'Are you comfortable with progress?', 'Are we progressing as you expected?', 'Is there anything else you'd like me to be doing?', 'Do you have all the information you need?' Even where this occurs, though, I've seen very few project status reports that record the level of sponsor satisfaction, and I think that's a mistake.

Ahola and Kujala (2018) comment, 'There is a very limited amount of study that focuses on impact of customer satisfaction in project-business. It can be also argued that in project-business each customer relationship is specific and...involves a very high risk of making wrong conclusions'. That this is the only paper I can find that relates to measuring customer satisfaction in project management tells you everything you need to know about the importance it is given by suppliers of delivery services (internal or external).

Returning to the example I began with, I spent four weeks interviewing both customers and project managers and found that no trust or respect existed, but, worse still, neither party had tried to develop the relationship. This led to a sort of project stand-off where the customer felt they had no choice but to bring in their own people. They had money, and for the most part the time factor wasn't critical. They were frustrated by the constant shifting of the goalposts and the fact that the processes employed by project managers appeared to be getting in the way of progress.

At the end of the engagement I made a couple of tweaks to the way the project was initiated and reported, which completely changed the emphasis of the relationship. Knowing the satisfaction of the customer was as important as the time, scope and budget ensured that no activity was undertaken without the collaboration and decision-making input of the key stakeholders.

Project leaders put service to their stakeholders at the very heart of what they do, because they know they are the only people who can provide feedback on whether or not they've been successful.

ACTIONS

DO: Meet with your stakeholders regularly and get their feedback on what's working well and what's not, or else use a tool to do the work for you.

READ: 'Measuring the Service Provided by Project Management' by Colin D. Ellis.

POST: Stakeholder satisfaction is the most important measure in any project. #ProjectBook

CHAPTER 37

GOSSIP: THE CULTURE KILLER

We've all done it, and even being the best versions of ourselves, we continue to do it. We don't usually mean to be destructive when we do it, yet it has the capacity to destroy everything, including the way we feel about ourselves. We dress it up in all kinds of ways to justify it to ourselves. We're venting, getting things off our chest, not wishing to be personal. We even 'apologise' before we do it: 'I'm sorry, but he's an idiot…' And after we do it: 'I shouldn't have said that, sorry'. Yet we still do it.

It's a behaviour that for the most part is unconscious, but it's something that needs to be dealt with. A study by Teamworks found that 21 per cent of staff regularly gossip at work, with corporate challenges (including projects) accounting for 86 per cent of it. A gossip session averages 15 minutes and an active gossiper burns up 65 hours of productive time every year.

Gossipers are people we generally avoid and, in our turn, gossip about. We don't understand them, their views or 'just what their problem is'. Yet gossipers are people too, and quite often the things they talk about are valid and should be taken on board. There's a right way to do it, though, and whispering to a colleague in the kitchen isn't that way.

You'll recognise gossip when you hear the following openers:

- 'I shouldn't be telling you this…'
- 'Did you hear what he/she said to me?'

- 'I don't normally talk about people, but...'
- 'Don't tell anyone else, but...'
- 'How much do you think he/she earns?'
- 'Did you see him/her at the Christmas party?'

Gossip in a project, as anywhere else in the workplace, is a culture killer. It's like Dutch elm disease, silently eating away at your culture and setting it on a path to destruction. Gossip:

- causes pain and resentment
- decreases productivity
- undermines trust
- increases anxiety
- wastes time and energy
- compromises standards and professional integrity
- undermines confidence in management.

Project leaders should never engage in any kind of gossip and should be quick to stop it when they hear it. They should stay true to their leadership instincts, set an example and deal with anyone who behaves in a way that doesn't meet the expectations of the team.

If you find yourself gossiping you should stop, apologise, walk away from the conversation and write down your thoughts. Is there a problem that you're not addressing with your project sponsor, or do you need to talk to a friend outside of work about how the situation made you feel so you can do something about it?

By writing your feelings down or taking them outside the office, you're acknowledging the damage they could do if you share them with colleagues. Once you've done that, you are in a stronger position to do something about the situation. If there wasn't a situation to begin with, then you'll feel better about yourself!

When dealing with gossipers you need to handle them in a consistent way, once you've established that a principle of your culture is not to talk behind each other's backs. I've had to do this with members of my teams on numerous occasions. They will be defensive ('I'm not gossiping!'), bemused ('I wasn't aware that's what I was doing') or contrite ('Sorry'). Whatever their response, remind them of their obligation to the team culture and ask if there is anything you can do to help.

Gossip is an unwelcome distraction from your project. Stop it now before it spreads further.

ACTIONS

DO: Ensure that your team agrees to be honest with each other at all times.

DO: Call people out when you hear them gossiping. Not doing so will undermine your role as a leader and the culture you've created.

POST: Project leaders say nice things behind people's backs. #ProjectBook

CHAPTER 38
KEEP IT SIMPLE

Jason Fox, author of *The Game Changer*, says, 'If the concept is complicated, no one will understand what it takes to change'. In other words, if your project team is playing buzzword bingo during one of your meetings, then you've already lost the dressing room. Oh the irony of my mixed metaphors.

I thought I'd share with you some actual objectives that were written into project plans, along with my understanding of what they really mean. Authors and organisations have been protected (although for a bottle of single malt they're yours):

1. 'To clarify the extent to which the efficiencies will corporately cascade' (to find out who will lose their jobs and when)

2. 'To instigate a mechanism by which change responsibilities are understood and executed' (to get people to actually change this time rather than only paying lip-service to it)

3. 'To reimagine the internal mechanisms by which approvals are gained or rejected for external proposals' (to get better at choosing suppliers because we currently suck at it)

4. 'To uplift the capability such that stretch targets can be met' (to give our people the skills to meet our ridiculous targets—or at least stop crying so much)

5. 'To maintain velocity while implementing an innovation construct' (to give our people more to do and reduce the time for new stuff while saying there'll be time for new stuff)

6. 'To design, build and implement a CRM capable of flex' (to put all the information from that spreadsheet into something easy to maintain and read that we can add to in the future, if we're lucky).

Now I've had a little fun with the answers, but hopefully you get the point.

Australian software company Atlassian use a plain English policy, and one look at their values will show you they're serious! I'm not repeating them here; go look for yourself.

One of the biggest mysteries for me when I work with organisations on their projects is why they make it so hard to understand what they're doing. Not only that, but when I speak to their people, I find they don't understand either. Fifty-page business cases using language that even the smartest person can't understand—all to justify…something, to themselves. It's all efficiency-this, and capacity-that, and other big words to try to convince themselves this is a great thing to do. It's needless. Not the justification—that's obviously important—but the 20000 words and 60-page PowerPoint presentation, when a sheet of A3 would probably do.

In Deloitte's 2015 *Human Capital Trends Report*, 75 per cent of senior leaders admitted their organisations were too complex (in their structures and language), yet only half had practices in place to simplify. Complexity disengages staff. It causes them to stop and question the 'why' and gives them the opportunity to use a lack of understanding as an excuse for not getting involved.

Leonardo Da Vinci said, 'Simplicity is the ultimate sophistication'. There's no easier way to demonstrate your sophistication than by using language that everyone (and I do mean everyone) can understand. Project leaders take the confusion out of their projects. They make the goals easy to understand, the conversations quicker and progress more transparent. They shun acronyms or at least make sure they're recognisable to their audience. They understand that complexity is hardwired into organisations, and they never stop questioning what things mean and choosing to demonstrate what simplification looks like.

If you want a place to start, you could follow the example of the Department of Foreign Affairs and Trade in Australia, who held an acronym-free day. Everyone paid a gold-coin donation to participate and another every time they used an acronym. They kept things simple, had fun and raised lots of money for a children's charity. Wouldn't it be great if every working day was like that? It's just a pity they didn't make it an acronym-free year. Now *that* would have facilitated an innovation environment worthy of government recognition.

ACTIONS

DO: Think carefully about your words and messaging. Are they fit for every audience?

READ: Atlassian's values on their website.

POST: Da Vinci said that 'Simplicity is the ultimate sophistication', and from today I'm getting sophisticated! #ProjectBook

CHAPTER 39

HAVE SOME FUN

I've got to be honest, as soon as someone tells me something is going to be fun, my immediate thought is, 'No it won't. It won't be because you're telling me it has to be fun. So it's not spontaneous fun but fun by design, and it's being designed by you. Mr No Fun'.

Okay, so maybe I'm not that bad, but you get the point. Fun can't be forced. It just happens when we take the time to find out what each of us finds funny. If it were an equation it would look something like this:

Challenge + success + recognition + team morale x project leader / humour + work environment x trust = fun

If none of those are happening or one piece of the equation is missing, there'll be little to smile about.

Fun is expected much more these days than it used to be. When I first started work, there were many managers (white, middle-class males, obviously) who ruled by fear. We called certain managers 'sir' and we couldn't be seen enjoying ourselves at our desks. We could let ourselves go in the staffroom (and sometimes the stationery cupboard, but that's a whole other book) and that was about it.

According to a recent BrightHR survey, 79 per cent of Millennials entering the workforce believe that fun is important for getting things done. The 21st Fortune 100 companies survey backs this up, with 81 per cent of the employees at these organisations saying they were fun places to work. And it works, as the combined profits in these companies were up 22 per cent on the previous year. So here's a new equation:

Fun + productivity = success

One of my favourite Mark Twain quotes (I've got two and I forget the other one) is, 'The human race has only one really effective weapon, and that is laughter. The moment it arises, all our hardnesses yield, all our irritations and resentments slip away and a sunny spirit takes their place'. So how do you go about building that sunny spirit? Well first, you need to embrace your own sense of humour (see chapter 12). Second, you have to stop taking yourself so seriously. Yes, you.

At every training session or workshop I run, I write 'Remember rule number six' on the whiteboard or flipchart. (It's based on a story told by Benjamin and Rosamund Stone Zander in *The Art of Possibility* whose message is 'Don't take yourself too seriously'.) Whenever I do this someone will ask, but what's rule number five? My answer, of course, is, 'Remember rule number six'.

Thirdly, get the team together and ask them — informally — what makes work fun for them. A great working culture is the sum of us all, so for it to be fun for all, we need to find out what makes people laugh. For some it's *Monty Python*, for others it's cat videos, and for one person in the world it's *Mrs Brown's Boys*. Whatever it is, find out. Project leaders I've known have used the following in their cultures:

- desk decorating
- crazy sock day
- bring your pet to work day
- humour hour
- dress-up Friday
- 'the way we were' photos of team members
- movie nights
- paper plane competitions
- the blame game (you get to blame everyone else but yourself — for everything — for one minute)
- board-game lunch hours
- team sports events.

The list goes on and providing the work gets done — that's still really important; this isn't *Police Academy* — you'll create something that people will want to be part of time and time again.

I read a statistic about babies recently. I'm a dad, so I do that every now and then. It was in a paper by Mary Rau-Foster and it said that the average pre-schooler laughs or smiles 400 times a day. That number drops to only 15 times a day by the time they reach age 35. The irony was, it made me sad to read that statistic.

Who told us to stop laughing and smiling in the office? Who's creating these work cultures that are sapping the humour from our brains? Who's got the power to change that?

Project leaders don't act like pre-schoolers, but they understand the value that laughter brings to individual wellbeing, team morale and project success.

ACTIONS

DO: Remember rule number 6.

READ: *The Pleasures and Sorrows of Work* by Alain de Botton.

WATCH: Every episode of *The Office*. It's funny because it's true (but don't do any of it!).

POST: Having a laugh is so important to helping us do our best work. #ProjectBook

CHAPTER 40

RUN MEETINGS THAT DON'T SUCK

We have a problem with meetings. Most of them suck. Like, really badly, and for some reason we seem reticent to do anything about that.

Some fear challenging the existing culture, others have decided to become part of the current culture, and a last group just don't know how to do it well because the meetings they attend, well, suck.

In the US alone over 25 million meetings are conducted every day and the unproductive ones cost, on average, US$37 billion annually. If ever there was a statistic to persuade us of the need to change the way we do them, that's it. It's like buying a membership to a gym, turning up every day, then never exercising. I've definitely never done that, and I know you haven't either.

Meetings are generally unproductive for three reasons:

1. The emotional intelligence of the attendees is low.

2. The attendees are not engaged in the subject matter.

3. The meeting has no structure.

Meetings will fall into one of the following quadrants (overleaf).

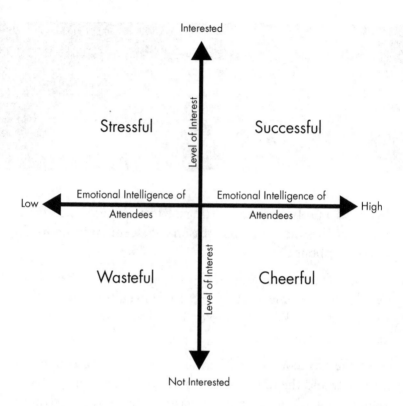

- **Wasteful** meetings are those that just shouldn't happen at all. These are the ones we call 'meetings for meeting's sake'. Either that or they're talkfests that take 10 minutes of content and spin it out into an hour. They're a waste of time, energy and, for some, emotion.

- **Cheerful** meetings are those where we spend the first half hour talking about anything other than what we actually should be talking about. Then when we do get around to the subject matter, we smile and pay it no more than lip-service. No actions, no decisions, no problems.

- **Stressful** meetings occur when people arrive late and spend the entire time on their phone/laptop/tablet. Or else someone talks for much longer than they should, there are frequent arguments, and you leave the meeting no closer to discussing or resolving the issues at hand.

- **Successful** meetings are those in which you feel you understand the purpose, your role, the content and the expected outcome. They run exactly to the agenda and finish on or before time. To hold successful meetings, every time, you need to put thought into the approach required to resolve an issue, get a decision or provide an update to a team. Meetings reflect your leadership, the culture you have created and your ability to deliver a project in a timely manner. They need to be good.

Ensure that your meetings have the following features:

- There's a reason for the meeting (not every conversation has to be a meeting).

- There's an agenda that's adhered to.

- If there's pre-reading, it's succinct and has been sent out with enough time to give attendees the chance to read it.

- The meeting starts on time and ends early or on time (having achieved its objectives).

- You only invite people—usually no more than six to eight—who will participate (no 'FYIs').

- The meeting is well managed and the chair addresses behavioural issues when they occur.

- Guests attend for their slot on the agenda only, not for the whole meeting.

- Devices are put away or on silent, unless being used to take notes (see chapter 8 on active listening).

- Actions are decided on and recapped at the end of the meeting so the owners understand what they have to do.

- There is an element of fun — and preferably chocolate biscuits. Everyone attends meetings in the hope of chocolate biscuits.

- Ensure you use a range of meeting styles and environments, depending on the situation.

The agile software development approach (see chapter 43) has brought the stand-up meeting into the mainstream, which is great. The Japanese have been doing this in manufacturing for years.

I used the *Chourei* (literal translation 'morning-bow') to run every morning meeting with one team I managed. It was a 20-minute opportunity for me to disseminate information from the meetings I had attended the day before, to talk about the work we needed to get done that day, and to check in with the team to ensure they were okay and there were no issues that required resolution.

At another organisation I used a similar approach, but we would go for a walk. Exercise and information — the perfect combination!

Agile stand-ups (as they're known) introduced visual accountability — in the form of cards — that are updated every morning, so the whole team is aware of progress. At the meetings, held around a large wall that carries a list of the tasks that are time-boxed to 15 minutes or less, individuals provide an update on what they're currently working on. The meetings are held daily to ensure momentum isn't lost. This wouldn't work for all meetings, but it should be considered for those that require a short, sharp appraisal of progress or to ensure the stakeholders know where you're at.

Regardless of where the meeting is held, how long it lasts or whether you're sitting down or standing, you need to ensure that all meetings have the characteristics outlined in the previous pages and that they are productive. If your meetings are not achieving their objectives, learn and change the approach for the next one.

Oh, and stop starting them on the hour or at half-past the hour. Microsoft Outlook is to blame for that. Start them at ten past the hour instead, and the attendees may have a chance of getting there on time.

ACTIONS

DO: Adopt one characteristic and implement it at your next meeting. Suggest that others join you in making your organisation's meetings more productive.

READ: Dermot Crowley's podcast 'The Six Ps of Productive Meetings'.

POST: Our project meetings make a difference — yours can too! #ProjectBook

CHAPTER 41

CELEBRATE SUCCESS

'The more you praise and celebrate your project,' Oprah tells us, 'the more there is in your project to celebrate'. Okay, so she said 'life', not 'project', but I'm pretty sure she wouldn't mind me twisting her words ever so slightly. (If you do mind, Oprah, let me know through the usual channels — that is, the letter from your lawyer.)

The FA Cup is a football institution in the UK. It's a competition that every single football club in the country can enter. The dream for amateur players is to make it to the 'third round proper'. This is where the big teams (Everton, Arsenal, Manchester United, Manchester City, Spurs and so on) enter the competition, so there's a chance that postmen, butchers and joiners could end up playing against millionaires in front of 40 000 people.

Football fans and players around the country celebrate every cup win as if it were the final itself.

They do this for a number of reasons:

- **Confidence**. A winning team is a confident team. Every win builds confidence that the next round can be won, regardless of the opposition.

- **Unity**. They come together to celebrate what has just been achieved and to build team spirit.

- **Optimism**. It gives them the chance to focus on the positives in what's just happened.

- **Break from the norm**. They may not be doing well elsewhere, but this win gives them the chance to celebrate something different.

- **Reward**. For some it may be financial, for others the recognition or admiration is enough.

- **Motivation**. It builds team morale ahead of the next challenge.

- **Reminder**. They review what they've achieved and what they're aiming for.

Look for ways to mark the milestones.

Very few projects receive trophies or admiration on implementation. In fact, you may be lucky to get a thank you, yet all the reasons above apply. Project leaders ensure that each significant milestone is celebrated in unique and different ways.

Applying the seven reasons to celebrate listed above, here are some examples of what you can do:

- Personally congratulate those who were involved in achieving the milestone.

- Have a morning or afternoon tea, a walk in the park or a drink at the pub.

- Highlight what went well. Have a 'Great stuff!' or 'Ways we're smashing it!' board.

- Give people an opportunity to get away from the tasks that currently consume them by changing the pace of work.

- Buy coffee, lunch, a gift or vouchers—just make sure you're not too generic with your generosity.

- Use the success as a launching pad for the next challenge, and take the confidence into that.

- Keep a visible progress chart you can tick off, or if you're using agile techniques (see part III: Methods), move a card to 'done'.

ACTIONSok

Nothing says 'winning team' better than one that consistently celebrates its successes and milestones, no matter how small they might be. Celebrate your cup run while it lasts.

ACTIONS

DO: Make the time to celebrate success. Who doesn't want to be on a winning team?

WATCH: 'Celebration' by Kool and the Gang — go on, wig out!

POST: Celebrating success is critical to building team confidence. #ProjectBook

PART III
METHODS

Methods, processes and techniques are important in guiding project managers towards the right approach to take to deliver projects to the stakeholders' expectations.

They provide a pathway to completion, show where key decision-points are and help project managers determine the information they need to be successful. These tools are often referred to as the technical side of project management. They are the things you can get certificates in, if you're that way inclined.

You should learn about PMBoK, visual facilitation, mind-mapping, work breakdown structures, Kanban, six-sigma, PRINCE2, Scrum, estimating, investment logic mapping and other techniques. Almost everything about the technical side of project management can be found on the internet or in books, so start by hitting your local library. There's no need for you to pay thousands of dollars for courses for this stuff—save that for the more important 'soft skills' training, although there are some techniques that are best learned from a trained facilitator.

Be relentless in your search for techniques that can both liven up your approach to delivery and provide much-needed clarity or speed of resolution on some of the issues you face.

Design thinking is a recent example that provides a framework for creativity and innovation.

The chapters that follow provide you with an overview of the two main approaches that projects can take, which are styled as *waterfall* and *agile*. Each has pros and cons and I've done my best to give you insights into these. Neither one is better than the other; their strength lies in how they're applied and scaled. For any project method to work it has to be tailored to suit your organisation, and your stakeholders need to understand what's required of them too.

We'll also look at a couple of techniques that are identified time and again in project management surveys as 'weaknesses' and yet that I believe all project managers should know, regardless of the method being employed.

Too many organisations (including those that provide advice on project management) still think that simply implementing a method or sending everyone on a certification course will guarantee delivery on time and to budget. It won't. This is like giving everyone a medal for crossing the finish line, regardless of their time or whether they cheated to get there.

Great project leaders build cultures that recognise the importance of methods, processes and techniques and therefore never need to be told to use them. These are the people who win the race, and they never stop running.

Shakespeare's Hamlet said, 'Though this be madness, yet there is method in't'. When it comes to project management, however, too often there's only madness in the application of methods. Don't fall into that trap.

CHAPTER 42

WATERFALL

What is meant by a *waterfall* project? The waterfall model entered the corporate lexicon in the 1970s to describe a design approach in software engineering by the TRW Defense and Space Systems Group. It was used to signify the cascading of customer requirements towards implementation (see diagram below).

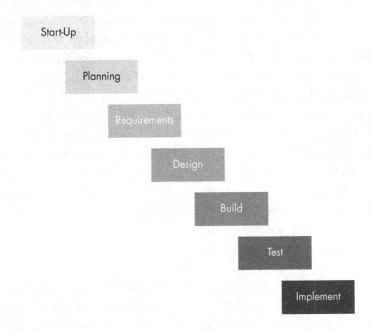

Bell and Thayer (1976) concluded that 'problems with requirements are frequent and important. Differences between types of requirement problems is quite small between projects. Improved techniques for developing and stating requirements are needed to deal with these problems'.

Amazingly, these issues still exist today, more than 40 years on.

Essentially, the waterfall approach requires that you gather everything up before you start the project: the needs and priorities of the customer; the design of how it will be built and put together; how it will be tested to make sure (a) it works and (b) the stakeholders are happy; and how it will be maintained once the project is completed.

The best way to think of it is like a big Lego set. You have everything in the box—all the pieces, the instructions, the tools (if required). Then all you have to do is review the design and estimate who you'll need to be involved, how long you think you'll need, the quality expectations and how much it will cost. Led by my son, the people required for this project would be him, with my support for larger, more complex sections. The time taken would depend on the size of the set—anywhere between 30 minutes and four hours. The quality expectations are that it will look exactly like it does on the front of the box while all the moving parts should work perfectly. The cost for his time would of course be $0 because he's 10 and has nothing better to do, although he'd be looking at $2000 per hour (or part thereof) for my help. What? I'm self-employed, time is money.

Well, you get the idea.

For a waterfall project to work you need to know a lot up front and should start with an idea, not a solution. If you start with a solution in mind, then the components of the approach are weighted towards what you've seen, not what's most important for the organisation.

The more you know up front, the less a project should cost (in theory), as there'll be little rework required towards the back end of the project, when everything gets more expensive.

It requires more work in the planning stage to collect information and will likely have to go through a series of 'stage gates' to ensure it will still deliver what was promised in the business case. It needs a dedicated sponsor and a steering committee who can help guide decision making, a definition of the culture required and, of course, a project leader to ensure that change is well controlled throughout.

Current thinking around the world is that waterfall projects don't work and organisations are falling over themselves to implement more 'agile' ways of working. Yet some of the best projects I ever worked on were waterfall projects. For an organisation to achieve its strategic objectives, and for its projects to be continually successful, it will need to consider and be great at delivering both kinds of approaches.

Pros and cons of the waterfall project

Pros	Cons
It's broken up into distinct stages, which aids thinking and communication.	It can be too rigid (i.e. you can't start B because A isn't yet finished).
Because you understand the needs up front, you're able to better plan for the unexpected.	In the wrong hands, it can be overly bureaucratic.
Some people like the certainty of a linear approach (i.e. A+B+C+D=E).	If there's too much change, the waterfall can start flowing upwards.

CHAPTER 43

AGILE

Agile is the current buzzword in organisations worldwide. If you're reading this in 2025 (hey, you never know), then you're probably wondering what all the fuss was about.

Essentially, we're currently rubbish at delivering projects because—some would say—we try to define too much at the start (using the waterfall method) and it doesn't allow for the customers' confusion, whims or dramatic U-turns.

As a concept, agile has been around for a while, but it came to prominence in 2001 with the signing of the Agile Manifesto after 17 software developers met at the Snowbird ski resort in Utah to discuss better and quicker ways to get products to market. Agile values include:

- individuals and interactions over processes and tools
- working software over comprehensive documentation
- customer collaboration over contract negotiation
- responding to change over following a plan.

These values are supported by 12 principles for developing 'agile software'. There are numerous agile methods, and software developers can get into really heated discussions about which is best. The most popular ones are Scrum, Lean, Kanban, XP (Extreme Programming) and DSDM (Dynamic Systems Development Method).

Compared with the waterfall method (A+B+C+D=E), agile approaches are much more fluid, often comprising a series of shorter projects within a project, with the product being developed iteratively. This means a team of people works on the requirements, design, build, testing and implementation of one smaller component to create the first iteration of the product, usually called a 'sprint' — A=E version 1, A+B=E version 2, A+B+C=E version 3 and so on.

Agile projects still require strong leadership and the development of a different culture. Contrary to what you might think, there still needs to be a plan. As Alistair Cockburn (one of the signatories of the Agile Manifesto) said at a conference in Melbourne, 'If people think that agile is a way to rid ourselves of project managers, they're wrong. On the contrary, we need good ones more than ever'. What sets those who lead agile projects apart from those who deliver waterfall projects is their mindset.

While there is a structure to agile methods such as Scrum, there's also a fluidity to product delivery that you don't find in waterfall projects. Those leading and sponsoring agile projects need to be open to constant change and comfortable with ambiguity. People who are good at managing waterfall projects may not necessarily make good agile project managers, and vice versa. However, as with most things in our world, you can learn the skills, providing you have the right mindset and the determination to do so.

Pros and cons of agile project management

Pros	Cons
Agile is much more flexible in its approach to scope (i.e. there's no need to understand every detail up front).	It's often used as a way of short-cutting projects more suited to a waterfall approach.
You get to see your product develop (usually every two to four weeks).	People think it's a silver bullet and will tell you it's the only way to succeed. It's not.
The process is much more collaborative.	Stakeholders don't realise the time commitment involved.

CHAPTER 44

NO PLAN, NO PROJECT

One of the biggest problems that project management now faces is that it's losing the art of planning. That's a worry because if you don't have a plan, you don't have a project. It really is that simple. A plan is the foundation for *all* activity. Whether you're using a waterfall or an agile method, you still need a plan. For an agile project, you may plan only the next two to four weeks, while for a waterfall project you'll be looking at the first three months at least.

A plan is a critical prerequisite when seeking to justify an investment and create some excitement and momentum around a project because, as leadership expert John Kotter says, 'The plan is where you build your guiding coalition to support your activities'. Building the plan is the most important project activity.

Almost every organisation I've worked with wants to spend too long justifying a project (to itself, usually) and almost no time on planning a project. Then they wonder why their project gets into trouble almost immediately.

Whenever I started a new job and reviewed its projects, my first question of the project manager was, 'Can I see the plan, please?' Too often that was met with a blank look or, just as worryingly, was confused with a schedule (that's a list of tasks, not a project plan).

ME: 'Can I see the plan please?'

PM: 'Yes, it's here in Microsoft Project.'

ME: [*Sigh!*]

A recent Google survey asked, 'Which processes would derive the greatest benefit from increased collaboration?' The number one answer was *planning*.

A federal review of US government-funded technology projects determined that 352 projects, totalling about US$23.4 billion were poorly planned.

Less than a third of project managers interviewed for the 2015 Project Management Insight survey said they always submit their project plans to their stakeholders for approval prior to work commencing. You get the picture. It's a mess and it needs to change if the project management profession is to regain its credibility.

Building the plan should be your first involvement as a project manager and you should grab the planning activity with relish. Insist on being given the time to do the work properly so the team can deliver the best possible output(s), and demand access—nicely, of course—to the right people.

First of all, get every single stakeholder together and say, 'Right, how do you want to do this?' Of course, as the project manager you have a multitude of approaches up your sleeve, but if you want collaboration (see chapter 30) you need to get the team to agree on the approach.

Note that I didn't ask, 'Who wants to be involved in the planning?' Those tumbleweeds you see in office corridors are a result of that very question.

It's too easy for those accountable for initiating a project to wash their hands of it the minute you get approval to proceed into planning, because there's a lot of work involved. If that happens you're already on the slippery slope to failure. For most projects, it's the project manager's job to pull the plan together based on the input of others, not to provide the input themselves.

As mentioned, the level of planning activity required will depend on the approach the project will be taking, with more upfront information being required for a more traditional (waterfall) delivery approach. However, the plan should never be so big and detailed that no one will ever read it. It needs to contain enough information to provide everyone with confidence that the products delivered will satisfy the customer's expectations.

To that end, the invitation to take part in the planning activity should be extended to absolutely everyone who has an interest in the project's success. Project leaders do this. They know that only with input from the people who will help implement the project can they possibly finalise:

- the benefits expected post-project
- the timelines for the project
- the scope
- the risks
- the stakeholders
- the objectives
- how it will need to be communicated and reported
- how the changes will be managed
- what the stages are
- who the project team will be and when they'll be needed

- what the cost for delivering the project will be

- the culture principles.

The schedule is built in throughout the planning activity and finalised at the end. It's introduced at the start of a project only when you've done something similar before and want to determine any differences this time around.

Without question, the plan (whether visual or printed) is the most important document in any project. It's more important than the business case, as it will demonstrate whether you can actually do the thing you want to do within the constraints you have. If it demonstrates that you can't, then you will have managed to save your reputation. Most organisations don't choose to do this. Project leaders insist on it.

ACTIONS

DO: Plan, plan, plan. Producing the plan is your job.

DON'T: Let anyone persuade you to skip planning or to rush it.

POST: The plan is the most important document of any project, so don't ask me to rush it. #ProjectBook

CHAPTER 45

WHY THIS? WHY NOW?

Here's the thing about the benefits of your projects: if your senior managers care — and I mean *really* care — about them, then their realisation won't be an issue. You deliver projects, and they have actions in place to get the benefits. Easy. As project leader, you get to see the fruits of your team's labours and the stakeholders get to reap the rewards. Everyone is happy.

I've worked for and with organisations where this has been the case. Not getting the benefits from projects just isn't a thing. They're in business plans and people's performance objectives and they're taken seriously. If the benefits are compromised, then the project is stopped or just never started.

From day one, as soon as the benefits are declared in business cases, senior managers need to be on the hook for them. If they declared cost savings, then these should be immediately deducted from the following year's budgets. If they're undertaken to mitigate risk, then at the conclusion of the project, the risk is no longer something you have to worry about.

At one organisation where I headed up the project division, we worked with the CFO to add 'budget line to be reduced' to the business case to stop senior managers erroneously declaring cost savings to make business cases look financially better. Within three months we'd changed the behaviour.

Unfortunately, for most organisations the realisation of benefits is still seen as unachievable.

Indeed, a KPMG survey of over 100 organisations in New Zealand found that only 21 per cent consistently achieve benefits from their projects—an appalling statistic and a clear failure of senior management.

Benefits are a big part of decision making. Without a realistic 'why', it's hard for the project leader to create the vision, passion and momentum needed to make the project a success. Executives often don't realise just how important realistic benefits are to a project manager and the planning process.

The expected benefits are the things you will always come back to when making decisions about what needs to be done. Whether it's designing, building, implementing or changing, every decision is driven by the stakeholder's expectations of the outcomes. If you don't know these at the start of the planning process, how will you ever really know what to build? Then, during implementation, how will you know that the change you make will add to the benefits expected by stakeholders?

They really are that important. A recent Gartner paper on healthcare IT systems stated, 'Projects are generally driven by a need to realise specific benefits through structured change. Benefits management and realisation seeks to move forward from the traditional investment appraisal approach and focus on the active planning of how benefits will be realised and measured'.

Project leaders get clear on the 'why' at the start and keep checking all the way through the project that they're on track to achieving it.

ACTIONS

DO: Take the time to understand and document the outcomes expected by the stakeholders.

DO: Continue throughout the project to track that the benefits will be achieved.

DON'T: Overcomplicate benefits.

POST: Knowing and tracking the benefits is critical to the success of the project. #ProjectBook

CHAPTER 46

SCALE FOR SUCCESS

'Despite more than 50 years of history and countless methodologies, advice and books,' noted the global research firm Gartner in 2015, 'IT projects keep failing'. I really enjoyed this report because although it talked about the things we haven't done to improve the profession in the past 50 years (something many commentaries do), it especially drew attention to the fact that organisations continue to make it hard for themselves.

This is something I talk about a lot when speaking to corporates. The reason organisations are burdened with 150-page business cases and endless layers of documentation is because they put them there—no one forces them to do it. They put them there because someone went on a 'best practice' course and decided that's what needed to be done to provide consistency. Some put them there because they think, as a government department, it's necessary to justify the spend. I worked in government for eight years and met regularly with auditors and regulators, who just wanted to see sound justification and be sure that sensible approaches had been adopted in delivering projects successfully, not that there were 150 pages of documentation.

In his book *Agile Project Management*, Jim Highsmith comments, 'Many project management practices and project managers are focussed on compliance activities not delivery value'. Of course, the statistics prove that implementing complex processes as a means of gaining consistency of delivery doesn't work (and never has), and that only through great people and great cultures can you achieve consistently good results. Despite this, millions of dollars continue to be wasted every year on process maturity assessments, which tell you how great the processes are that people aren't using.

The key to a successful framework is, of course, to keep it simple and to scale it for each project.

In a 2011 blog post on Oracle's 'Unified Method', Tom Spitz made three interesting observations:

- 'Too much method can be as risky as too little.'
- 'Don't serve the method, make it serve you.'
- 'The output of a task needn't be a document.'

Inflexible methods are a thing of the past. Every project demands a unique approach. Think about what absolutely needs to be done to deliver the project successfully. Do you need a 30-page business case or can you do it more succinctly?

The same goes for your project plan. Does it need to be in a document or can you put its components on a wall (and I don't mean a Gantt chart!) to make it visual? Do you need monthly rather than weekly meetings? Would 20-minute stand-up meetings work? If your organisation has a program management office (PMO), the greatest value it can add is in helping you create a unique and scaled approach for your project.

The methods we use to deliver our projects are a guide. You can't shortcut the justification for a project or the need for a plan and project controls. You can, however, scale these approaches so you only ever produce what Matthew Lyon calls 'Minimum Viable Documentation'.

ACTIONS

DO: Tailor your approach to each project you lead.

DO: Work with your PMO to improve the way each approach is scaled.

POST: I make sure my method is fit for purpose. #ProjectBook

CHAPTER 47

ESTIMATING

How long do you think it will take you to finish this book? I'm talking about actual reading time, eyes on the page. Four hours? Six hours? Two weeks? Some of you may choose to read just one chapter a day, in which case it'll take you 10 weeks or so. Whatever your calculation, it is likely that your estimates will be based on your:

- *history*—reading books of this length typically takes you five hours of reading time over two weeks

- *expertise*—as an experienced book reviewer you know that books of 250 pages take 3.5 hours a day over six days.

Shortcutting the estimation process—for waterfall projects especially—is one of the most common causes of problems later on in a project. A major PwC study in 2012 listed poor estimation as its number one reason for project failure, while another survey in 2016 had 'Improve resource planning and forecasting' as its number one priority for project managers.

Poor estimation is a result of poor project management. Good estimation comprises collaboration, transparency, repeatability and comparability. The more information that's available, the better the estimate will be at that point in time. It's your job to ensure that the estimates are the best that they can be. You'll know if you've done enough work because you will have complete confidence that the task will be completed on time and use the people you identified. If you don't have that confidence, then you haven't done enough work.

Estimates usually have four parameters:

1. **Role.** Who will do this?
2. **Effort.** Physically how long will it take to do it?
3. **Duration.** Over what period of time?
4. **Cost.** At what cost?

For the most part, you'll use history and expertise to get to the estimate. More experienced project managers may use some flashy algorithms. In order to build the right culture for your project, however, you should always look to involve the right people in the estimation process.

HISTORY

This approach is especially useful if you have delivered comparable projects recently (within two years). The benefits of this approach are:

- You will have a good idea of the time and cost before you start the project.

- The estimate is based on running the project in your organisation, so it takes into account the way your organisation does things.

- It's easily understood by senior managers, as evidence already exists.

For this approach to be effective the project needs to be truly comparable and recent enough to be relevant.

EXPERTISE

In the absence of a historical precedent, you'll need to get the right people in the room to provide you with the knowledge and experience required to build an accurate estimate. The benefits of this approach are:

- With the right people in the room, you'll get the best possible estimate.

- It engages people in the planning process and provides a detailed view of what's involved.

- It's applicable to all stages of the project.

The schedule is the last part of the project plan to be completed, and the confidence that the team and stakeholders have in it is directly attributable to the estimates you've provided.

ACTIONS

DO: Involve the right people at the right time.

READ: Any case study you can find that can help improve your expertise around the project subject matter you're working on.

POST: I don't estimate in isolation — it's a team sport. #ProjectBook

CHAPTER 48

MANAGE RISK

There isn't a single project in the world today that isn't threatened by some level of risk. It's one of the constant sources of distraction for project managers, and if it isn't for you, then it should be!

According to the 2015 PMI *Pulse of the Profession* report, poor risk management accounted for 30 per cent of project failures. It appears the warning went unheeded, because in the same report in 2016 only 28 per cent of organisations surveyed said they used risk management practices all the time.

All too often, risk management is seen as an administrative exercise rather than being critical to the role of project management. Worse, having gone through a risk identification exercise, some project managers fail to take appropriate action, thus increasing the likelihood of a risk becoming an issue.

Issues are the last things you want in your project, so you must do everything you can to avoid them. Sometimes this involves spending time and money, and that's why it's important that they're added to your schedule.

The five important steps that project leaders use to identify and manage risk are:

Identify → Plan → Schedule → Action → Assess

IDENTIFY

This starts in the planning stage and continues throughout the project. It involves getting the right people in the room and asking them to identify the things that could go wrong (or that you could potentially benefit from) throughout the life of the project.

Don't forget to tailor your communication approach to the personalities invited (see chapter 9), as you'll want to glean information from some attendees prior to the meeting.

The identify step ends only when you can't think of any more risks. It doesn't end when the meeting-room booking ends. If you need two, three or four sessions to identify the risks, that's fine. You can capture the identified risks in a register or similar document. It doesn't have to be a complicated document full of formatted cells and whizz-bang formulas. What you need is something simple that will allow you to maintain and update the status of a risk weekly.

PLAN

Having identified the risks, you need to plan how you're going to address each of them. Typically there are four approaches, which I call the four Ts:

- **Treat.** You'll spend time and money to ensure this risk doesn't become an issue.

- **Transfer.** You don't have the knowledge, time or the control to manage this risk, so you're going to transfer it to someone else (insurance is the best example of this approach).

- **Tolerate.** Where risks are of low probability and impact you may choose to tolerate them.

- **Terminate.** You may terminate once the possible risk event has passed. Alternatively, you may decide to de-scope that particular item because of the level of risk it exposes you to.

SCHEDULE

Once you've decided on the course of action to take, you need to add them to your schedule. This step is often overlooked by project managers hoping that identifying and planning the risks is enough. It's not. Treating risks takes time and costs money, so it needs to be added to the schedule.

ACTION

Having added the actions to the schedule, you need to make sure they happen when you need them to. If they don't, you've introduced new risk to your project, which you definitely don't want to do.

ASSESS

Having taken action (or not), you need to assess the risks regularly, ensuring their likelihood or impact has been reduced as a result of the actions you've taken. If the likelihood hasn't changed, then you may need to do more work.

Risk management should continue throughout the project. We need to move away from a culture of managing issues to one of managing risks. That means constantly monitoring what we're exposed to and taking relevant action to reduce this exposure.

Simply applying risk standards doesn't work; it needs to be a part of the fabric of what we do. In his report into projects in the Australian Public Service, 'Learning from Failure', Peter Shergold summed this up neatly when he said: 'Legislation doesn't change culture, people and their actions do'.

When it comes to risk, project leaders take action and never stop until the project is closed.

ACTIONS

DO: Plan the actions you need to take to lessen the effects of risk, and add them to your schedule.

DO: Follow the five-step process for managing risk.

POST: The culture we build needs to be one of risk management, not risk avoidance. #ProjectBook

CHAPTER 49

DEAL WITH ISSUES

Left unchecked, issues (like risks) have the ability to kill your project off quickly. Not only that, but if you don't have mechanisms in place to control their impact they can give you sleepless nights and even affect you personally.

The project management method PRINCE2 defines an issue as 'a relevant event that has happened, was not planned, and requires management action. It can be any concern, query, request for change, suggestion or off-specification raised during a project. Project issues can be about anything to do with the project'.

Issues can relate to people, the things you're building, money or the suppliers you're using. Like managing risks, managing issues is a key requirement of a project manager.

To be able to manage them, you first need to know about them. That sounds obvious, I know, but I've known project managers who have been unapproachable, which has led the team either to try to work around them or, worse, not to tell them of any problem.

If you've read this book sequentially and have decided to practise everything you've read in chapters 1 through 41 (good for you, by the way), then approachability is not going to be an issue. If not, you'll need to work on this quickly. Only once you know about an issue can you act on it, and act you must.

It is essential that you seek to clarify the problem and identify its root cause, which may not be as easy as it first seems. You'll need to draw on the people closest to the problem to get clarity on its nature and seriousness.

Once you have done that, you need to write it down. Leaving it to fester in your head isn't good for you or your project and will block you from taking the next important step, which is to compare it to all the other issues you currently have.

If this is your first issue, then the priority is pretty clear. If it's your fifteenth or sixteenth, it's not so straightforward, but the last thing you want to do is to waste time resolving this particular issue, if the people and time are better served elsewhere. 'The key is not to prioritise what's on your schedule,' says Stephen Covey, 'but to schedule your priorities'. Once you know what to work on first, then you can gather more information about what it will take to change something.

In projects where you're using an agile method, change can happen quite late. One of the principles of the Agile Manifesto is, 'Welcome changing requirements, even late in development. Agile processes harness change for the customer's competitive advantage'. It's likely, therefore, that you'll have a different approach to managing change in these projects, but you still have to manage it.

For waterfall projects you need to estimate how much it will cost to introduce the change, what the impact will be on the end product and expected outcomes of the project (it should enhance them), and how long it will take.

You should also identify the trade-offs required to deliver it within the planned time and cost. Saying yes to every change request is project management's equivalent of opening Pandora's box—you could end up releasing all the world's evils, along with any hope of successful delivery.

Once you have all the information, you need to make a decision. If it's not your decision to make, then escalate it to the responsible person so they can make it. Either way, the decision needs to be made, and the answer should be 'no' as often as it's 'yes'.

In a 2012 review of large-scale IT projects, McKinsey identified change control as one of the core project management practices necessary to deliver projects on time, to budget and at value.

Projects don't fail because of scope creep, they fail as a result of poor scope control. Project leaders are in control at all times.

ACTIONS

DO: Prioritise your issues so you understand what's important and what's not.

DO: Ensure that change is managed in a timely manner.

POST: I need to control the changes in my project and say 'no' as often as I say 'yes'. #ProjectBook

CHAPTER 50

REPORT HONESTLY

Let's get one thing clear: project reporting is not administration. It's an opportunity to take a step back from what you're doing, update the controls you have in place and assess what needs to be fixed. It's your honest assessment of progress to date and it provides you with an opportunity to formally escalate issues for decision.

The issues you highlight should have already been communicated to the sponsor or stakeholders, who shouldn't therefore be surprised when they receive the report.

All too often the report is not a true reflection of the project; in some instances it reflects changes from what the project manager produced!

In a 2007 study by a group of US researchers, 56 experienced software project managers reported writing biased reports 60 per cent of the time and that this bias was 'more than twice as likely to be optimistic (that is, to make things look better than they really are) than pessimistic'.

The danger here is communicating to your stakeholders and to your team the illusion that all in the garden is rosy, when it's fairly obvious that it's not. This undermines your credibility and will drive your culture into the pleasant or combatant quadrants (see the introduction to part II: Culture).

Status is not a debate. Having written your honest appraisal of the project, any attempts to change it—regardless of who requests it—should be rebuffed. You're best placed to assess the progress of the project, so don't let anyone undermine your integrity. You wouldn't let anyone else report on the state of your life, so don't let anyone do likewise with your project. Reporting is part of your job. No one should have to remind you to do it and it should always be honest.

ACTIONS

DO: Your report — it's important!

DON'T: Let anyone change it, but take on board any feedback and concerns that others may have.

POST: Reporting is an important part of my job — it allows me to assess where we are at. #ProjectBook

CHAPTER 51

SUCCESSES ARE THE BEST LESSONS

Lessons learned is an expression we hear a lot of in project management. Typically, though, organisations and project managers wait until the end of the project to share them, by which stage it's too late, as there's a good chance that those mistakes will already have been repeated.

And repeating mistakes is something we're great at in our projects. In 2011 the Victorian Ombudsman conducted a review of ICT-enabled projects in Victoria, Australia. They found the common themes for failure were:

- leadership, accountability and governance
- planning
- funding
- probity and procurement
- project management.

Every single project they reviewed made mistakes that organisations have been making for the previous 10 years. In the five years since the report was released into the public domain, every one of the mistakes they outlined in their report has been repeated by organisations not just in Australia but worldwide. Pick any project management survey or report you can find from 1995 onward and you'll see what I mean.

It seems that sharing bad news stories doesn't work, so how about we start to share good news stories instead? 'What went well' always gets less airtime than 'what went badly', and project leaders can change this.

In her book *Broadcasting Happiness*, Michelle Gielan writes about the positive effects that good news can have on us, as opposed to the bad news we're continually exposed to. She found that three minutes of negative news in the morning makes viewers 27 per cent more likely to report having had a bad day six to eight hours later. Those who were exposed to transformative stories, on the other hand, reported having a good day 88 per cent of the time.

While Gielan's book focuses on the media industry, the same principle is surely true of our organisations. The best lessons that project leaders can help other people learn are those around 'what went well'.

Create a visual success wall, where people can put up cards displaying the things they've got right. Call out success on your corporate collaboration system or intranet. Capture your successes in a document to be shared with all project managers as they start new projects. Or just talk about the things that went well. All the time.

This is not a call for arrogance, as project leaders don't look to take the credit for successes. In trying to change the project management game, we want to stop the rot of continually repeating mistakes of the past by continually repeating the successes instead.

ACTIONS

DO: Share your good news stories so others can learn from them.

READ: *Broadcasting Happiness* by Michelle Gielan.

POST: Any success story you have! #ProjectBook

CHAPTER 52

MEASURE YOUR SUCCESS

If you have put the time and effort into being the best leader you can be and have developed an inclusive and diverse culture, then the success of your project leadership (not your project) can and should be measured in a number of different ways.

STAKEHOLDER SATISFACTION

I talked about this in earlier chapters: you should be seeking regular feedback about the way you are leading the team, and face-to-face is the best way to gather this information. However, if you don't have time to ask the questions of four to six people a month, then using a simple survey tool to capture their feedback can help. Make sure it takes no longer than 90 seconds to complete, though, or people won't take the time to do it.

Project managers should never be measured on the time and cost of their projects, as these are the very things that will change in accordance with stakeholder wishes. Your stakeholder satisfaction score is the only true measure of your ability as a project leader.

STAFF ATTRACTION/ATTRITION

I'm currently working with the project managers of two unpopular projects. Unpopular projects introduce tools or structures that existing employees are likely to resist. The project manager's job is to create something that demonstrates their value to the organisation so people both understand it and wish to contribute to it.

If you've been successful in doing that—and both project managers I'm working with have done a fantastic job at it—people will be asking to join your team. They'll be volunteering to be a pilot site or you'll find them reading up on your project and following its progress.

You'll also find that your team members won't want to go back to their day jobs or move off onto another project. The team will be stable throughout the project and you'll find growth opportunities to repay that loyalty.

MENTORING REQUESTS

When you get it right, others who are leading projects will approach you for help. This is an acknowledgement that they're following the good work you're doing and the behaviours you're exhibiting. They'll ask for your opinions and guidance, and for you to share your knowledge with them, so they can find equal success by adopting your approaches.

Project leaders will downplay their roles, placing emphasis on the good work the team is doing. However, they should be quietly pleased to be seen as an example to others in their position.

INTERNAL REWARD AND RECOGNITION

Nothing says 'you're doing a great job' like being recognised by senior managers. This could take the form of an email, a meeting with a member of the executive or, best of all, a promotion or pay rise. Both of these are granted as a result of hard work and exhibiting great behaviours. Again, project leaders never seek reward and recognition, but consistently attribute the success of the project to the hard work of the team.

EXTERNAL RECOGNITION

The final measure of your success takes the shape of external requests for your time and expertise. You'll be asked to do keynote speeches or to take part in conference panel discussions, or you'll be headhunted. A friend of mine was headhunted for a role as Transformation Director for a large corporate in Europe, but she turned it down to finish the work she'd started in developing her team—which made her even more desirable as a candidate!

All of these forms of recognition serve as reminders that you're doing the right things as a true project leader, making a difference in the world.

ACTIONS

DO: Measure the level of stakeholder satisfaction with your project leadership.

DON'T: Focus purely on time and cost as measures of your success.

POST: I look beyond time and cost to measure the success of my projects. #ProjectBook

SUMMARY

So there you have it. Hands up if you thought project management involved all of these things? Okay, seven of you ... that's a start.

Of course, reading the first section of this book was the easy part. You now have to go away and put all of these ideas into practice, but here's the rub: the triumvirate of leadership, culture and methods must be applied in equal measure across the life of a project for you to be successful as a project leader. And it's a balance you need to get right.

TOO MUCH LEADERSHIP

Project leadership, done well, is a great thing to behold. It's like Simon with Garfunkel, Morecambe with Wise, Hall with Oates and, er, Turner with Hooch. It picks us up, it's energetic, it gets us involved, it tells us we're great and we need to get better still. It's honest, forthright and inspiring. However, if that charisma isn't backed up with the knowledge of how to get things done, you'll soon hear, 'Graeme is a lovely guy, but ...'

If you place too much emphasis on charismatic leadership and not enough on the culture or mechanisms for productivity or progression, in no time at all you'll find yourself as 'Head of Special Projects'.

Project leaders build cultures and are aware of the processes and tools available. They then make good use of both to capture the information necessary to support the successful completion of milestones.

194 THE PROJECT BOOK

'Charisma is a sparkle in people that money can't buy,' says Marianne Williamson in her book *Elements of Leaders of Character*. 'It's an invisible energy with visible effects.' But without building a culture and the know-how of techniques and process to guide the team through delivery, that sparkle will lose its lustre very quickly.

TOO MUCH METHOD

While too much leadership can be bad, what we see more of in project management is too much method. Unfortunately, for the past 15 years method has been used as a silver bullet by organisations (and many continue to do so), despite the frequent failure of waterfall projects. We are now witnessing the same results with agile projects. I read a book recently that said that if you apply agile principles to every project, you'll be successful every time. There is no evidence whatsoever to support this claim, but much to suggest the opposite. The Standish Group's 2015 *Chaos Report*, for example, noted that only 39 per cent of agile projects were successful.

To be fair to those who promote these methods, they go to great lengths to point out that they don't work in isolation. After all, a fool with a tool is still a fool. Yet this proviso goes unheeded time and again. In my many project leadership roles, I would frequently come across project managers more interested in the structure of the templates than the people. That way failure lies.

TOO MUCH CULTURE

As strange as it may seem to many (especially those working in environments that drain their creativity), too much culture can also be a bad thing. And in some instances, nothing brings a team together like a bad project manager. The culture is formed through a shared disaffection or lack of respect for the very person who should be building the team. In these instances, the team starts working around the project manager rather than giving them or their line manager feedback that they are not performing the role effectively.

In rare cases, where a team has worked together before, there can also be too much familiarity, and that's a tough one for a project manager to handle. That camaraderie is a great foundation for project culture but what worked before won't always work again. It's a mistake to assume that the team can reuse the same approaches regardless of the project and the person leading it.

GET THE BALANCE RIGHT

Many organisations, individuals and consultancies still think too simply about how to develop great project management, which is why practitioners like me find it hard to convince them that achieving it is more than just a week-long training course.

Great project leadership is no accident. It requires time, effort, feedback, mistakes, self-awareness, education and change. It can be achieved aged 18 or 80, and it never stops evolving. Getting the balance right, and successfully delivering every project you lead, is your challenge as a project leader.

I believe you can do it—you should too.

PROJECT SPONSORSHIP

For all of our good intention with regard to projects, it's a fact that most organisations still aren't very good at them and haven't been for some time. Attempts to build new products or fix existing problems are continually met with expanded time frames and budgets, often leading to disappointed stakeholders and, in some instances, front-page horror stories.

And it's not just 'some' projects that fail. Most research put failure rates at between 50 per cent and 75 per cent. The upshot of this appalling statistic, according to the Project Management Institute (PMI) in their *Pulse of the Profession* report in 2018, is that a million dollars is wasted every 20 seconds on projects around the world.

One of the main reasons projects fail is that senior managers are fully engaged only in those projects in which they have a vested interest. In my experience, these 'pet projects', as we call them, very rarely add any material value to the organisation, yet they consume countless hours of precious people time.

In fact, as I've noted, there are only two reasons for project failure: poor project management and poor project sponsorship. This part of the book addresses the second of these reasons to provide senior managers with a blueprint for continual success, just as the first part did for project managers. Every reason we can come up with for project failure (and reports and statistics frequently list between 14 and 16) comes back to these two reasons.

To put a much-needed positive spin on our challenges, The Standish Group identified the three key success factors for projects as:

1. executive sponsorship

2. emotional maturity

3. user involvement.

In my experience, these are all critical and are all within the control of the project sponsor and project manager.

Committed executive sponsorship is still (as it has been for a while) the biggest contributor to project success. Every project needs a senior manager to identify a problem that needs to be fixed, to stand by it through the justification and planning process, and to push the project manager to deliver. Without such a champion, the project simply won't be given the priority it needs to be successful.

There is a common and misplaced assumption, however, that people in senior management positions will necessarily understand what it takes to sponsor projects to success. Project sponsorship is just another line on the job description, and few know how to do it competently and consistently. So organisations establish project management offices (or PMOs) to take the responsibility away and only put in the effort once a month at governance meetings or in reviewing reports.

A quick look at some of the major projects occurring around the world right now shows a clear lack of ownership. I see lots of grand, bold statements of what will be delivered and when, even *before* the planning has been completed, which immediately sets the project up for failure.

The fact is that projects, by their nature, continually change and evolve. Senior managers who understand sponsorship know this. They provide their energy, ideas and unequivocal support to ensure that the needs of the stakeholders are met and that those leading projects are doing their bit to drive for results. Too many have become apathetic when it comes to this last point, accepting mediocrity as the norm, crossing their fingers and hoping for the best.

At least half of an organisation's activities every year will be project-based. Organisations have for years been investing in the wrong things and wondering why nothing has improved and there's no demonstrable return on investment.

Great project sponsorship and management can become a strategic competency for success only when organisations stop resorting to quick-fix certification programs as a mechanism for lifting its capability and start focusing on what's important.

WE NEED TO INVEST IN THE CAPABILITIES TO HELP ORGANISATIONS EVOLVE

I run year-long capability development programs with a number of organisations to help build strong and successful cultures of project management, and they are achieving levels of success that others can only dream of. Long experience has shown me that what makes projects successful is the people who lead them and the environment we create for staff to do their very best work to deliver to stakeholder expectations.

It's time for senior managers to put time, effort and real money into developing a capability that is both fit for purpose and capable of evolving as the organisation grows. One that understands that at the heart of great projects are sponsors and executives who do the right things, at the right time and in the right way.

Senior managers have to realise that investing in methods as a way of solving the project failure puzzle doesn't work.

Agile is the current method being peddled as a silver bullet for improving project delivery. Organisations think that simply implementing a method such as Scrum will work. It won't. Indeed Chief Information Officers in the UK estimated in late 2017 that 93 per cent of agile projects had already failed. The same report estimated that agile project failure alone would cost the UK economy £37 billion. Lack of senior sponsorship was identified as one of the key reasons for failure.

These methods, whether waterfall or agile, are only as good as the people who use them and the teams that are created to develop the products. In other words, the methods aren't the problem; the mindset, competencies and behaviours of those who are leading them are.

The best projects are a result of the people who lead them and the environment they create. In short, leadership and culture. If you want to be successful in all of your projects, this is where you start. You then use the methods to support you in creating the right approach and capturing the information necessary to help you stay on track. Only in this way can a project sponsor and project manager jointly ensure that projects meet stakeholder expectations around time, cost and scope.

Make no mistake, though: successful delivery starts and ends with you as sponsor, however this role is defined. To implement something new, you have to lead from the front and show everyone how it's done. Throwing it over the fence to the person who has responsibility for delivering the project just doesn't work. Neither does skipping the planning stage and just getting on with it.

A 2015 survey by PMAlliance found that only 17 per cent of project sponsors and managers agreed on key criteria such as benefits, objectives, scope and deliverables. Don't add to this problem. Get close to your project manager at the start, work together to build a culture for the team and a plan that everyone buys into, then remain visible and make decisions throughout.

MORE THAN JUST GOVERNANCE

There are many (and I do mean *many*) books in the project management marketplace on the subject of governance. I know because when writing a book you have to read everything else written on the subject. And to be fair, most of the advice they offer, if followed, could add real value to an organisation, particularly when it comes to clearly articulating what a project sponsor should do. Not so much if you want said people to understand *how* they should do it.

Now let's get the jargon, or at least some of it, out of the way early. The project sponsor or *project executive* heads up the steering committee (or *project board*) and is the figurehead of the project.

The senior responsible owner, or *program sponsor*, is the person accountable for a *program*, not a project. A program is a collection of projects. Depending on the size and complexity of a program, each project contained within a program could have its own project sponsor (or project executive), who together would form a program steering committee (or program board) in support of the program sponsor.

This part of the book covers the roles and responsibilities of a project sponsor, not the program owner. That said, if you're a budding program owner, you'll find lots in here to help you.

The agile world (and I'm using Scrum as an example here) can be confusing, as some organisations try to shoehorn the roles into traditional ones we're familiar with. However, when I've implemented agile, the sponsor was a key person for both the product owner and the Scrum master to defer to for decisions, and therefore generally fit neither of these two roles. The sponsor's role is therefore almost unchanged in terms of accountability.

For consistency I'll be using the term *project sponsor* here, although the information is equally applicable to project executives or anyone who is ultimately accountable for the delivery of a project or initiative.

I'm afraid this is rapidly turning into a *Monty Python* sketch, so it's time to move on. The problem is people are very good at defining what a project sponsor should do, but very few project sponsors know how to actually do it. Reading through numerous reviews, reports, articles and transcripts, and drawing on my own experience of what I've seen, I've identified five broad reasons for this:

1. Project sponsors don't fully understand what's expected of them.

2. Those who are designated as project sponsors don't have the time to fulfil the role to the best of their abilities.

3. Those who are designated as project sponsors don't accept the role they've been given.

4. Those who are designated as project sponsors lose interest in the project or are distracted by other 'priority' work.

5. Project sponsors don't know how to carry out the tasks they've been assigned.

In all these cases the projects invariably failed, and I use numerous case studies throughout this part of the book to demonstrate how this happened.

The role of a project sponsor is not an easy one, particularly if you are already time poor or have had no previous experience of managing or governing a project. Sponsors often rely on a project manager or central function such as a PMO to coach them in their role and ensure they make timely decisions so the project progresses as planned.

The danger with this approach is that it becomes too easy for the project sponsor to lose focus or interest, and the project manager ends up becoming both judge and jury on the project, which is to be avoided at all costs.

As with project managers in the first part of this book, I want to give project sponsors a full rundown of how to undertake this role, rather than just listing the responsibilities. I've broken down the role into specific areas, so project sponsors can dip in and out of the book and learn specifically what's expected of them at different stages and how to meet these expectations. These are all things I've learned and practised successfully throughout the course of my senior management career.

PROJECT SPONSOR'S LIST OF RESPONSIBILITIES

For those looking for a simple list of responsibilities as a starting point, I've created one for you to use. I constructed this list with the help of the following resources:

- Project Management Institute: *The Project Management Body of Knowledge* (PMBoK, 6th edition)
- Project Management Institute: *Governance of Portfolios, Programs and Projects: A Practice Guide*
- Axelos: *PRINCE2 (2009)*
- Axelos: *Directing Successful Projects with PRINCE2.*

These four books complement each other. Some line items are mentioned that I have yet to see in practice, so for simplicity's sake I have removed these or collapsed them into other responsibilities.

Here is my list:

- Appoint the project management team, including the project manager.
- Oversee the development of the business case, ensuring it's aligned to corporate strategy.

- Clarify and monitor corporate priorities.
- Act as a role model for the project, gaining buy-in from stakeholders.
- Secure funding for the project.
- Ensure suppliers are well managed.
- Ensure the benefits promised in the business case can be delivered.
- Manage the project manager.
- Ensure the risks associated with the business case are identified, assessed and controlled by the project manager.
- Monitor and control the progress of the project at a strategic level, ensuring consistent alignment to the business case.
- Escalate high risks and issues to corporate management as appropriate.
- Make decisions on escalated issues, with particular focus on continual business justification.
- Organise and chair project steering committee meetings.
- Ensure overall business assurance of the project.

This list of responsibilities falls into the three categories of stewardship, decisions and results that I introduce in the parts that follow. Each responsibility is critical to performing the role of project sponsor effectively.

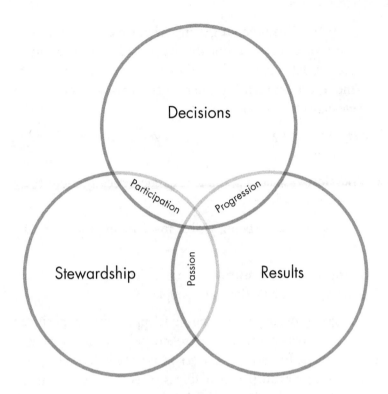

- **Stewardship**. Literally, this is the act of managing and taking care of something; here it also embraces the behaviours required to role model what great project sponsorship looks like.

- **Decisions**. It's critical to projects that decisions are made quickly to ensure that progress is never held back by indifference and that projects that cease to add value aren't unnecessarily continued.

- **Results**. This is about getting what we expected from our projects. If you thought the statistics for successful project delivery were bad, they pale in comparison with the record on realising the results (benefits or outcomes) we expect from our projects.

These three key areas are bound together and supported by three elements:

- **passion**—speaking and acting energetically about the project

- **participation**—being visibly involved in project activity throughout

- **progression**—ensuring the right decisions are made at the right time by the right people.

As a project sponsor you have a unique opportunity to positively affect the lives of others and to create a lasting legacy to inspire others. In his book *Outliers*, Malcolm Gladwell writes, 'Cultural legacies are powerful forces. They have deep roots and long lives. They persist, generation after generation, virtually intact, even as the economic and social and demographic conditions that spawned them have vanished, and they play such a role in directing attitudes and behaviour that we cannot make sense of our world without them'.

As a sponsor and senior leader it's your job to create and evolve a culture of successful delivery. Every project starts and ends with you.

PART IV
STEWARDSHIP

In the navy, the Chief Steward's job is to supervise the operations and maintenance of the galley and living quarters of both officers and crew while at sea. This is a great metaphor for our projects, because as soon as they're 'launched' it's the project sponsor's job, on behalf of the 'officers' or executive team, to ensure that the project remains aligned to its business case while ensuring that the 'crew', or project team, has everything it needs to keep the ship afloat.

Unfortunately, most project stewards resemble characters out of *The Love Boat* or *Carry on Cruising*. Well-meaning and nice people, but often ill-equipped to deal with the job in hand and frequently resorting to inappropriate actions or behaviours.

Providing project stewardship means more than chairing meetings well and actively listening to what you're told. It's about being a role model for others to follow, caring wholeheartedly about what the project is trying to do and recognising the role of every member of the team in their successes. It's about being clear on what's important for the organisation, providing others with opportunities for development, keeping it simple, and adding a healthy dose of inspiration and humour when it's needed most.

A sponsor must become a leader to provide effective stewardship of projects. Leadership isn't a given just because 'leader' is included in your title or job description. Taking a leadership course won't make you a leader either, I'm afraid. In one survey McKinsey estimated that US companies alone spend US$14 billion per year on leadership development, yet only 7 per cent of respondents felt their companies developed leaders effectively enough to generate improved results.

All too often, leadership is equated with achieving a particular position within the hierarchy, rather than becoming a role model for change for others. The certificate you got might look nice in a frame, but how many habits or behaviours have you changed since you received it? How have you kept in touch with the changing nature of project and operational delivery? How much more productive are you than before? How much more engaged is your team than they were before?

This is what it means to lead. To know when to step up and when to step in, and that includes future-proofing the organisation.

Leaders should exist at all levels and be nurtured by those who carry the scars of failure (see chapter 73). These stories and experiences are critical if we're to develop the next generation of project sponsors who know how to do the job well. Apathy is just not an option.

The Ketchum Leadership Communication Monitor listed the top five attributes of leaders as follows:

1. Leading by example
2. Communicating in an open and transparent way
3. Admitting mistakes
4. Bringing out the best in others
5. Handling controversial issues or crises calmly and confidently.

If you're looking for a leadership blueprint, this is a great place to start. Get feedback from your peers and direct reports on how you perform against these attributes and what you can do to improve, then work hard to do just that. You don't need to go on a leadership retreat, you need to make some hard choices and change some habits.

These attributes will stand you in good stead when you take the reins of a project because (you may have noticed) projects — and the governance of them — don't have a great reputation. In a recent survey undertaken by the Governance Institute of Australia, 73 per cent of its members said that governance is a drain on productivity! That's like three-quarters of car manufacturers saying cars are bad for the environment! (They are, by the way.)

Don't be one of these people. Governance should help, not hinder, a project and as the sponsor, your job is to demonstrate what great stewardship looks like and be on top of what's happening, always.

What you need to avoid at all costs in your projects is blame — something we see a lot of. In Australia in 2016, there was a project to collect Census information online. For the most part, the project was well communicated, although practitioners like me were secretly hoping it had been tested properly to ensure personal data wouldn't be lost. To cut a long story short, the system was hacked and personal data compromised. This was a hugely disappointing outcome for everyone involved.

What I wanted to hear from the Prime Minister and accountable steward of the project, Malcolm Turnbull, was that he was sorry. I wanted to hear that they'd got it wrong. They'd made mistakes in the governance, project management, supplier management and security aspects of the projects and would seek to rectify them quickly. That despite years of project failure in the public service, this was the project that would change everything, given how critical it is that public servants are seen acting in the best interests of the general public.

None of that happened. Instead he blamed the supplier, IBM. Who then blamed the government, and within a few hours the whole project had been reduced to a couple of kids acting tough and pushing each other around in a kindergarten.

As soon as the finger of blame is pointed you create factions and lose the ability to act effectively. You create a situation in which you can no longer proactively learn from failure, but instead just try to prove you were right and they were wrong.

The irony is that no one wins in this scenario and your role as steward is undermined. L. David Marquet comments in his book *Turn the Ship Around!*, 'Focusing on errors is a debilitating approach when adopted as the objective', while Seth Godin, in his excellent book *Tribes*, observes, 'What people are afraid of isn't fear, it's blame'.

To avoid this failure, you need to fully understand the sponsor role that you're being asked to undertake and to push back when you have too much on your plate already. Understand that it will take time you may not currently have and that there are many tough decisions to be made. Honesty and humility will be needed in spades in order to do this in the right way.

The sponsors I've met whose projects have failed did the opposite: they didn't delegate work; they failed to make decisions at the right times. They saw the role as 'just another thing to do', rather than an opportunity to nurture, build, guide and direct. They felt they just needed to show their face at a meeting or register their name on the minutes—and bad-mouth their colleagues behind their backs.

Every project an organisation undertakes represents an opportunity to enhance the corporate culture. To try different things. To provide time for innovation. To run meetings how they're supposed to be run and to be part of a high-performing, fun-loving team that's talked about for years. It's not the project manager's responsibility to make sure you're doing your job correctly—it's yours.

So if you don't know where to start, ask for help. Take a training course that focuses less on the process and methods and more on the behaviours and mindset required, that informs you about the different stages of projects and the key deliverables you should expect from each. A course that gives you a full rundown of what the project manager should be doing and how to distinguish the good from the bad, one that leaves you inspired to use a project as a vehicle for organisational good.

So in assuming the role of chief steward, this is your opportunity. Turn up, tune in and make sure you don't drop out. The ongoing steadiness of the ship depends on you.

CHAPTER 53

THE BUCK STOPS WITH YOU

Let me be clear from the start. In becoming a project sponsor, you accept full accountability for the project. You understand how it links to the organisation's vision, you give it your wholehearted support and you commit to seeing it through to the end, with the realisation of the benefits that justified the project in the first place.

Or, as Professor Peter Shergold stated in his review of how the Australian Public Service continues to get projects so badly wrong, 'Having a single point of accountability is a cornerstone of project management...'

The project starts with the appointment of the sponsor and ends with the sponsor's ensuring that the benefits of the project are realised. You're in it for the long haul, through thick and thin, light and dark, good times and bad... You get the picture.

It may seem like an obvious statement to make in a book on project sponsorship, yet time and again senior managers fail to fully grasp that if the project sinks, they go down with it. In a 2016 PMI report, only 27 per cent of organisations specify executive accountability for project success. Put simply, senior managers aren't stepping up and doing their bit for their projects.

Endless reviews into project failures around the world say the same thing. For example, a 2012 Victorian Ombudsman investigation into ICT-enabled projects (all of which had failed, I hasten to add), reported, 'Too often there was muted acceptance that all ICT-enabled projects go wrong; responsibilities were so diffused that it was difficult to identify who was accountable; or there was a tendency to blame those previously involved'.

We saw this play out five years later, when the aforementioned online Census submissions project was hacked by a foreign country. Here a complex project led from the very highest levels of government ignored 15 years of lessons learned (including the Victorian Ombudsman's report) and failed embarrassingly.

In the US, Housing and Urban Development (HUD) is responsible for a $45 billion housing program each year. In a 2016 report to Congress on its $35 million financial systems implementation disaster, the Government Accountability Office pulled no punches over who was at fault ('The failure of the project was due to management weaknesses') and outlined where the sponsor could have taken corrective action and demonstrate strong accountability.

Accountability is one of those words we hear a lot in our organisations, yet people rarely stop to think about what it actually means. The *Oxford English Dictionary* defines it as 'the fact or condition of being accountable; responsibility', which frankly isn't helpful at all and only adds to the confusion. The Japanese use the expression *setsumei sekinin*, the literal meaning of which is 'duty to explain'. I like this better.

When you are accountable for a project, it is your duty to explain the progress of the project to anyone at any time. Most sponsors see this as a project manager's job, when in reality it's a shared responsibility. It is the project manager's job to plan, lead and motivate a team of committed people to deliver the products required to achieve the benefits as described in the business case. A business case that you, as the sponsor, own. It's your job to make sure all of that happens—in the right way and at the right time, in line with corporate policy.

If it's starting to sound like hard work, then that's good, because it is. Nothing great was ever easy.

As a project and program manager myself, I thought the transition to the role of project sponsor would be easy. After all, I was the guy who made sure my sponsor knew what their role was and what was required of them. I fed them the right information at the right time and kept them informed of the things that could potentially go wrong. How hard could it be to make a bunch of decisions on some projects?

The difference was that as a project manager I had a maximum of three projects to manage and —personalities and product-building issues aside—keeping track of them all was relatively straightforward. I mostly knew what was happening and when, and I knew if I needed help I had a willing sponsor on hand.

As a project sponsor, however, I had three projects that I was accountable for as well as a day job that seemed to take up at least four of the five days I was in the office. Where was I going to get the time to fully immerse myself in each project? To meet with my project managers? To drop in on the teams to find out how things were going? To get involved in the planning, celebrate the successes, and seek feedback and input from my peers?

The short answer was that I had to change, because the role of sponsor isn't something you can half-commit to.

I had to delegate more of my business-as-usual work in order to accommodate the project work, not the other way around. Projects are the vehicles through which we deliver transformation and achieve the goals we set our organisations.

Often bonuses or performance pay is linked to our projects, and if it's not, it should be in my opinion. To turn around the numbers outlined in the part introduction, you as the sponsor need to take the role seriously. I'd love for your organisation's vision or purpose to ignite this fire, but we tend to use money instead. So be it.

Better still is a visible demonstration that you own the project. Former AT&T Chairman Michael Armstrong once said, 'The ancient Romans had a tradition: whenever one of their engineers constructed an arch, as the capstone was hoisted into place, the engineer assumed accountability for his work in the most profound way possible: he stood under the arch'.

Are you prepared to take all of the blame and none of the credit? Are you prepared to defend the decisions you've made and manage poor performers? Are you prepared to fight for your project when the organisation wants to chase shinier objects instead? Can you personally guarantee success? Are you prepared to 'stand under your arch'?

The team need to know you're 100 per cent in from the start, whatever it takes. The project is yours and the buck stops with you.

ACTIONS

DO: Take public accountability for the project from day one.

READ: *Turn the Ship Around!* by L. David Marquet.

POST: I'm the sponsor of the *[insert project name]* project. The buck stops with me. #ProjectBook

CHAPTER 54

VERIFY PRIORITIES

I remember my favourite project prioritisation session vividly. I was head of projects for a large government agency and asked each member of the executive team to provide a one-page summary and 30-second speech for each initiative they wanted to undertake the following financial year. Then they took turns to stand up and present these to their peers.

I gave them a sheet that enabled them to grade each key element of the project being presented and at the end (before we left the room) I collated the scores and produced a list of the 82 projects. Their goal was then to agree on the top 10, top 25 and top 50. We had proved the previous year that we had enough permanent people to complete 55 projects, but the record of meeting stakeholder expectations was poor, so I set the number at 50.

The whole process took three and a half hours. There were laughs, verbal jousting, howls of derision, structured discussion and some well-conducted arguments. We confidently published the top 50 and set about delivering them the following year.

Halfway through the year, we re-evaluated what had been completed and talked about what was left to do. Each sponsor took it in turns to present their progress and why it was important that we continue to invest (or plan to invest) in each of their initiatives. Numbers were re-verified and time frames clarified. We killed some projects in order to add some new ones and each sponsor gave the team confidence—or not—in the value of their projects.

That year we delivered 57 projects and met stakeholder expectations on 76 per cent of them. We were able to do this because people believed in what was being done and were confident we could achieve everything we planned.

If you don't run a similar process in your organisation, there are a number of dangers:

- You don't have a shared view of what's important and what's not.
- You may be undertaking 'pet projects' that have little ROI.
- You're planning to do too much.
- You end up doing the wrong projects in the wrong order.
- You overpromise on the benefits of your projects.

What I see often in the organisations I work with is a willingness to deliver but an overreliance during strategic planning on a complex spreadsheet full of weightings to tell you what's most important. Once they get into the financial year, there's no consensus on what needs to be done, and the benefits have been talked up to the point where there's no belief that we can achieve what we promised. Money and time is wasted and staff morale and culture suffers.

Like most issues in the project management world it's completely avoidable, and as a sponsor you have a responsibility to ensure your organisation gets it right from the outset.

When it comes to prioritisation, there are a number of tools available to help senior managers decide on the most important projects to undertake. In my experience, however, multi-column spreadsheets and weightings introduce more complexity than clarity.

I've always believed in face-to-face conversations that focus on what's urgent and what's important. If you're not familiar with it, I recommend you apply Stephen Covey's First Things First model from his excellent book of the same name.

Dr Covey explains that things that are 'important and urgent' are things that are broken or likely to affect business as usual. These also include anything that's deadline-driven (legislative projects, for example). Any project that helps you exploit an opportunity needs to be addressed in the first one to six months. In reality, if you want to start these projects on 1 July, then you need to have the planning completed by 30 June or you'll start behind.

Most work should be 'important but not urgent', as this allows for good planning prior to execution. This includes, for example, risk management, relationship building and the opportunity to continually review a project against its projected ROI. It also allows for a proactive rather than a reactive culture.

Anything that is 'not important but urgent' should be scheduled towards the end of the financial year. Providing you haven't overcommitted people, these are the projects you can bring forward should they become important. You should only ever plan to commit 75 per cent of your capacity in order to accommodate the unknowns.

Finally, those things that are 'not important and not urgent' should be dropped altogether. Everything here could potentially be a pet project and should be put on an 'if we get the time and money, we'll do it' list. However, if you want to be more efficient, you should kill these at the strategic planning stage and look to bring them back next year—or not at all!

Your job as sponsor is to be absolutely clear on your priorities and then to stick to them.

According to the PMI's 2014 *Pulse of the Profession* survey, only 52 per cent of organisations routinely prioritise projects.

And in a joint survey undertaken with PwC the same year, only 17 per cent of executive leaders viewed their projects as being strategic.

When this is the case, you end up with too many projects that need the same people or funding at the same time, and almost nothing gets delivered in line with the expectations of the stakeholders.

I talk a lot about the need for organisations to under-promise and overdeliver, because as it stands today the opposite is true. I don't mean we shouldn't stretch the organisation to achieve a sustainable level of change, I mean we shouldn't overstretch it.

The Standish Group management consultancy, producers of the annual *Chaos Report* into worldwide project failure, identified the number one 'deadly sin' that organisations make as 'Overambition. A strong desire to execute a significant project to gain fame, fortune or power through the impact of overreaching goals'.

I'm pleased to say I've seen only a few cases of this at an individual sponsor level, but I've seen it many times at an organisation level, where it means just one delay can derail the entire strategic plan. It also means that if you want to introduce new projects to fix things that are broken or to exploit market conditions, then you have nowhere to go.

Jason Fried and David Heinemeier Hansson in their book *ReWork* similarly recommend that we plan to do less. 'Embrace the idea of having less mass. If you keep your mass low you can quickly change anything. You can make mistakes and fix them. You can change your priorities, product mix or focus.' As a member of the senior management team and a committed project sponsor, your role is to make sure this doesn't happen. It's to make sure you set aside your personal desires and goals and challenge your peers to do likewise to ensure the organisation is the real winner.

Once you have a clear view of the priorities, you can get busy on carrying them out. As Dr Covey puts it, 'Effective leadership is putting first things first. Effective management is discipline, carrying it out'.

ACTIONS

DO: Ensure the leadership team is clear on their priorities.

DO: Continually review projects for ongoing viability.

POST: We stand by our priorities and constantly review them. #ProjectBook

CHAPTER 55

SHARE THE BURDEN

The first thing I did as a project sponsor was appoint my steering committee (or project board). I usually did this before selecting my project manager as I wanted the team to have a say in the decision-making process. On more than one occasion we selected a person from one of their departments.

The steering committee is a crucial function that any project requires and is a key support mechanism for you as a sponsor. The authors of *Directing Projects Using PRINCE2* go a step further to assert, 'The project board is accountable for the success or failure of the project. Being accountable means accepting and demonstrating "ownership" of the project. The project executive is seen as the focus of accountability for the project and accordingly retains the ultimate decision-making authority'.

For its part, the PMI advises that 'project governance should involve the least amount of authority structure possible'.

I agree with both of these points. The steering committee needs to 'own' the decisions made, and we need to ensure there are as few people as possible involved in that process. After all, there's only so much leadership love you can share.

One project steering committee I was asked to sit on had 19 members. It was a relatively large transformation project, yet only six people represented what I would call the 'core' project steering committee. Everyone else was either presenting a paper or there as an 'FYI' (I think that means 'I can't be bothered listening, so please can you come along and take notes so I don't miss anything', though I'm happy to be corrected on that interpretation).

Whatever the size of the project, in my experience, a steering committee of six to eight people works best. The individuals may change through the life of the project, depending on the phase or the activity being undertaken.

The steering committee is made up of two distinct groups of people: users and suppliers. This is PRINCE2 terminology, but I think it works really well in identifying the different stakeholder groups.

Users are the people who define the requirements, get to use what's built and realise the benefits stated in the business case. For example, if your organisation is building a bridge, the users in this scenario might be represented by a traffic manager, or similar person responsible for ensuring that traffic routes are kept clear, as well as members from signalling and maintenance. If you're implementing a new finance system, then a finance manager would likely represent the internal users (assuming the Chief Financial Officer is the sponsor).

Suppliers are the people who support the build and development of the product to meet the users' needs. They supply people, expertise or assets to help deliver the products. As an example, IT is a supplier (never the sponsor) for every technology-enabling project to ensure that the product they buy or build meets the needs of the users.

With me so far?

Quite often, external parties are contracted as suppliers and I recommend inviting a senior member of their team (or partner) onto the steering committee. It's critical that they invest their time and are party to the decisions being made. It will also ensure that they're included in the culture of the project.

The final element of leadership I would share is that of assurance. A person with the responsibility for assurance will keep the steering committee honest and ensure the right things are done at the right time. They'll have no allegiances and will ask the questions that aren't being asked by those accountable for delivery. Often this is an external person who provides you with a level of challenge that isn't available internally.

Unfortunately, most steering committees start as snowballs—small, compact and perfectly formed—but very rapidly become avalanches, out of control, with the power to destroy.

As the sponsor you need to keep the membership of your steering committee fluid and to ensure you have the right people demonstrating the right behaviours at every meeting.

The Victorian Ombudsman's report into the top 10 IT projects, which was extremely critical of the role of the steering committee, concluded, 'The steering committee must not only have relevant experience, it must challenge the project manager about failure to meet milestones and ask the hard questions in order to drive the project to success'.

As the chair, it's your responsibility to ensure that this happens throughout the life of the project and that the members are committed to its success. This will mean taking the time to review any papers or updates presented to the committee and asking questions of the project manager when performance isn't as expected.

There has to be clear delineation and separation of responsibility from you the sponsor, the board and the person responsible for leading the project, the latter of whom is not part of the steering committee but reports to it.

When this delineation exists, projects are ultimately more successful, as each party is clear on its responsibilities and able to hold the other to account. Former New South Wales Auditor General Peter Achterstraat noted in 2013, 'In successful projects there is usually a clear distinction between the person or team that provides the long-term leadership for the project and the team that manages the project'.

Remember, it's critical not only that you get the right people around you, but that they consistently behave in the right way.

Motivational speaker Jim Rohn famously suggested that we are the average of the five people we spend most time around. So if you find you're low on energy or inspiration, or are having negative conversations that aren't focused on resolving the challenges you face, first you need to look at the people around you.

Although you as the sponsor are ultimately accountable for the success of the project, it's really important that you share the leadership love with a team of committed people, people you can rely on, who can ensure you remain the best version of yourself.

If you get the right people in the right roles at the right time, then decision making will become easier and you'll be able to quickly remove roadblocks so the project manager can meet expectations.

Your job is to ensure that everyone works in this way all of the time (and that they don't lose interest as the project progresses). It's also your job to ensure the project manager continues to meet expectations. When you have both of these things working in harmony, you'll experience what it's like to be surrounded by leaders who love what they do.

ACTIONS

DO: Take the time to ensure you have the right people around you to aid the decision-making process.

READ: Melia Robinson's interview with Tim Ferriss on surrounding yourself with good people (*Business Insider*, 14 January 2017).

POST: I need a team of committed people around me to keep me honest. #ProjectBook

CHAPTER 56

SAY THANK YOU

'Cultivate the habit of being grateful for every good thing that comes to you, and to give thanks continuously,' counselled Ralph Waldo Emerson. 'And because all things have contributed to your advancement, you should include all things in your gratitude.'

The last organisation I worked for as a permanent employee in the UK had a lofty vision to snatch back all it had lost in terms of market share and sales and establish itself as a digital giant. The fact that it achieved its goals in the time frames it set was testament to the stewardship provided by the then managing director.

A person of knowledge, integrity and humour, he was determined that the organisation would succeed through the efforts of its employees, not the leadership team. He was encouraging, motivating, flexible in his thinking, empathetic and prepared to take risks, and he delegated appropriately. Yet when I think back to those fantastic days, the thing that stands out for me was the credit and gratitude he gave to others when it would have been easy for him to take all the glory.

In every town hall meeting he held, every interview he gave, every one-on-one interaction with staff, he was quick to thank the thousands of people who were making this transformation a reality. Even in the days when we weren't making the expected progress he was quick to acknowledge the good intentions and efforts of others, before talking about the collective work that *we* had to do to get back on track.

SAY THANK YOU 229

He knew that the success of the program depended fundamentally on the people doing the real work and that the leadership he brought must recognise this. Although over 10 years ago now, the leadership example he gave continues to be a source of inspiration for me.

Saying thank you is a little thing you can do as a sponsor that can create huge benefits to the project. Amy Morin, writing in *Forbes* magazine, lists seven proven benefits of gratitude:

1. **Better relationships**. The relationships we build are the foundation for the success of all projects, so it's critical that we do everything we can to continually strengthen them. This was something I learned to do late in my career and was key to building loyalty for what we had to achieve. A simple verbal acknowledgement or handwritten card can mean so much to someone who has put time and effort into completing a task.

2. **Improved physical health**. A 2012 study indicated that people who show gratitude experience fewer aches and pains and report feeling healthier than others. As you'll be juggling multiple projects alongside your day job, anything that can help you feel physically better should be embraced!

3. **Improved psychological health**. Gratitude reduces negative emotions and increases our empathy towards others. It helps people focus on the good that others can offer and encourages feedback that can further improve performance.

4. **Enhanced empathy and reduced aggression**. From the Greek word *empatheia*, empathy means literally to 'feel into another person', or to be able to see and feel things from their perspective. It is a skill that all leaders should develop and practise daily.

Empathy is the key difference between leaders and managers. It influences the way we communicate to the team, the way we assign work, the way we manage expectation and performance; it helps us to spot when team members may be anxious, stressed or worried. This personal connection helps us see them as fellow human beings, and as a result reduces any aggression we might otherwise show if something is done in a way we don't like. Our world is full of anger and frustration — those who choose not to succumb to it are the ones who make the difference.

5. **Improved self-esteem.** Oprah Winfrey once said, 'Be thankful for what you have; you'll end up having more. If you concentrate on what you don't have, you will never ever have enough'.

   Being grateful for the things you have or the progress you've made will undoubtedly make you feel better about yourself. When I was the sponsor of a large and particularly stressful technology project I kept a journal to capture everything I was grateful for. It helped remind me what we had, despite the issues we faced, and helped keep me focused. Whether you keep a gratitude journal or verbalise it to others, it can do wonders for your self-talk.

6. **Increased mental strength.** Amy Morin writes, 'Recognising all you have to be thankful for — even during the worst times of your life — fosters resilience'. She draws on psychological studies to demonstrate how gratitude helps overcome stress and perhaps trauma too. Ensuring the right decisions are made at the right time requires mental strength and acuity.

7. **Improved sleep**. In 2007, Arianna Huffington (founder of *The Huffington Post*) collapsed as a result of exhaustion, hitting her head on her desk with such force that it broke her cheekbone. Following that chastening experience she became a passionate sleep advocate, which led her to research and write her best-selling book *The Sleep Revolution*.

   In it she talks about the benefits she has experienced from getting a regular eight hours of sleep every night. One of the things that helps her sleep is knowing she has shown gratitude to others throughout the day. This has become a core part of her 'Thrive' program utilising Oxford psychologist Mark Williams' '10-finger gratitude' exercise: once a day count 10 things you're grateful for, and never miss an opportunity to show gratitude to others.

Showing that you're grateful for the work another person has done isn't just something that's nice to do—it's critical to providing the level of support and stewardship necessary to make a project successful.

President John F. Kennedy said, 'We must find the time to stop and thank the people who make a difference in our lives'. By making time, you'll find that others do the same.

ACTIONS

DO: Make time to show gratitude to the team.

READ: *The Sleep Revolution* by Arianna Huffington.

POST: Anything that thanks those around you! #ProjectBook

CHAPTER 57

BUILD TRUST

'The secret of life is honesty and fair dealing,' Groucho Marx declared. 'If you can fake that, you've got it made.' Of course, it's very hard to do that all the time — trust me, I've tried!

What makes you trust this statement? Was it because I asked you to trust me? Or maybe you've met me! Trust is a word we use a lot. For most of us it's a core value that we uphold in both our personal and our working lives.

In a recent Atlassian survey on the impact of Artificial Intelligence on teamwork, the statistic that caught my eye concerned trust. According to the survey, 78 per cent of those interviewed said they didn't trust their teammates, while an even larger proportion — 86 per cent — didn't fully trust a teammate to adapt to changing situations. A 2018 PwC CEO survey found that one in five respondents had 'extreme concern' about the lack of trust in business.

These are pretty startling statistics when you consider that our workplaces, projects and relationships depend on shared trust. So where did all the trust go?

Too often we think of trust as a given. 'I've been in this role for 15 years, so they should trust my judgement.' 'The plan says it will be delivered by next Friday, so they should just trust me on that.' And so on. Yet, author Simon Sinek says, 'A completed checklist doesn't guarantee trust'. And he's right. Trust must be earned.

Trust depends on having confidence in a person that they will deliver. It is a product of history, experience, honesty and the relationship we have with the person. As a sponsor, if you want to earn the team's trust you have to work hard for it. You have to behave consistently well, provide energy and do things when you say you will.

Back in the 1980s, Ratners jewellers were a dominant retail force on the English high street. The chain sold good-quality products at great prices. We believed the company's marketing and trusted its guarantees on quality.

Then in 1991, owner Gerald Ratner stood up on stage and told an audience of business leaders, 'People say, "How can you sell this [decanter] for such a low price?" and I say, "Because it's total crap"'. As if that wasn't bad enough, he went on to add that his stores' earrings were cheaper than a Marks and Spencer prawn sandwich, but 'wouldn't last as long'.

For the reward of a few cheap laughs, Ratner completely undermined the trust customers had invested in his brand and almost overnight wiped £500 million off the value of the company. Within two years he was fired by the new chairman. And 'doing a Ratner' became a byword for making a fatal public communication gaffe.

Each organisation has a duty to act honestly, ethically and responsibly in order to gain the trust of its employees. By doing this, they create the right kind of environment for staff to be the best version of themselves and to work collectively to achieve their goals. In projects, this starts and ends with the sponsor.

When the team trusts you, they're much more likely to be loyal, challenge outdated ideals and put in extra effort to get the work completed. They're also more likely to come up with ideas to further enhance the project and the reputations of all of those working on it.

In her book *The Creativity Formula*, Dr Amantha Imber suggests, 'Employees who trust that their employers are looking after their best interests are much more inclined to offer ideas and engage in other innovative behaviours'. In *Uncommon*

Sense, Common Nonsense, Jules Goddard and Tony Eccles go one step further: 'If senior executives put their career on the line—for example—by making jobs and rewards contingent upon the success of a change program, they will earn the trust of their people. Otherwise it's just posturing'.

One organisation I worked for insisted on keeping certain projects a secret, citing 'sensitivities' and 'delicacies'. In reality, what they were saying to staff by doing this was 'I don't trust you with this information'. I was able to get them to change their approach on the grounds that everyone was talking about the projects anyway!

To collaborate successfully to achieve project or organisation goals, trust is critical. Trust that you'll all uphold the behaviours you've agreed on. Trust that you'll deliver on your promises. Trust that you'll listen to and respect new ideas. Trust that you'll be honest at all times. Trust that you'll help each other and say only nice things behind people's backs. When you act in this way, collaboration is high and so is performance. When you don't, targets are missed, great employees leave and stakeholder confidence in your project or your ability to deliver it dissipates or is lost altogether.

Honesty and fair dealing should never be faked. You can trust me on that.

ACTIONS

DO: Take the time to build trust through your actions and behaviours.

READ: *Uncommon Sense, Common Nonsense* by Jules Goddard and Tony Eccles.

POST: I'm working hard to earn the trust of others. #ProjectBook

CHAPTER 58
SIMPLE IS BETTER

In his book *The 8th Habit*, Stephen Covey discusses a poll of 23 000 staff from multiple companies and industries. One of the most surprising statistics to emerge was that only 37 per cent of respondents said they had a clear understanding of what the organisation was trying to achieve and why.

That's right, only a little over a third of staff knew what they were working towards!

In a 2015 report, Deloitte found that 75 per cent of organisations said their organisations were too complex but, more surprisingly, only 50 per cent of them were doing anything about it.

When I first started work (for a bank in the UK) in 1987, my then boss told me the two hardest challenges were going to be learning how to use the machinery (huge Burroughs cheque-sorting terminals) and understanding the language that was used. I mastered those Burroughs terminals in the first week, but I'm not sure I ever got my head around the language. It was something I'd experience at every organisation I worked for. Upon arrival I'd be given a set of HR policies to read and a copy of the acronym dictionary—it was actually called that, and I needed it to interpret the HR policies.

When organisations do this it's a clear statement that they—and their leaders—haven't taken the time to remove the complexity from the working language and have allowed acronyms and jargon to multiply like rabbits.

Like so much in leadership, keeping your language simple is a choice you make every day. Even if your organisation generally uses complex language, you don't have to. You can be the difference and show everyone else how it's done. The things we build may be complex, but that doesn't mean our language has to be. Or, as famous Dutch footballer Johan Cruyff once put it, 'Playing football is very simple, but playing simple football is the hardest thing there is. To make something simple, you have to master the complex'.

Keeping things simple just isn't something we take seriously in projects. We're too busy insisting that people fill in forms and follow processes. Every project name is given an acronym that no one understands; even the documents we use are identified by acronyms — PID (project initiation document) instead of plan, for example.

Storytelling expert and best-selling author Gabrielle Dolan, on a mission to remove jargon from the office, has launched Jargon Free Fridays (www.jargonfreefridays.com). 'We are drowning in a sea of corporate jargon, acronyms and bullet points,' she laments. 'We are confused and bewildered by leaders who are not prepared to say it as it is and talk in a way that is more real. Every time we use jargon and acronyms we disconnect and isolate people. Let's take a stand and make a change.'

Organisations that keep it simple are reaping the rewards. Uber is one such example, according to Richard Koch, author of the book *Simplify*. Writing in *Entrepreneur* magazine, Koch credits Uber with creating something so simple that most people who now use it hadn't even known they needed it.

Koch believes Uber's key advantages are a result of the following:

- **ease of use** — simple ordering process; reduced uncertainty around which kind of car is arriving; transparent price; easy to split the fare

- **usefulness**—security and peace of mind; app works the same in cities around the world; automatic receipt; choice of services

- **art**—the experience is a revelation compared with other taxi services.

Uber took a complicated traditional model and simplified it to the point that people who used to take public transport for their journeys, now 'book an Uber'. While price is important for some, simplicity is important for all.

Ford is an example of a traditional company that decided to take a stand against complexity. In 2006, incoming CEO Alan Mulally found himself in charge of a company that had eight brands and 40 different vehicle platforms.

At the end of 2007, Ford recorded a loss of US$2 billion and set about simplifying the organisation. It reduced the number of brands from eight to six and reduced the number of platforms and models by 50 per cent. This in turn allowed the company to reduce its supplier numbers by half, lower the headcount and move from a complex regional organisation structure to a simpler global model.

In 2011, Ford earned US$20 billion, a shift of US$22 billion in just four years.

If Ford can do it for an entire organisation, you can do it too. You just need to want to do it. Often managers are too quick to point the finger of complexity at others, when they're just as bad. Goddard and Eccles believe, 'Successive managers try to safeguard their jobs by making things more complex—how many turkeys would vote for Christmas? Organisations should take simplicity as seriously as quality'.

So what can you do to make projects simpler to understand? Be clear on why you're undertaking the project. A strong 'why' statement will allow those internal and external to the project to be able to connect the dots between what they do from day to day and how it contributes to the organisation's vision.

Be specific on how you'll measure the outcomes of the project. I'm so tired of hearing 'the project will save us $5 million', with no data to back this up. Declarations like this are ambiguous and demotivating for those involved. What are you going to get, when are you going to get it, and how? List what the project will and won't do. This is a task for the project manager, although as the sponsor you need to be involved.

Ambiguity is continually reduced through project planning to the point where you're as certain as you can be about what needs to be built before building it. Be clear on the priorities so everyone working on the project always knows what the most important things are, both internal and external to the project. Don't give your project an acronym or fancy name. It's not profound or clever—it's a sign that you're trying to confuse.

Learn how to phrase your messages for a 7-, 17-, 37- or 70-year-old. I was first introduced to this idea a couple of years ago by leading Australian motivational speaker Matt Church, who broke it down as follows: 7 = simple; 17 = inspirational; 37 = practical; 70 = wise. Recording videos in which I tried to explain my work to my 10-year-old son (you can find them at www.talkswithted.com) was one of the hardest things I've ever done!

Make sure the project manager breaks the project up into stages that are easy to manage and communicate, rather than taking a 'big bang' approach to delivering the project.

Steve Jobs famously said, 'Simple can be harder than complex: you have to work hard to get your thinking clean to make it simple. But it's worth it in the end, because when you get there you can move mountains'.

You need to take a stand and be the difference, to ensure that you, the project manager and the project team keep it simple. The more people understand, the more engaged and invested they will be in the work to be done and the outcomes to be realised.

Would your project pass the 7-year-old test? Give it a go. It's a fun exercise, and you'll be surprised at how refreshing the team find it.

ACTIONS

DO: Take the complexity out of your language and the way you do things.

DON'T: Give your project a fancy name or acronym!

POST: We're keeping it simple to make everything easier. #ProjectBook

CHAPTER 59

BE PRESENT

Recently, following a project steering committee meeting I'm part of (as an independent adviser) for a large infrastructure program, I had to take an executive director to task for checking his phone throughout the meeting.

I'd tried to catch his eye a number of times, to give him a disapproving 'Put. The. Phone. Away.' look, but he was too engrossed in whatever was on there. Afterwards, when I asked what it was, he said that he was swapping texts with his wife about furniture. The message he sent to the project manager running through their report was one of indifference and, frankly, disrespect—and unfortunately it's something we see a lot of in our organisations today.

Baby boomers (born 1946–1964) and Generation X (1965–1984) often associate addiction to phones with Millennials (1985–2004), reproving them as the 'Distracted Generation'. One 2016 report on internet trends estimated that teenagers check their phone at least 150 times a day. Yet Nielsen's *Global Survey of Generational Attitudes* produced some surprising results—for instance, on the percentage of meals that were *not* technology free: Millennials (40 per cent), Generation X (45 per cent), baby boomers (*52 per cent*).

Distraction is clearly a problem for all generations, not just Millennials. For some, technology has become their master and they're glued to their phones at the dinner table, on the train, while waiting for their kids at school, even when talking to others! It's a problem that needs to be addressed, and we all have a responsibility to make better choices.

As a project sponsor, you'll notice this most when you're chairing a steering committee meeting.

This meeting offers you and your trusted advisers the opportunity to come together once a month (or more, depending on the requirements of the project) to appraise your progress and ensure the project manager is on track to deliver as expected.

You organise and chair the meeting—you own it. You set the tone by making clear what's acceptable and what's not. What's not acceptable is steering committee members showing a lack of respect to the presenters by checking phones, laptops or tablets. If they do, not only does it send a message that those people are not listening to what's been said, it also reflects on your leadership of the meeting.

Phones should be off the table and switched to silent (not vibrate). Is that too much to ask for an hour?

Being present demands more than not being distracted by your device; it demands that you switch on your ears and fully immerse yourself in what's being said.

Active empathetic listening, introduced by Tanya Drollinger and Lucette Comer in 2005, is a technique I've practised for a number of years now. It's a great way to stay alert and present in any conversation, workshop or meeting. It comprises three elements:

- **Sensing.** What is the person saying, what emotions and expressions are they using, and what are they implying but not saying?

- **Processing.** Take the time to write down and think about what's being said, the emotions demonstrated, how the person would normally react, and the themes or messages being conveyed, then summarise them back.

- **Responding.** Take the time to acknowledge what they've said, give an appropriate response, ask more questions or provide reassurance.

Maintain eye contact through all three stages and use body language such as head nods to demonstrate active listening. I often write notes, though not necessarily during the conversation itself. There's no need always to offer an immediate response. One leader I worked for who was a great listener would often ask for some time to digest it (even if only five minutes) before offering a response.

As a project sponsor, much of your time will be given up to others, and that means there'll be lots of listening.

Julian Treasure, in his TED talk '5 ways to listen better', offers this advice:

- **Silence.** Practise being silent for at least three minutes a day. I use a meditation app (Headspace) to do this and find that by being silent for 15 minutes I'm much calmer, and clearer too.

- **Channels.** Rather than being distracted by conversation and noise, look for the channels in the things you hear. These may be rhythmic patterns or you may get better at noticing the silence in between the noise.

- **Savouring.** Treasure uses the example of a washing machine as a noise he's come to appreciate. (Mine beeps relentlessly at the end of its cycle, which drives me mad, so I don't necessarily recommend that!) However, I've come to appreciate office noise as a sign of a healthy culture and other people's music as a sign that 'noise' is pleasurable.

- **Listening positions.** As in active empathetic listening, Treasure recommends that we develop different listening positions—from passive to active, reductive to expansive, critical to empathetic. By shifting positions, you're likely to hear different things every time.

- **RASA (the Sanskrit word for essence).** Receive, appreciate, summarise, ask. This final piece of advice is the easiest to adopt right now. Pin the word up to remind you how important listening and being present is. Being present and listening also focus our minds on what's important and encourage a positive 'can-do' mindset. The times we're distracted become vacuums in which negative thoughts breed.

In *The Art of Possibility*, Benjamin and Rosamund Stone Zander sum it up like this: 'When our attention is primarily directed to how wrong things are, we lose our power to act effectively. We may have difficulty understanding the total context, discussing what to do next, or overlooking the people who "should not have done what they did" as we think about a solution'.

At a time when we seem to be losing the art of talking and listening, it's important to remember that conversations are the conduit through which change is delivered. As project sponsor you have a responsibility to be part of the dialogue, not merely watching from the sidelines.

ACTIONS

DO: Put your device down and listen to what's being said.

WATCH: Julian Treasure's TED talk '5 ways to listen better'.

POST: Only by actively listening can I find out what's going on. #ProjectBook

CHAPTER 60

ROLE MODEL WHAT YOU EXPECT OF OTHERS

As the figurehead of the project, it's your responsibility to share the vision, demonstrate the behaviours, communicate in the right way, and uphold the organisation and project culture principles. If the project is to achieve what it needs to be successful, you have to be a role model for transformation.

In their book *First, Break All the Rules*, Marcus Buckingham and Curt Coffman put it like this: 'A manager has got to remember that he is on stage every day. His people are watching him. Everything he does, everything he says, and the way he says it, sends off clues to his employees. These clues affect performance. So never forget you are on that stage'.

This idea sits uncomfortably with many people, who simply want to attend a few steering committee meetings and read a few bits of paper, and allow themselves to be consumed by back-to-back meetings.

Being a role model requires self-awareness, continual feedback and a determination to be different from those around you. It requires that you understand the difference between leadership and management and that you are able to change roles as required.

Leadership involves a choice. It's a choice to be different and not conform to the way things have always been done.

It's a chance to learn from past mistakes, to encourage and incorporate new ideas, and to constantly strive to be the best version of yourself. The key to success as a leader is difference, not deference.

In *The Art of Possibility*, Benjamin and Rosamund Stone Zander describe leadership as 'a relationship that brings the possibility to others and to the world, from any chair, in any role. The "leader of possibility" invigorates the lines of affiliation and compassion from person to person in the face of the tyranny of fear. Any one of us can exercise this kind of leadership'.

The road to becoming a leader is a rocky one, and without full knowledge of the things you're good at and your opportunities for improvement, you'll remain in management limbo. This is fine if you're happy to remain as a task-focused subject matter expert, but as a project sponsor you have to practise what you preach and be relentless in your desire for development.

Continually seeking feedback is key to this self-knowledge, as quite often we're held back by the way we talk to ourselves. Martyn Newman, in his excellent book *Emotional Capitalists*, says, '95 per cent of our emotions are defined by the way we speak to ourselves', while Steve Pressfield, in *The War of Art*, reminds us, 'Our job in this lifetime is not to shape ourselves into some ideal we imagine we ought to be, but to find out who we really are and become it'.

Quite often we are forced into this position as sponsors by the urgency of the change ahead of us. A great case study of a CEO who did this really well is Paul Geddes, of Direct Line Insurance in the UK. In 2008, following the global financial crisis and after receiving £45 billion in aid, the Royal Bank of Scotland (RBS) group was ordered by the European courts to break up its businesses. Geddes, who at the time was leading the RBS insurance business, became CEO at Direct Line

Insurance in 2009, when more than 30000 staff had been impacted by the changes required by the courts. Geddes had to reassure staff as well as customers and shareholders, and to set about a painstaking separation of the business from RBS.

In an interview with *Marketing Week* magazine in the UK, he talked about the great value of good communication, especially given the impact on staff and their jobs. 'It was an important experience for me in really communicating well with your people so that they understand what you're trying to do as a business.'

He oversaw cost-saving measures of US$160 million, 1400 staff redundancies and a halving of the number of offices used.

Of his leadership style as the figurehead of the project, he said, 'You have to show people that you can think commercially about delivery and hitting hard KPIs, not just soft KPIs. You never forget the stuff you're good at but you need to add to it the stuff that you're less proven at—or that people might suspect you're not good at'.

They don't suspect—they know! To be an effective leader and become a role model, you have to keep working at the stuff you're not good at.

Not good with reading lots of detail? Learn how to analyse and look for hidden risks. Not good at showing you care for others? Learn how to build relationships and show empathy. Not good at negotiating? Find an approach that works for you then put in some deliberate practice. Not good at public speaking? Book yourself on a Toastmasters program or find a good mentor to work with.

No one is born a leader. The people who achieve it are self-aware and work hard to fill the gaps. One of the biggest mistakes I see sponsors make is in the way they communicate. As humans we naturally default to delivering a message in our own preferred medium. As a social person, I always prefer face-to-face and rarely send emails; conversely, one of my former colleagues did everything by long email. In both cases, if the people we're communicating with don't receive the message in their preferred medium, it's most likely to fall on deaf ears and the work will never get done.

A project sponsor I'm currently mentoring thought the way to inspire action was to show his frustration through bad language. This approach only works with people of a similar personality, and even then the words used could be misconstrued, inflammatory or offensive and reflect badly on your leadership style.

Dianne Gottsman, an etiquette expert based in the US, believes using bad language is a communication habit worth breaking for the following reasons:

- Clean language makes you more promotable.

- It demonstrates grace under pressure.

- Others look up to you and will ape what they see.

- You appear immature when you use bad language.

- You are showing respect when you communicate to others in a way they appreciate.

It's the last point that's most important, in my opinion, because it applies to all forms of communication with the project team and beyond. To be a role model for transformation and to fully engage an audience, you have to be able to consistently deliver a message in four different ways:

- **Detail.** There has to be a significant level of detail (facts, figures, case studies and the like) to reinforce the message.

- **People.** You have to be able to demonstrate empathy, understanding, vulnerability and humility.

- **Action**. You have to show passion and a determination to get things done by removing roadblocks and getting on with the job.

- **Social**. You have to be able to network internally and bring energy, humour and an open mind.

Becoming a leadership, transformation and project role model is one of the hardest things you'll ever need to do, but no one who has done so has ever said it wasn't worth it.

ACTIONS

DO: Understand that you're a role model and people will copy what they see.

DO: Watch your language and learn to control your emotions.

POST: Only when I'm the best version of myself can others aim to do likewise. #ProjectBook

PART V
DECISIONS

While your stewardship charts how you behave, lead and communicate, it's the decisions you make that will ultimately be the key differentiator between success and failure in a project.

Writing in the *Harvard Business Review*, Daniel Goleman notes, 'A person who lacks self-awareness is apt to make decisions that bring on inner turmoil by treading on buried values. The decisions of self-aware people mesh with their values; consequently, they often find work to be energising'. Not just energising, but inspiring too. Self-aware individuals can talk eloquently about the vision of the project and how its deliverables will bring that vision to life. You want to create a feeling in other people that you are passionate and positive about the possibilities the project brings to the organisation.

Seth Godin says in his book *Tribes*, 'Leaders commit to a vision and make decisions based on that commitment'. It's important to ensure that the project manager shares this passion and vision and that you both clearly understand who makes what decision and when. This sounds easy, but in practice I consistently see organisations suffer from decision confusion (who makes it and when) or, worse, decision avoidance (that's not my decision to make).

Decision making lies at the heart of good governance, yet when you turn to the textbooks it's no wonder people get confused. The Project Management Institute, in its *Governance of Portfolios, Programs and Projects — A Practice Guide*, declares, 'Governance typically focusses on who makes the decisions (decision rights and authority structures), how the decisions are made (processes/procedures) and collaboration enablers (trust, flexibility and behavioural controls), thereby defining the governance framework within which decisions are made and decision-makers are held accountable'.

It goes on to say, 'Confusion exists in distinguishing the governance needs at different levels of portfolio, program and project management'. Is it any wonder? It's well-meaning advice, but it uses language that alienates the reader, rather than clarifying the why and how decisions that need to be made to support continual project progress. In my experience, this confusion exists because important conversations between the various leaders (project sponsors and project managers) weren't held up front; the focus is on following a framework rather than having a conversation in which it's agreed who will do what.

This is neatly summed up in a paper on governance from LexisNexis: 'One of the benefits of good governance is getting the right decision-making authority and accountabilities at the right points in the organisation. This facilitates faster, better and more transparent decision-making'.

By being clear and transparent, those delivering the project can be confident in times of crisis because the important conversations were had before the project started. And make no mistake, each project will have its moment of crisis.

The decisions you need to make will come thick and fast, and not just on the important components of a project — budget, time, scope and quality. They start with deciding whether it's something you should actually do and end with the decision to bring everything to a controlled close.

You need to have a say in the selection of the project manager, how to deal with poor performance or behaviours, the culture of the team and which benefits have greatest priority. You'll also need to work closely with the project manager on the management of suppliers.

While the day-to-day responsibility for checking progress against an agreed schedule of work sits with the project manager, you need to be clear on your communication strategy should performance standards dip or milestones be missed. The Victorian Ombudsman's report into failed IT projects specifically discusses the sponsor's lack of decision making in this area: 'Senior officers in agencies were often reluctant to make critical decisions about projects such as placing them on hold or terminating contracts'. This is as true in the private sector as in the public sector.

On one project where I was the sponsor, the project manager and I agreed to terminate the contract of a supplier within two weeks of our starting the project as they weren't able to produce the basic project management artefacts to give us the confidence that they knew what they were doing. This set our project back six weeks, but we got a much better outcome. These are the kinds of decisions you need to make.

In that particular instance, the project manager and I drew on a mix of rational and emotional information to make our decision. The rational information included no schedule, no risk register, late for meetings, unanswered phone calls and missed targets; on the emotional side were broken promises, lack of respect, no confidence in their project manager, their inability to 'speak our language' and poorly run meetings.

While evidence is of course important, not every decision will be a rational one. It's important to have the emotional conversation too: *How does this make you feel? What is the team's level of confidence? Does it feel right for the organisation to be doing this at this time?* Daniel Goleman, in his book *Emotional Intelligence*, called this 'feeling vs. thought': 'As we all know from experience, when it comes to shaping our decisions and actions, feeling counts every bit as much — and often more — than thought'.

It's your job to make decisions, make no mistake about that, but in order to do so, you need to be the best version of yourself, analyse the information, then trust your instincts. If you make the wrong decision, you acknowledge this for what it is, show humility and ensure corrective action is taken to get the project back on track.

No one gets fired for making a wrong decision... Actually that's not true, a fair few people have been fired for just that. What I mean to say is no one gets fired for apologising for making a bad decision... Actually, even that's probably not true in every case. How can I simplify this...

Decisions are important and you need to make them in order to succeed.

There. That's better.

CHAPTER 61

WHAT'S THE PROBLEM AND THE OUTCOME?

When I was seven I broke my left leg. I'd come home from a family visit, kicked the football in our backyard against the wall, 'scored' a great goal and celebrated by swinging on the washing line that was hung between two metal posts in the yard.

Now, washing lines in those days weren't security-minded, childproof arrangements. That is to say, it was a bit of blue plastic slung between a couple of green posts concreted into the ground, so when I leapt up and grabbed it, it broke. By the laws of gravity I came down hard on the concrete and landed awkwardly on my leg, which ended up sticking out at an unnatural angle.

I don't remember much after that except for being in the hospital for what seemed like 12 hours, before Dad picked me up (with my freshly plastered leg), insisting to the doctor on duty that 'he's not staying here'. I got to go home and stay up late and watch *The Battle of Britain* on TV. They were good days, apart from the broken leg of course.

So what does this trip down memory lane have to do with getting clear on the problem?

When I arrived at the hospital it would have been obvious to anyone that my leg was broken. Still, instead of simply giving me a painkilling injection and putting my leg in plaster (that's what they did in 1977) the doctor did five things:

1. He asked for a detailed account of what happened, how I fell onto the leg and whether I'd had any previous leg injuries (Dad could answer the last one).

2. He asked me to stand up and put some weight on the leg and to tell him when and where it hurt (through the tears obviously — I was only seven!).

3. He poked different parts of my leg to find out which bits hurt and which didn't and checked whether I still had feeling in my toes and heel.

4. He sent me off to X-ray for a picture of the leg, thigh and ankle.

5. He checked the X-ray carefully and consulted another doctor.

Only then did he decide on the course of action to be taken: 12 weeks in plaster, followed by exercises and regular check-ups at my local GP to get my leg working properly again and to resume my dreams of playing for Everton (which, at 50, I still have).

One of the big reasons that projects fail is we don't take enough time to get clear — and I mean X-ray clear — on the problem to be addressed or the opportunity to be exploited. We rush headlong into building or buying something, then scratch our heads when the stakeholders don't get what they were expecting.

Too often organisations and project sponsors start with a solution in mind, rather than focusing on resolving a problem. At one organisation I worked for, we had a finance system that didn't produce the reports the finance team needed to be able to accurately analyse and forecast our operational spend. Our Chief Financial Officer had been to a sales presentation, fallen in love with the system demonstrated to him and insisted we buy it.

In total we spent around $500000 on the project and even then the company had to write and code the reports that the original system would have provided. We could have spent a month and $20000 to solve the actual problem we had. Instead the project became about buying a solution to problems we didn't have. And of course we never did get the benefits promised in the business case to justify the spend in the first place.

To get everyone to buy into a project from the start you need to ensure the problem is clearly articulated and that you're not creating more problems in doing the project. In traditional projects a person or persons will work with the stakeholders to collect information on what they need to solve the problem. It will be a series of questions designed to thoroughly challenge their thinking and ensure they're focused on problem resolution.

For complex projects, this could (and should) be a lengthy exercise culminating in a clear, concise document that can act as a basis for building a good plan.

Often business analysts will use a method such as MoSCoW (Must, Should, Could, Would) to get clear on the priorities of the requirements in order to build only what's needed. Only once it's finished can you start looking at the possible solutions.

Other methods I've used include Scrum and *design thinking*. Scrum is a popular agile method, used largely on technology projects, where workable products are designed, built and shipped in short time frames (known as sprints). Its creation is credited to Jeff Sutherland in 1993, though the term itself was first used by Takeuchi and Nonaka in a 1986 study in which they likened high-performing, self-organising teams to rugby scrums.

Using this approach, the stakeholders work together to identify a wish list of requirements to fix the problem, which is called a *product backlog*. The product owner (who represents the users) ensures the requirements are understood and the list is prioritised, so the team can work on the most important things first. They then combine these into a sprint, which is a concentrated work package that is usually delivered in between two and four weeks.

The entire process is overseen by a *scrum master*, and your job as the sponsor is to ensure that the product owner and scrum master are doing what they need to do to ensure maximum value is delivered to the business. This approach works best where time frames and budgets aren't fixed and teams are self-organising and motivated to deliver.

The design thinking method is generally credited to David M. Kelley, the founder of design consultancy IDEO in the US in the 1990s, and is a method for practical, creative resolution of problems and creation of solutions (courtesy of Wikipedia). The method has six phases: definition, research, interpretation, idea generation, prototyping and evaluation. The first three of these phases concentrate solely on defining the problem, challenge or opportunity. From defining the problem into a very clear statement, to researching, surveying and observing, to analysing data and looking for patterns.

Only once all these phases are completed can you begin the process of generating the ideas to solve the problem, address the challenge or exploit the opportunity.

Design thinking can be used in conjunction with traditional and agile project methods. If you'd like to know more, Emrah Yayici's book *Design Thinking Methodology* is a great place to start.

Regardless of the approach you use, it's critical that the stakeholders are involved from the start and that you make no assumptions as to what you think they want.

As the sponsor, it's likely you're the direct beneficiary of the post-project outcomes, so it's absolutely critical that you ensure this exercise is done in the right way. Everyone needs to understand the problem and how it will be addressed *before* you start designing or building.

Once you understand the problem, you can define the benefits you expect. It's always that way around.

The benefits (or outcomes) are the reasons we undertake projects in the first place and they need to be unambiguous, time-bound and achievable.

In a State of the CIO survey, 63 per cent of CEOs interviewed said they preferred projects to make money, while only 37 per cent preferred to save it. So you have to be able to demonstrate the tangible gains for the organisation and back this up with detailed analysis of how you'll achieve that.

KPMG New Zealand estimate that only 21 per cent of projects consistently deliver the benefits they promise. Like most statistics around projects, this is appalling. A joint McKinsey/Oxford University study found that IT projects specifically deliver (on average) 56 per cent less value than initially expected.

The New Zealand ministerial inquiry into the Novopay project, an initiative to replace 2457 education payroll systems, predicted that the project 'was unlikely to ever achieve the benefits it promised', this despite spending over $100 million on the project.

There was a similar case at an organisation I once worked for. When I started I initiated a review of the benefits expected by the projects we had on the books. Half the benefit statements I read could have been written by the Brothers Grimm. Most of the numbers were pure fantasy, and new to the business though I was, even I knew they were unachievable and that as a (high-profile) business, we were setting ourselves up for failure.

So I did what anyone would have done. I asked the CFO to review them all and, where financial savings were declared, the executive responsible had to declare which budget line would be reduced the following year. Nine projects were immediately cancelled and we instilled a completely different mindset into those sponsoring projects.

Often projects lose steam because no one cares anymore. Maybe it was a good idea to begin with, but now it just feels like something someone else wants and the benefits don't seem relevant—and I'm not just talking about the tangible numbers here, but also the intangibles, such as how it will make lives easier.

If you have continued business justification and a good 'why' statement, then don't panic! You're in good shape and just need to reassert your why, demonstrate the value the project offers and get the team back on board. What you can't afford to do is hope they'll eventually see the light and start supporting you again.

In their paper 'What We Know about Leadership', Hogan and Kaiser found that high-performing leaders who fought for what was right added significantly to their organisation's value, in one case providing an additional $25 million. So you need to keep the faith, and help others to keep theirs too.

Solving a problem and realising the benefits are the reasons we undertake projects in the first place. If you're not clear on them at the start, then it's unlikely you'll ever see a return on investment either financially or in the time you've invested. You've got to do it properly from the start.

ACTIONS

DO: Take the time to understand the problem, rather than looking to buy something new.

READ: *Design Thinking Methodology* by Emrah Yayici.

POST: This project will be different — we'll deliver the outcomes! #ProjectBook

CHAPTER 62

NEGATE THE NEGATIVITY

As the sponsor, you have to be positive about the project delivering the benefits promised when you said it would. All of the time.

It sounds fairly obvious, and it would be great if I could just end this chapter here, yet I find myself reminding senior managers about this far too often, so it's worth going into a bit of detail on how to keep the big bad negative wolf from your project's door. Let's start with an important fact.

If you're negative about the project, everyone else will be negative about the project so it won't get done.

Okay, that's not strictly true. Sometimes the team will get it done by finding a way around you. After all, nothing brings a team together like a poor manager, but this is definitely not where you want to be.

So it would make everything better if you could decide to adopt what Carol Dweck calls a growth mindset, rather than a fixed mindset. Having a growth mindset builds motivation and encourages productivity. Those with a growth mindset believe that they have the ability to achieve anything. Conversely, having a fixed mindset sees only problems and issues. Those with a fixed mindset believe their abilities are fixed and nothing new can be learned or taught.

Of course, you can't be upbeat and energetic all the time. That's just not realistic as you'll end up burning yourself out or making yourself ill. However, as long as you demonstrate a mindset focused on what's achievable, others will follow. Having said that, you need to be able to back the mindset up with facts.

You have to be crystal clear about why you're doing a project, ensure it continues to be viable, surround yourself with the right people, and continue to challenge sceptics and cynics and the negativity that will rear its ugly head from time to time.

As the sponsor, you must constantly look beyond the challenges and remain focused on the opportunities that the project offers. The positivity people feel will stem from the mindset you have, the actions you take and the language you use. Issues in projects are as inevitable as the setting of the sun each day; it's how you (and the project manager) respond to them that's important. As soon as you call something a 'problem' or 'roadblock', that's exactly how it will be perceived.

Pioneered by Richard Bandler and John Grinder in the 1970s, Neuro-linguistic Programming (NLP) connects the ways we speak (our language), how our brain processes information (neurological activity) and our behaviour (programmed by experience), which we have the power to change.

As with everything that promises to fundamentally change the way people think, NLP has had its fair share of detractors and promoters. Speaking as someone who has applied its principles for the past 10 years, I can only tell you that from my experience it works — principally around the way we talk.

An NLP tenet is that we have three ways of processing information:

- auditory (hearing)
- visual (seeing)
- kinaesthetic (feeling).

Auditory people focus on the words and take the time to think deeply about what you've said. Visual people look for hand gestures, eye contact or smiles, while kinaesthetic people put their trust in how they feel and the sensations they are aware of.

Incorporating all three of these approaches in a challenging situation would require that you keep facial expression soft and your language focused on addressing the challenge, while asking people how they feel about the suggested course of action, or better still, encouraging them to propose solutions.

Benjamin and Rosamund Stone Zander suggest that to overcome negativity we should 'speak from a position of possibility'. When you speak from the centre outwards, you help people to see what they can do to address a challenge (not a problem) they face. Ask people to use the word *and* instead of *but*, to reframe sentences positively or to propose solutions to enhance the current approach.

When you focus only on the problem (or the person who created it), it takes much more effort on your part to lift people up to where they need to be to solve it. Having said all of that, there'll always be cynics who are looking to undo the good work you are doing, and there's nothing worse than a cynic. I'm okay with sceptics who just need to be convinced that something is doable. Cynics, on the other hand, suck the life out of a room and everyone in it. Leadership guru Seth Godin nailed it when he said,

> Cynics are hard to disappoint. Because they imagine the worst in people and situations, reality rarely lets them down. Cynicism is a way to rehearse the let-downs the world has in store, before they arrive.
>
> Someone betting on the worst outcomes is going to be correct now and then, but that doesn't mean we need to have him on our team. I'd rather work with

people brave enough to embrace possible futures at the expense of being disappointed now and then.

Unfortunately there are still too many cynics in our projects and organisations. According to a Gallup survey, these actively disengaged 'CAVE dwellers' (Consistently Against Virtually Everything) cost US businesses alone US$350 billion a year in lost productivity, and they do that because we let them. For too long we've let these people get away with this kind of behaviour and some of them, frankly, just need to go and be negative elsewhere.

When you remove the cynics, when you negate the negativity and build a team of people focused on positive outcomes a project can bring, the paybacks in terms of morale, engagement and productivity can be huge. And if you're cynical about everything you've read here, then maybe, just maybe, you're the problem.

ACTIONS

DO: Talk from a position of possibility and demonstrate how to be positive.

READ: *Mindset* by Dr Carol Dweck.

POST: I'm positive about the success of the project and am helping others to be the same. #ProjectBook

CHAPTER 63

HIRE AND PICK YOUR PROJECT MANAGER

Axelos's *Directing Successful Projects with PRINCE2* guide is really, really clear about one thing: 'One of the most important decisions a newly appointed [sponsor] will make is who to appoint to manage the project'.

All aspects of a project need to be taken into consideration, it adds, including its complexity, the political environment in which it exists, its size and a clear understanding of what's required, before matching it to an appropriate—and available—person.

One of the most important decisions.

That's how essential it is for your project that you get exactly the right person to lead it. Not the person 'given' to you by IT. Not a member of the accounts team because no one else wants to do it. The *right* person. A person who knows what it means to lead, build a team, create a strong plan, manage upwards, find ways to get things done in order to meet the expectations of you and your steering committee.

What you don't want to do is pick someone who isn't any of those things or who will simply tell you what you want to hear. Seth Godin calls these people Sheepwalkers. Staff who've been 'raised' to be obedient. That's the last thing you need on a project.

In his book *Start with Why*, Simon Sinek says, 'The goal is to hire people who believe what you believe'. Richard Sheridan, in his book *Joy Inc.*, suggests you 'hire humans, not polished résumés'.

For the past 10 years résumés are just how we've hired project managers. We've focused our attention on the badges they've attained (PRINCE2, PMP, Scrum and so on), rather than their resilience, attention to detail, ability to plan or, crucially, how they treat the people who work with them. A P2 Consulting project management survey found 'no correlation between the organisations that report high levels of certification and those organisations that achieve positive results'.

Of course it's important that people have these technical skills. This isn't just about certification, though. It's easier to filter out people who lack certificates than to use more 'subjective' measures such as the leadership they provide, the teams they create or the stakeholders who have been delighted with the experience they've had.

Finding the best fit means asking better questions.

Some of the best project managers I've ever hired haven't had a special certificate or even much experience. Indeed, my best hire had previously been an executive assistant, as I describe in chapter 33. To find these people I ensured that the information they provided as part of the recruitment process gave me the opportunity to assess their leadership potential. By this I mean they included statements about the skills they've applied to be the best version of themselves, the environments they have created and how they have consistently used feedback from stakeholders to improve their performance.

As with project methods, there's no best practice when it comes to hiring project managers, since each organisation is different. The following are five useful practices you can adopt. Certainly they may add time and cost to the recruitment process (even for internal hires), yet the goal has to be quality as only this will deliver the results you're looking for.

1. Ask for written recommendations from stakeholders. How many reference checks have actually told you something you hadn't already picked up in the interview? Instead, why not ask for written recommendations from project sponsors or stakeholders that you can follow up on to be reassured of their credentials before wasting more time and energy on interviews?

2. Ask them about their values. The very best project managers have a set of values that they exhibit in every piece of work they undertake. This is what drives their performance. You want to know that their values match up with your expectations before they start, so get them to list them in their application.

3. Ask them about the best team they created and how they did it. Get the candidates to describe in 200 words or less the best project team and culture they ever created, how they did it and what was so good about it. Also ask them how they'd go about recreating something similar in your organisation. Forget all those 'describe a time when...' prescribed answers in interviews. Find out how simply they can provide information about one of the most important parts of project management before you set them loose on your project.

4. Ask them to describe the biggest thing they learned
   about themselves on their last project. Great leaders
   (and the best project managers are great leaders)
   will constantly strive to better themselves, and that
   sometimes means learning from their mistakes. Find
   out how self-aware they are by asking them to share
   what they learned about themselves on their last project.
   You might also ask them how they bounced back
   quickly from failure. One candidate once told me that
   in six years as a project manager he'd never failed. The
   interview ended at that point.

5. Ask them about a time when they received great
   feedback and how it made them feel. We all like
   praise, and project managers are no different. The
   most tangible evidence of how well a project has
   been managed and governed is the feedback provided
   by stakeholders. Asking them about feedback
   demonstrates that they're able to see the good in the
   cultures they create, which in turn creates teams that
   are a positive force for good.

Finding great project managers isn't easy, as the talent pool
has been much watered down by people who've only got a
certificate and nothing else. Indeed, Ernst & Young recently
removed the requirement for new graduates to hold a degree
and have moved to human-centred questions instead. This
clearly demonstrates the critical importance of relationship
building and communication skills, especially for those in
customer-facing roles.

There are plenty of great project managers out there, and
when you find one you have to sell them your vision as a
sponsor. You have to be clear about the value the project can
bring to the organisation and how they have a critical role in
leading a team to achieve just that.

In his book *Creativity Inc.*, Ed Catmull points out, 'The obvious payoffs of [hiring] exceptional people are that they innovate, excel, and generally make your company—and by extension you—look good'. Who doesn't want that?

ACTIONS

DO: Take the time to find the right person for the project.

READ: Part I of this book, which outlines what a project leader looks like.

POST: I'm investing time to find the right person to lead my project. #ProjectBook

CHAPTER 64

BE ETHICAL

A former boss of mine, who was also the sponsor of one of the largest transformation programs we were running, got sacked for approving a six-figure contract with a consultancy who'd flown him around the world on a speaking tour. Everyone knew the deal was going to happen — especially the consultancy, who didn't even submit the correct paperwork.

When I quizzed him on whether it was the right decision to employ the consultancy — ethically, this was my responsibility — he said that the value they offered far outweighed that of the other applicants, and given our current working relationship with them, it was too risky not to engage them for this larger piece of work.

All of that, of course, might have been true. They might have been the best option, providing the best people and delivering the most value. However, by sidestepping the process and accepting an all-expenses-paid trip, he had undermined his own integrity, which put all his actions under scrutiny.

It didn't take the audit team long to uncover other issues including gifts, golf days and other trips. The consultancy hadn't done anything other than demonstrate a very old-fashioned way of working (which is still alive and well in some businesses). My boss, though, had demonstrated a lack of ethics by putting himself before the organisation.

Ethical decisions start almost as soon as the project starts. Over the life of a project or program you will face severe ethical tests, so you should always start as you mean to go on.

If you've followed the advice in this book so far, then you're off to a good start, but you need to be acutely aware of your actions at all times, because responsibility for your ethics cannot be delegated to someone else. Not to a project manager or to an assistant — no one.

If you're new to ethical responsibility or need a reminder, then let me summarise what it means. The *Oxford English Dictionary* defines ethics as 'the moral principles that govern a person's behaviour or the conducting of an activity'. Put more simply, it is doing things in the right way.

This includes, but is not limited to:

- **treating people in the right way** — displaying empathy, being calm under pressure, not talking about people behind their back, not apportioning blame, role modelling behaviours

- **adhering to the code of conduct rules and regulations** — health and safety, human resources, financial, contracts and negotiations, being transparent and honest, understanding the law

- **making decisions based on facts and what's considered best for the project** — not on favours or personal bias

- **performing in line with your role** — accepting accountability, giving autonomy, managing performance, overcoming bias and promoting fairness, rewarding good behaviour.

This all sounds quite 'basic', yet anything can happen in the heat of a project, so it's important that you keep ethics front of mind. The Governance Institute's Ethics Index scored Australian organisations as only 'Somewhat Ethical'. They list the top five ethical issues as:

1. corruption
2. company tax avoidance
3. misleading and deceptive advertising
4. bullying
5. discrimination / executive pay (equal fifth place).

They named the top five elements that ensure ethical conduct as:

1. accountability
2. transparency
3. whistleblower protection
4. a strong legal framework
5. financial penalties.

Ethical decision making in projects is no different from that in organisations. The PMI's excellent 'Ethical Decision-Making Framework' (or EDMF, because they obviously had to give it an acronym) is aimed at guiding people through the project management profession, although it's equally valuable for sponsors. It sets out the five As of how to make sound ethical decisions:

- **Assessment.** Make sure you're armed with all the facts pertaining to the decision you need to make before proceeding. Ask yourself:
  - Does it comply with federal legislation (or the legal framework in which we're doing business)?

- Does it abide by the organisation's code of conduct?
- Does it align with the cultural values of the project or organisation?

- **Alternatives.** Ensure you've considered all available choices. Ask yourself:

  - Have we considered all the pros and cons for each available solution to the problem?
  - Is our decision biased as a result of an existing relationship or situation?
  - Has everyone had equal and fair opportunity to present to me?

- **Analysis.** Identify your decision and test its validity. Ask yourself:

  - Does it take differences of opinion and viewpoint into account?
  - Am I free from external influence?
  - Am I in a sufficiently calm state of mind to make this decision now?

- **Application.** Apply ethical principles to your decision. Ask yourself:

  - Will my decision result in the greatest value for our project and organisation?
  - Is my decision fair and beneficial to all concerned?
  - Do I stand to gain in any way personally from this decision?

- **Action.** Make a decision. Ask yourself:

  - Will it seem like a good decision a year from now, given what I know today?

  – Would a peer make the same decision based on the same information?

  – Could I make the decision public and still feel good about it?

Millennials place a high value on ethics. The Deloitte Millennial Survey placed 'ethics, honesty and integrity' as the second most important thing they looked for from an organisation, after fair treatment of people.

Here are some examples of how I've seen unethical behaviour play out in projects over the years:

- Accepting gifts (including meals) from organisations bidding for work

- Asking project managers to change the commentary on reports to make it seem more 'favourable'

- 'Hiding' underspend of the project budget in the hope of using the balance for something else

- Telling project managers to skip or shortcut a process

- Making a decision that's weighted towards your preference immediately before leaving a role

- Selecting an option that doesn't have the best interests of the organisation at heart

- Favouring males or certain ethnic groups in a recruitment process

- Displaying behaviours that aren't aligned to the role or cultural values

- Not making decisions transparent.

Acting in the best interests of the project and organisation, and ensuring that others do the same, starts with the sponsor. There are many examples of individuals and organisations who have made decisions for personal gain, only to fall on their sword at a later date. Don't add to these statistics. Be ethical, not rueful.

ACTIONS

DO: Be wary of your behaviours and actions.

READ: PMI's 'Ethical Decision-Making Framework'.

POST: I understand that I'm an ethical role model and consider my actions carefully. #ProjectBook

CHAPTER 65

MAKE QUICK (NOT HASTY) DECISIONS

Victor Vroom and Arthur Jago believe the most effective leaders are able to make prompt decisions in times of crisis and uncertainty. They cite the example of Admiral Horatio Nelson's decision making 'under the almost unimaginably difficult and confusing conditions of a sea battle' (Pocock, 1987). But, they go on, 'decisiveness is also important under normal conditions. Mintzberg (1973) observed that managers are involved in decision making all day long, and the quality of their decisions accumulates when they act decisively'.

I remember speaking to a peer of mine not long after I'd been promoted to my first senior management position. Our boss had been pressing us to make decisions quickly and decisively as we had a large transformation program to deliver and couldn't afford to mess around. The conversation went something like this:

ME: 'How do you make quick decisions?'

HIM: 'One word.'

ME: 'What's that?'

HIM: 'Experience.'

ME: 'How do I get experience?'

HIM: 'Wrong decisions.'

Which filled me with a huge amount of confidence. The point he was making—in a not very helpful way, it has to be said—was that in order to make quick decisions, you're going to get a few wrong from time to time.

That's not to say that you make hasty decisions—that's a different kettle of fish.

Paul C. Nutt based his important book *Why Decisions Fail* on an examination of decision making over a 20-year period. In his view, entrepreneurs were responsible for a great deal of poor decision making in the 1980s and 1990s because they perpetuated a myth that all decisions needed to be made quickly, which in turn led to many catastrophic decisions. Just think of all those who went out and bought a pair of MC Hammer pants or a Sinclair C5 electric car. Huge mistake.

And the problem, as he sees it, is compounded now that we're expected to respond immediately to emails and texts, without having time to think about the consequences. Nutt believes more than half the decisions we make will fail for one reason or another. He offers some useful guidelines on how to make quick but measured decisions:

- **Personally manage your decision-making process.** Decisions are most successful when managers take control of them based on the information they receive, rather than leaving it to the subject matter experts.

- **Search for understanding.** By getting more detail on the issues being addressed and what it is that needs fixing, you reduce the risk of reacting to something that may not be the root cause of the problem.

- **Establish your direction with an intervention and an action.** Intervention establishes the reasoning for action; an objective (the stated outcome, such as *we need to have something built in one month's time*) opens up the possibilities for other ideas.

- **Identify more than one option.** The more options you have, the better the decision you'll make. Every option you discard enhances the value of the option you've chosen to explore further. As Simon Sinek reasons in *Start with Why*, 'Our behaviour is affected by our assumptions or our perceived truths. We make decisions based on what we think we know'. Gathering more options mitigates this risk.

- **Stress idea creation and implementation.** It's not just about getting things done quickly; it's also about ensuring there's no bias towards one idea when another might be better (for example, reusing something you already have rather than developing something new) before implementing.

- **Deal with barriers to action.** The best way to do this is to involve everyone in the decision-making process from the start. However, where there are still barriers you need to act swiftly to remove them in order to progress.

The Agile Manifesto expands on this need for quick decisions. The 12 principles that underpin the manifesto are as follows:

1. We trust intrinsic motivation.

2. We proof by working product only.

3. We prioritise customer delight.

4. We welcome change.

5. We prefer face-to-face communication.

6. We deliver early and often.

7. We grow a system.

8. We make no mistakes—we learn.

9. We thrive on daily collaboration.

10. We design technical excellence.

11. We sustain a constant pace.

12. We love simplicity.

What agility requires more than anything else is a different mindset—what Carol Dweck calls a growth mindset. One that thinks anything is possible, that challenges convention and looks for better, smarter ways to do things. This is never more needed than in decision making.

For those who like to understand all the details before committing, it's important to know just enough to inform a good decision. Using the agile principles as a guide, delivering early and often requires quick decisions, as does sustaining a constant pace. Organisations that crave agility (not just a shortcut) need to embrace quick decision making and support a solution-focused culture.

For the most part, you'll use your steering committee as a sounding board and even involve them in this decision-making process. Some organisations require a voting system (a quorum) when it comes to decisions, so it's important for you to get clear on the rules. When everyone has the same information it can work really well. However, demanding that you take action only when everyone is in agreement can cause problems. It might have worked well for the Beatles (four positive votes were required in 1966 for them to agree to something, which is why they stopped touring), but it's not so efficient for projects.

With quick decisions, you take as long as you need and no longer to make the best decision you can. So please, please, please me and make quick decisions, well.

ACTIONS

DO: Keep your project moving even if you have to revisit a decision.

READ: *Why Decisions Fail* by Paul C. Nutt.

POST: I make quick decisions to keep my project moving. #ProjectBook

CHAPTER 66

DEAL WITH POOR PERFORMANCE

At some stage in your project, the project manager will let you down. Hey, we're all human and we make mistakes; it's a fact of life and how we grow. Unless they're provided with feedback, and expectations are reset, however, there's a good chance they'll continue to let you down and the project will slowly die.

I firmly believe that if, over the past 15 years, sponsors had been more engaged in projects and had actively managed the poor performance of project managers, the statistics around successful delivery wouldn't be as bad as they are today. Nonetheless we are where we are, so let's draw a line here today and resolve to be different.

Managing poor performance isn't something we're all immediately good at. It often takes time and a process to get better at it. Indeed, some of the most stressful situations I've ever been in have involved performance management, but I didn't avoid them. I embraced the requirements of my role and sought to get better at it.

Here are four things I've learned when it comes to managing the project manager.

1. CREATE A SHARED UNDERSTANDING OF WHAT'S EXPECTED

Managing poor performance starts with setting expectations when everything is good. Victor Lipman, author of *The Type B Manager: Leading Successfully in a Type A World*, writes, 'Managers will have day-to-day expectations about employee behaviour, collaboration and culture—the ways in which team members should interact with one another. Clear expectations are a manager's best friend. Without them, clear results can prove elusive'.

Setting clear expectations requires that you put time and thought into defining the role of the project manager with respect to the stakeholders they'll be working with, the time frames or the funds they have at their disposal. If you're using metrics to measure their performance, Dan Pink, in his book *Drive*, suggests 'you make them wide ranging, relevant and hard to game'.

Being specific about what's expected ensures that the project manager is clear from day one on what the baseline is with regard to performance. From here you can build a strong relationship based on this shared understanding.

2. COMMUNICATE IN THEIR PERSONALITY PREFERENCES, NOT YOURS

Most people will tell you they are good at communication 'at all levels'. This can be achieved only if you can tailor your messages accordingly. As I mention in chapter 9, there are

282 THE PROJECT BOOK

four types of project manager and to be able to manage their performance effectively, you need to ensure you deliver your messages in a way that engages their personality. The four types are as follows:

- The *Detail Project Manager* likes lots of information. They prefer to communicate by email and will often send long ones to make a point. They prefer short, sharp meetings and to fully immerse themselves in the detail of the project they're managing. They like order and completing documents, but are less likely to be able to inspire people to change. They prefer the formality of a meeting, and for you to present them with a clear list of what needs to be done and when.

- The *People Project Manager* has the welfare of their staff at heart. They like teams, harmony and recognition for the results of their efforts. They are the glue of the project team and will be great advocates for the project, providing they fully understand 'why' it's being undertaken in the first place. While they enjoy having some rules to work with, they may not fully embrace the controls they need to maintain (schedule, risk register, budget and the like). These project managers want your attention and require more of a 'personal touch' than the other types.

- The *Action Project Manager* is direct. They have a drive to get things done and have little time for 'fluff and nonsense'. They don't settle for traditional ways of doing things if they see them as getting in the way and will establish their 'authority' early in a project. These project managers are more disposed to take risks in order to get things done quicker, and while they'll maintain good project documentation they may downplay risks and get frustrated if decisions are delayed. These project managers just want to be left to get on with the job and for you to make decisions quickly to aid progress.

- The *Social Project Manager* provides energy and inspiration. They love to bring people together and revel in creative workshops. They are trusting and will often use stories to emphasise a point or motivate an individual. They love new ideas and constantly strive for innovation. They're often not great on the documentation front, but will know how the project is progressing based on the mood of the team.

To be truly great, each one of these project managers has to be able to adopt the personality traits of the others, and it's your job as a sponsor to ensure they do the things that don't come naturally to them. For example, as a project manager I was very much the social PM. My sponsors did an excellent job at reminding me that a regularly updated plan and risk register inspires confidence in those around and above me, and that I too needed to set clear expectation in order to get the results we needed.

3. NIP IT IN THE BUD

As soon as you don't get what you expect (having done 1 and 2 really well), you have to deal with it immediately before it gets out of your control. The Office of Personnel Management in the US has concluded that early feedback is critical to improving performance. It suggests that the feedback needs to encompass three elements:

1. **specific** — directly relating to the issue at hand (don't dance around it)
2. **timely** — don't wait too long before addressing it
3. **manner** — delivered in a way that will best improve performance.

This last element relates directly to the personality of the project manager and is crucial in ensuring they understand what they need to do to improve.

Once you've done this, you reset expectation and wipe the slate clean again.

4. TAKE ACTION

If you have covered points 1, 2 and 3 well and things still haven't improved, ignoring the problem and hoping it will go away or improve without your input isn't an option. You have to take steps to remove the project manager and bring in someone more suited to do the job. Remember, as the project sponsor it's your job to ensure that the project's products are delivered in such a way that the business can get full value from them. If one cog in the project machine isn't working, it has to be replaced quickly. You have to make these tough decisions. Once you've done all you can to set the right expectation, manage them to that.

In *Emotional Intelligence*, Daniel Goleman says, 'Leadership is not domination, but the art of persuading people to work towards a common goal'. Taking off from this point gives you the perfect opportunity to get things right from the start so performance management isn't needed, because prevention is always better than cure.

ACTIONS

DO: Set expectation properly.

DO: Deal with performance management issues decisively.

POST: To be successful we need to be tough on poor performance. #ProjectBook

CHAPTER 67
FAIL QUICKLY

Failure is something that happens to us all and it can happen on a daily basis. It needs to become something that we're comfortable with and learn from because resilience is an important quality required in projects.

Every year more than two-thirds of projects are considered failures, and most organisations would not be surprised by this statistic. In most cases, however, failure was the result of not making a hard decision.

In the project management world we are excellent at finding reasons for failure and dehumanising their root cause. For example, here are the 16 identified 'Primary Causes of Project Failures' from the PMI's 2015 *Pulse of the Profession* report:

1. Change in organisation's priorities
2. Change in project objectives
3. Inaccurate requirements gathering
4. Opportunities and risks were not defined
5. Inadequate vision or goal for the project
6. Inaccurate cost estimates
7. Inadequate/poor communication
8. Inadequate sponsor support
9. Poor change management
10. Inaccurate task time estimate

11. Resource dependency

12. Inadequate resource forecasting

13. Limited/taxed resources

14. Inexperienced project manager

15. Team member procrastination

16. Task dependency.

Remember, though, *there are only two reasons for project failure: poor project sponsorship and poor project management.* And given that the buck stops with you (see chapter 53), you could argue there's only one reason for project failure.

Here's the same list paired off with the person responsible for making sure the failure didn't happen:

1. Change in organisation's priorities *(project sponsor)*

2. Change in project objectives *(project sponsor)*

3. Inaccurate requirements gathering *(project manager)*

4. Opportunities and risks were not defined *(project sponsor and manager)*

5. Inadequate vision or goal for the project *(project sponsor)*

6. Inaccurate cost estimates *(project manager)*

7. Inadequate/poor communication *(project sponsor and manager)*

8. Inadequate sponsor support *(project sponsor)*

9. Poor change management *(project manager)*

10. Inaccurate task time estimate *(project manager)*

11. Resource dependency *(project manager)*

12. Inadequate resource forecasting *(project manager)*

13. Limited/taxed resources *(project sponsor and manager)*

14. Inexperienced project manager *(project sponsor)*

15. Team member procrastination *(project manager)*

16. Task dependency *(project manager)*.

Every excuse we come up with in reports, reviews, post-mortems and investigations can be linked back to the person responsible. Every time I sit down to read the latest project management survey, I dread what new horror story lies within.

I noted in the Preface that The Standish Group's 2016 *Chaos Report* identified three key success factors for projects as (1) executive sponsorship, (2) emotional maturity and (3) user involvement. My experience bears this out. Furthermore, it confirms that all three factors are within project sponsor and project manager control.

But how do we get to the point where we accept that the project isn't going to either deliver what we expect or give us the return on investment we require, and 'fail' the project? What will it take? Put simply, we (by which I mean you as the project sponsor) need to be more courageous.

You need to get better at interpreting the data you are presented with, asking the project manager the right questions, getting feedback from the team on what's working and what isn't. With this information you can take appropriate action.

Part of the problem is that we take project failure personally, seeing it as a stain on our reputation. It's worth remembering that while a project may fail, this doesn't make you a failure as a leader. In fact, the research shows that those who embrace failure become much more resilient and make better decisions as a result, so in that sense failure can only be a good thing.

Yet we waste so much money on failed projects.

The License Application Mitigation project in the US State of Washington offers one example. The project, to automate the state's vehicle registration and licence renewal system was originally estimated to cost US$15 million and take five years. Two years later the costs had risen to US$41.8 million; the following year they rose to US$51 million, and three years after that to US$67.5 million. At this point, it became obvious not only that the cost of the project was out of control, but that the cost to operate and maintain it would be six times more than the system being replaced. The project was stopped with US$40 million already spent.

We could find at least one such example in any country, in any year, and it just has to stop. The number one principle of the PRINCE2 project management methodology is that a project should have continued business justification. Yet this principle is forgotten time and time again.

Failing fast is a concept used in the software development industry and one we see used well in agile projects, where iterations of the software being produced are tested at regular intervals. When the tests fail, the project 'fails' and they go back to the drawing board.

Astro Teller, of Google X, shared in his TED talk that their engineers are so thirsty for a quick failure that they have developed a team whose sole purpose is to create adverse conditions for their 'moonshot' projects (the self-driving car being a good example) to fail.

In his book *Failing Forward*, John C. Maxwell argues that if we're not failing (as individuals and organisations), then we're not moving forward. In order to overcome the fear of failing, he offers up seven abilities that you, as the project sponsor, need to develop:

1. **Reject rejection.** Take responsibility for your actions, but don't blame yourself.

2. **See failure as temporary.** Personalising failure can cause you to get stuck. As an achiever you will see problems as momentary events.

3. **See failure as isolated.** Failing is not a lifelong event. Smile, because you can't win them all.

4. **Keep expectations realistic.** You have to mentally prepare for each obstacle you create. Each requires a unique expectation. Don't give up.

5. **Focus on your strengths.** Concentrate always on what you can do and where you are successful.

6. **Vary approaches to achievement.** Don't be shy about trying new approaches to problems, and don't allow others to make you feel like a failure.

7. **Bounce back.** You can't take failure personally—learn from it and move forward.

When a project is going to miss its targets, as the sponsor you have a choice to make: carry on as you are or stop and take stock. The latter is the right and courageous thing to do. Even though it may not feel like it at the time, you'll be doing yourself, the team and the organisation as a whole a big favour.

ACTIONS

DO: Embrace failure and pass on the learning to others.

READ: *Failing Forward* by John C. Maxwell.

POST: Failure is a demonstration that we tried something different. #ProjectBook

PART VI
RESULTS

I've noted that consistently good project results are hard to come by, yet most organisations continue to think they're doing a great job. It's got to the stage where project failure has become so commonplace that we've started to see it as success, or we just aren't seeing clearly at all. To illustrate this disconnect, in a recent KPMG survey of New Zealand businesses, 61 per cent of organisations surveyed believed project success rates were improving, despite the fact that they weren't!

Thinking every project will be successful is the root cause of many project problems; there is simply no data to indicate that will ever be the case. Indeed, IBM found that only 41 per cent of projects ever hit their project plan targets. For the New Zealand businesses surveyed in the KPMG study, the figure was 33 per cent.

Today we expect every single project to be successful, but even when they aren't we convince ourselves they are rather than admitting they failed!

The Victorian Ombudsman's report into failed ICT projects found, 'Too often, there was muted acceptance that all ICT-enabled projects go wrong'. This needn't be the case. It's important to recognise at the start that not every venture will be successful.

Maybe it's time we planned to fail more in order to succeed more?

In *The New Rules of Management*, Peter Cook uses a school analogy to highlight the folly of thinking that every single project will be successful: 'Failing 50% of your subjects or your exams is not a good strategy for school. So we learn to try not to fail anything. However for life, failing 50% of your projects is a great strategy. Aiming to fail 50% of your projects is the perfect way to embrace the risk inherent in any worthwhile project'.

I tend to agree. In my experience, we never delivered 100 per cent of the projects we promised we would at the start of the year. Every quarter the portfolio would be reviewed for ongoing viability and priority, which would often lead to widespread changes to meet the ever-evolving demands of the business.

Peter Cook again: 'Often we don't commit to serious goals and projects because of the risk of failing. What will it mean about me if I really go for it and don't get there? What will other people think? What will I think?' When it comes to results, failing a project may be the best result. The key here is that you gave it everything.

You may be unable to make a 100 per cent commitment for a variety of reasons. Here are three:

- **Workload.** You simply have too much on your plate, and adding another project — without being clear on your priorities — overwhelms you.

- **Lack of buy-in.** The project is the brainchild (or pet!) of someone else within the organisation and you've been asked to lead it, even though you're unconvinced it's something the organisation should be doing.

- **You don't know how to.** Let's face it, sponsoring projects is something everyone assumes you can do as soon as you are appointed to a senior management role. In reality, it's not just another hat for you to wear; it's a completely different set of clothes, and often there's no one there to help you choose and dress.

To achieve the results expected—both in terms of product delivery during the project and benefit realisation afterwards—it's absolutely paramount that you commit 100 per cent. Anything less and failure will undoubtedly follow. In *First Things First*, Stephen Covey suggests that this commitment is key but also observes that 'basing our happiness on our ability to control everything is futile'.

You need to establish what Covey calls a 'compass' and a 'clock'. Both are equally important, though each of us tends to favour one over the other. By *compass*, he means vision, values, principles, mission, behaviours, conscience direction (what we feel is important and how we'll work together). By *clock*, he means commitments, appointments, benefits, schedules, goals, activities (what we need to do and how we manage our time).

During the pre-project business case construction phase, organisations expend a lot of words articulating the clock—*burning platform, hard and fast deadlines, building capability, increasing capacity* and a load of other nauseating jargon to avoid establishing concrete measures around the $10 million in savings promised.

Generally, dates and costs have been estimated during strategy development and are based on best-case scenarios that almost never materialise. It's important to remember that any dates and costs at this early stage are indicative only and can quite easily change by +/− 100 per cent once you get into the project planning detail.

The planning phase is where you confirm the clock elements of your project. People (it's never resources), equipment, deliverables, dates, quality, costs, structures and objectives—these factors form the foundation for the project, but only when paired with the compass elements. Without creating a vision of the future, and agreeing how you'll behave and work together, delivery will be fraught, fractured and fragile. These projects are liable to break down at any minute, as the only thing holding them together is the paperwork created.

While it will be important for your project (and organisation) to ensure that certain forms are filled at certain times, this is no measure of a successful project. As Jim Highsmith reminds us in his book *Agile Project Management*, 'Compliance results are different'.

Compliance results may be important but are not an effective barometer on whether a project is achieving the expected results. That's not to say you should mistrust the reporting of project managers, but it should always be married with real-time feedback from those working on the project or involved in the building of its products.

As a project sponsor, you must involve yourself not only in regularly assessing the compass and clock results, but also in taking corrective action where there is the slightest deviation. On one project I was sponsor on, I gathered feedback on the performance of the project manager as well as checking the detail of the report. The report indicated that everything was rosy, but feedback on the project manager's performance was poor.

I advised the project manager of what needed to change and set him a goal of a month to make the corrections. Four weeks later, not only had the project manager addressed the behaviours, but he'd also empowered the team to provide monthly feedback on the things he could improve.

On a different project, the (contract) project manager didn't respond to the challenges the team had with his behaviours and I let him go. Our projects are too important to be held back by inefficient individuals or suppliers. This is just one example of where you'll have to make tough decisions to get the results you expect.

Traditionally we have only ever measured the clock elements of a project. McKinsey found that most leadership programs fail because businesses don't track and manage leadership performance over time. The same is true of projects, though I'm pleased to say that this is changing.

In his TED talk 'Being brilliant every day' Dr Alan Watkins suggests that 'in order to change the result or performance, you have to focus on the behaviour'. That will involve people changing how they think, feel and express their emotions. Being a project sponsor means being a role model and helping people to do this, not just approving a project status report.

Driving for and achieving results—through successfully delivering or failing projects—is your responsibility and a skill that every senior manager and project sponsor should have. Every decision you make should safeguard these results and support the organisation's strategic intent.

Never forget that you get the results your leadership deserves. Only you can affect that.

CHAPTER 68

CULTURE IS KEY, BUT SO IS STRATEGY

One of the most rewarding things about being a project sponsor is the opportunity to work with a project leader to create a vibrant, productive subculture within your existing organisation culture. A culture that people want to be part of. A culture that positively challenges the status quo. A culture that holds itself to account for its behaviour and promises. A culture that's talked about for decades.

The sad fact, though, is that most project sponsors spurn this opportunity in their zeal to 'get on with it'. They move from business case (why) to planning (what) without any thought to creating the environment in which great people can do great things (how).

Tomas Chamorro-Premuzic, writing in the *Harvard Business Review*, explains, 'Culture is key because it drives employee engagement and performance. However, culture isn't the cause of leadership so much as the result of it'. The best projects are a result of the person who lead them or the environment they create. This has always been the case and always will be.

I covered the culture model in part II of this book. It's important to understand that as the project sponsor you are a critical part of the project culture, as it represents the environment in which your project will be built. The project manager becomes the glue and your collective leadership style is critical in preserving and enhancing it.

You must also ensure that the project is important strategically, and remains so throughout its lifecycle. One of the most overused quotes is from Peter Drucker, who, in a conversation with then Ford CEO Mark Fields, said, 'Culture eats strategy for breakfast'. While culture is the *how* of work, you still need strategy to guide the *why* and *what*.

It's not good enough just to have a great culture, you need strategic intent too. Indeed I'd argue that you can't build a vibrant culture if you don't have a good strategy, as people will always say, 'Why are we doing this again?', leading to a loss of engagement.

The first strategy I was involved in building was set for five years. Given the advances in working practices and technology, that time window has narrowed significantly, so today anything over three years is considered ambitious.

The project portfolio identified as part of the strategy has to help the organisation achieve the goals it has set without compromising business-as-usual activity. This means ensuring you take on only as much work as your people can handle; otherwise, not only will you fail to hit your strategic goals, but business-as-usual work may be compromised too.

Throughout the year, your strategic goals should be continually reviewed, and should they change, the project portfolio will likely have to change as well.

STRATEGY

GOALS

BUSINESS AS USUAL
Run the Business

PROJECT PORTFOLIO
Grow the Business

CULTURE

It would be really wrong to think of culture as the only thing a project (or a business, for that matter) requires to be successful. You need a good strategy too.

ACTIONS

DO: Ensure that strategy is clear and that project cultures improve the way things get done in business as usual.

READ: *The Culture Code* by Daniel Coyle.

POST: Culture is important to my project, but strategy is too. #ProjectBook

CHAPTER 69
GET OFF TO A FLYER

Having established that culture is the most important element of your project, that's where you must always start. Resist the temptation to blunder straight into implementation without planning and take stock of what you have to do.

The start is the most important part of any race. Usain Bolt, the Jamaican 100-metre sprinter and multiple gold medal winner, was consistently slow out of the blocks, which meant he had to work twice as hard to catch up. This is a great metaphor for starting a project off in the right way. If you don't start with understanding how you'll work together as a team, you'll be constantly playing catch-up.

As the sponsor, think carefully about the people you need to be involved in the unique culture you're creating. Think about the detractors, passives and promoters, and invite them all to two days of culture setting. Or, as Simon Dowling recommends in his excellent book *Work with Me*, 'Throw a Starty Party!'

Two days of establishing a vision, agreeing behaviours and talking about how you'll work together (collaboration). Two days of discussing what works well within your current organisation, and what lessons you've learned from other projects and elements of your culture.

How will you gather information, talk and communicate with each other, and set your workplace up for success? Are you co-located (always the best option) or are you geographically distributed? How are you going to run your meetings — stand-up, sit-down or walking, 5 minutes, 15 minutes or 45? How are you going to use music (because headphones are a culture killer)?

How will you celebrate success and reward great behaviour, collaboration and innovation? How are you going to keep it simple and, most important, how will you ensure you don't take yourselves too seriously?

At the end of this two-day exercise you'll have defined the vibrant culture you need to best deliver the objectives and outcomes.

Netflix is an example of an organisation with a vibrant culture. Its well-publicised culture deck sets out exactly what's expected and sets the tone for how the work gets done. (Sheryl Sandberg, Chief Operating Officer at Facebook, has called the culture deck 'one of the most important documents to come out of Silicon Valley'.) It sums up its culture as follows: 'Freedom and responsibility instead of creating endless rules and processes', which is how most companies deal with major growth.

My personal favourite is its expense policy, which is just five words long: 'Act in Netflix's best interests'.

Netflix is just one technology company that fully understands the role of great culture in delivering great products. It is building on what Google, Apple, Microsoft and others have been doing for years, and that is to put their staff 'in control' of the way things get done.

A culture deck takes two days for a team to complete. I know this because this is the core of what I did and was a key output, produced at the start of the project, that defined *how* people would work together. Whatever you do, building a strong culture is a critical part of setting your project up for success. As Ed Catmull says in *Creativity Inc.*, 'One of the most crucial responsibilities of leadership is creating a culture that rewards those who lift our aspirations'.

As the sponsor you are a big part of this, and you need to ensure that it's built before the plan is developed. Your project manager or scrum team should be experts at building and evolving the culture to meet the changing demands of the project.

Once that's done, you should spend some time thinking about all the things that could kill your project. In essence, you're going to do a pre-mortem on your own project. The pre-mortem technique has been around for a while but continues to be underused by most organisations.

Think about all the things you need to do differently to ensure your project doesn't die early. Set aside a specific length of time (two hours always worked for me), ensure everyone who's going to be involved in the project is physically there (face-to-face is best) and have a great facilitator to ensure that the conversation keeps moving and good notes are taken.

Then follow this four-step process:

1. List everything that has gone wrong with previous projects in the organisation. This helps draw a line under some issues, shine a light on others and ensure everyone is fully aware of the mistakes you don't want to see repeated.

2. List anything that could possibly go wrong with the project. This can be quite a fun exercise, as people come up with the wildest ideas! The aim here is to challenge everyone to think about what could kill (or at least seriously harm) the project before you get started.

3. Now pick the top 10. The facilitator should capture every idea, while as a team you pick the biggest risks to your success that need to be addressed early on.

4. Come up with solutions. The team should work together to create solutions for these problems. This becomes a risk mitigation plan for the project manager, but its true function is to make everyone responsible for ensuring that these things don't occur.

No one wants to do a post-mortem, so addressing any potential issues early is critically important. If you wait until the end, it's too late. Getting the culture right isn't easy, but the best chance you have of establishing something that works (or at least can be built on) is at the start.

In *Finite and Infinite Games*, James P. Carse writes, 'Just as it is essential to have a definitive ending, it must also have a precise beginning'. Creating this precise beginning is your responsibility as project sponsor. Once you have an established culture, then you can pass responsibility to the project manager to ensure its evolution.

As the sponsor, you need to ensure that the project manager puts sufficient time and effort into ensuring this happens. In its culture deck, Netflix tells managers, 'We're a team, not a family. We're like a pro sports team, not a kids' recreational team. Netflix leaders hire, develop and cut smartly so we have stars in every position'.

Right now Netflix is one of the most successful companies on the planet, and they owe that dominance to the culture they have created. It's no accident. It takes time and strong leadership. Ed Catmull, current President of Pixar Studios, says, 'Quality is not a consequence of following some set of behaviours … rather it is a prerequisite and a mindset you must have before you decide what you are setting off to do'.

I'll leave the final words to Usain Bolt: 'I worked a lot on starting well. After that, when I get into my stride, I just let everything flow'.

ACTIONS

DO: Take time to build your project culture.

READ: *Creativity Inc.* by Ed Catmull.

POST: We're running a pre-mortem to set ourselves up for a successful start. #ProjectBook

CHAPTER 70

EVERY PROJECT NEEDS A PLAN

The evolution of the project culture starts with the planning of the project, which should follow immediately after the initial culture has been built. The role of a project manager is therefore to:

1. build a team

2. build a plan

3. deliver the project.

It's important to state at this point that the costs and times you have come up with in the business case (providing you have one!) are not the final costs or times the project will be delivered to. These are estimates. It is the planning process that will determine what can be delivered and when. Often the pre-planning business case can be out by plus or minus 100 per cent, which is why it's so critical that you make time for planning.

In my experience, so many organisations get this wrong. This is reinforced by the worldwide reviews and reports into project failure. In a review of federally funded projects in the US in 2008, the Government Accountability Office defined 413 projects, totalling US$25.2 billion as poorly planned, poorly managed or both.

Reviewing the top 10 IT projects in Australia, the Victorian Ombudsman found, 'None of the projects investigated [were] well planned'. The HealthSMART project included in this review was so bad it didn't even have a business case 'despite seeking over $300 million in funding'.

The e-Borders project in the UK cost the government £830 million and has still not delivered against its original vision. A key reason for this poor performance? Failure to set appropriate benchmarks from which to assess project progress.

PWC's 2016 Global Construction Survey found that most of the 500 major projects worldwide they assessed failed to come within 10 per cent of the time deadlines.

Money and time are consistently wasted because organisations can't be bothered to put the effort into completing planning properly. As a sponsor, you need to be aware of this issue and make sure you don't make the same mistake.

If your project is using a traditional or waterfall approach, then you must ensure the project manager is given the time they need to get the plan right. For a 12-month project, it can take up to three months to finalise the plan. You'll have clarity on the benefits, scope, deliverables, quality expectations, communications required, stakeholders affected, initial risk exposure and structures required to get the job done. I can't overstate how important this is.

A KPMG New Zealand project management survey found that only 33 per cent of organisations achieve the objectives they set out to. You don't want yours to fall into the same trap. Having a detailed plan—with phases such as design, build, test and implement—that the project manager can manage to will mitigate that risk. It's then your job to make sure they stick to it.

A couple of years ago I was asked to review a project that was being led by a subject matter expert. When I asked him where the plan was, he touched his head and said, 'It's all up here'. That's not good enough. It certainly wasn't for that project, which was eventually cancelled at a loss of $1.5 million. All for lack of a plan.

If your project is using an agile approach, then the plan will be much more fluid, with less certainty around time and cost. In *Agile Project Management*, Jim Highsmith identifies the following core values of agile project management (which mirror the values outlined in the Agile Manifesto):

- individuals and interactions over processes and tools
- working products over comprehensive documentation
- customer collaboration over contract negotiation
- responding to change over following a plan.

You can expect more uncertainty at the start, with the project gaining clarity as each sprint (or short cycle) is completed. If you're looking for these projects to follow established funding phases or to produce lots of documentation, then you've chosen the wrong approach. The planning in an agile project concentrates on getting to the end of the first phase (sprint), before assessing and re-planning.

That said, running agile projects isn't an excuse for removing the project manager, as emphasised by Alistair Cockburn in chapter 43.

Spotify is an example of an organisation that doesn't form traditional project teams, but instead creates autonomous, cross-functional, co-located, self-organising squads to get the work done. Interestingly, the company also measures success by how satisfied customers (internal and external) are.

If you're not bound by time or cost, or you aren't fully clear on the customer need, the agile approach is definitely a good way to go.

Whichever approach you take, your job is to make sure there's a plan that's comprehensive enough to provide you and the stakeholders with confidence around dates and costs and that evolves as the project progresses. Creating an initial plan isn't enough. You also have to ensure that the plan—owned by the project manager—is updated regularly to reflect the work that's been done and that has yet to be done. Your job as a sponsor is to keep pushing the project manager to deliver, not to sit back waiting for it to happen.

Many project managers have lost the knowledge of what it takes to create a plan. You cannot tolerate this. Again, their job is to build a team, build a plan and deliver the project. Without building a team you can't build a good plan. Without building a good plan you can't deliver the project. It's that simple.

Having said all that, project planning is not a straight-line process. It is a non-stop juggling and balancing act that requires flexibility, collaboration, attention to detail and a sense of humour! A regularly changing plan is not easy to manage.

Project managers who have taken the time to build a strong plan will defend it passionately and rebuff any attempts to change it. This is a good thing if the suggested changes don't contribute to the outcomes, but it can be a bad thing if they do.

I can't stress enough how important the planning process is. Like Chitty Chitty Bang Bang, when you're in control of it, it will take you exactly where you want to go. When you're not, you're grounded.

ACTIONS

DO: Get involved in the planning process — it's your project, after all.

READ: *Agile Project Management* by Jim Highsmith.

POST: We're planning to succeed, not planning to fail. #ProjectBook

CHAPTER 71

INNOVATION NEEDS MINDSET AND TIME

For many organisations innovation is still something they strive for, something they feel they don't have, something that will help them achieve the success they know they are capable of. They've seen the new kids on the block—Uber, Airbnb, Netflix and the like—come up with ideas that have disrupted entire industries and they want to do the same.

'We need to think and act like entrepreneurs.' 'We need to think outside the square.' 'We should buy a table tennis table, because all the most innovative companies have one.' 'Now, I need that four-page report in PowerPoint by Friday...' And they wonder why their people don't come up with ideas that challenge the organisation to be different and to unlock potential revenue streams and savings not previously thought of.

Innovation will never naturally occur in these organisations for two reasons:

- They don't give people time to work on different ideas.
- They don't have the growth mindset necessary to think that anything is possible.

Uber, Airbnb and Netflix have been successful because they had time to work on those ideas, got them to market quickly rather than waiting to achieve perfection, and—most importantly—are staffed by people who aren't held back by 'the way we do things around here'.

Some have interpreted this as 'going agile', and while agile approaches can change the speed at which organisations get products delivered, they still require a change of mindset from all involved if they're to be as effective as they can be.

3M popularised 15 per cent time in the US in the late 1940s in order to find ideas that would ensure they stayed relevant in the post-war world. They'd had great success in the 1930s with Scotch tape, the brainchild of employee Richard Drew, and were determined to encourage their employees to dream up similar (money making) ideas. This led them to the game-changing Post-it note. Their culture of allowing time for innovation continues to attract employees with great ideas, as do similar initiatives in organisations such as Google and Apple.

Another organisation that excels at innovation is Australian software company Atlassian. Organised by its Head of Engineering, Atlassian's 'Ship-It Days' give employees 24 hours to work on whatever they want. It's a way of generating product ideas that can be used immediately or in future planning. From changing light bulbs to developing brand-new software services, Ship-It Days have proved hugely successful and popular.

Projects should be role models for innovation. We should build in time for talented people to find better ways to do things, and we should create environments that aren't restricted by traditional structures.

A recent study found that senior executives of the most innovative companies were themselves innovators. And these leaders displayed 50 per cent more discovery skills than those in less innovative companies. The evidence is clear. If you want your project (or organisation, for that matter) to be successful, senior executives have to role model what that looks like.

Westfield has a fast-pilot, fast-scale, fast-innovation approach to getting projects delivered quickly. It also has a

Wall of Broken Dreams filled with ideas that haven't made it past the pilot stage or have failed altogether. It is this growth mindset that encourages an innovative approach, because, as Carol Dweck puts it, 'Exceptional people have a talent for converting life's setbacks into future successes'.

Staff with a growth mindset make the difference when it comes to high performance. They find ways to get things done and don't need to be told. They never stop looking for smarter or better ways. They are never held back by 'the way we do things round here' or by people who want to rush them through a task. This has nothing to do with personality and everything to do with attitude.

If innovation is part of your current culture, then developing an innovation strategy or set of principles is a good place to start. According to the 2016 Innovation Index, only 37 per cent of organisations have one. As well as defining a structure for capturing and testing new ideas, it also outlines the behaviours required to fully adopt the approach.

For if generating new ideas is to become the new normal, the Innovation Index suggests, the organisation and team need to demonstrate the following attributes and behaviours:

- positivity
- persuasiveness
- experimental
- willingness to take chances
- a broad, diverse network of people to share ideas with.

One approach some have found useful is Innovation Labs. The use of Innovations Labs has increased by almost 15 per cent recently among the world's top 30 companies and by 25 per cent among the top 10. Labs are used to test ideas quickly and to deliver value to the customer quickly. They are predominantly in-house units set up to complement existing ways of working, with specific projects selected to use them based on the needs of the customer or the speed at which value is required. These labs are led by executives and staffed by people with a growth mindset.

As a project sponsor, you need to ensure that you adopt an innovation approach for the right projects and that the project manager isn't holding talent back by implementing a rigid way of thinking and approaching problems. If you are to create the right solution to meet the needs of the customer, the project sponsor and the project manager need to build in time, lead by example and encourage a different way of thinking.

Here are some strategies that can help in getting this right:

- **Build on what you've already got.** Don't reinvent the wheel. If you have something that works, build on it to deliver value quickly.

- **Fail fast.** If your solution isn't going to give the customer what they're looking for, call a halt, and start again.

- **Anticipate future trends.** Keep your eye on what others are doing, anticipate what the customer may need and deliver more value than they were expecting.

- **Create something that surprises people.** Stray from the norm and build something worth talking about. Use a tool to capture ideas, provide some money (seed fund) for a prototype and invest in the things that add real value.

While innovation can be applied to any kind of project approach, it lends itself to the agile method much more than it does to the waterfall method. In agile, you get to build and test ideas every two to four weeks, when it's easier to fail them and try something new.

With the waterfall approach, much more certainty is created at the start of the process to ensure you get what you expect, which means there is much less room for innovation. That's not to say innovation approaches can't be adopted to help resolve issues, though.

As sponsor, you have to encourage innovation in others. Stretch your own thinking and mindset, be relentless in your search for smarter and better ways of doing things. Find a mentor who can help you build a growth mindset. Being innovative shouldn't be a 'nice to have'; it should be something every project and organisation does. All it requires is time and a different mindset. Get to it!

ACTIONS

DO: Develop a growth mindset and regularly challenge your own thinking.

WATCH: 'Mastering the Five Skills of Disruptive Innovators' (*HBR*, 20 October 2014).

POST: We're developing a growth mindset to find smarter ways to do things. #ProjectBook

CHAPTER 72

METHODS NEED TO BE UNDERSTOOD

If there's one thing we're good at in project management, it's confusing the hell out of people with terminology about methods. It has become a disease and it needs to be eradicated. Too often I hear (and see on social media) arguments about which one is best, how someone is applying it wrongly or why all projects are doomed if they use or don't use a particular method.

It's so unhelpful and, frankly, boring. What these method martyrs have lost sight of is the fact that in project management it's our job to deliver a product that satisfies a customer need and allows them to get the value they expect for their investment. Some 99.9 per cent of the time, the customer doesn't care how it's done, providing they get those things in the agreed time frame and within budget. Currently that's not happening, so the arguments about which method is best are misplaced.

I discuss methods in detail in chapters 42 and 43.

The biggest issue with methods is that for years senior managers have seen them as silver bullets to improve the way projects are delivered. This is lazy and fails to recognise that people and culture are the biggest determinants of project success or failure.

Changing culture and coaching or getting rid of people can be a long and laborious process, but that shouldn't mean it's avoided. It needs to be tackled head on if you want to improve things, because simply changing your method of delivery won't do this.

Most organisations are making the same mistake with agile approaches today. CEOs are making grand statements about going agile and being 'more like Spotify', rather than putting time and effort into evolving the culture and mindset of their people to meet future challenges.

Of course, it's fantastic that organisations want to equip their staff with knowledge of the latest method. However, the method of delivery has always been the least important contributor to project success. So simply to assume that everything will change when they 'go DevOps' is to repeat the mistake CEOs made in the early 2000s with PRINCE2 and PMBoK.

As a sponsor it's important that you understand the different methods for delivery and ensure your project takes the right approach. At no stage do you allow yourself to be dictated to by the project manager. Which route to take will be the subject of discussion between the two of you at the start of the project.

You don't need to go on a three-day course to prepare for this (although if time and money permit, it might help), but you do need to fully understand the way your organisation justifies its investments, plans its projects and delivers on the benefits.

It's your responsibility to present the funding papers to the executive committee using the right form at the right time (often called gates), and you need to take an interest in where these processes can be improved to deliver value more quickly to your stakeholders.

There's no such thing as 'best' practice, so don't let a project or program management office (PMO) convince you there is, because what's best for one project might not necessarily suit another. And beware those who tell you how it should be done yet who've never been a project manager themselves. These people generally value the system and processes over the people.

In his *Learning from Failure* report, Peter Shergold observed, 'Effective project and program management involves more than strict adherence to a prescriptive methodology. Leadership skills, judgement, common sense, initiative, effective communication, negotiation skills and a broad perspective on the surrounding environment are all essential. Project and program management is a creative and collaborative process'.

And that's true regardless of the method being used.

Remember, the best projects are a result of the person who leads them or the environment they create. Underpinning all of this, however, will be a system for delivery that both you and the project manager should know inside out and deliver consistently against. The 'rules' are there for you too, and breaking them will only undermine your role as a leader.

ACTIONS

DO: Take the time to understand the different delivery methods and how they should be used.

DO: Get familiar with your organisation's framework and ensure it's applied consistently.

POST: We're making sure there's no madness in our methods. #ProjectBook

CHAPTER 73

CELEBRATE GOOD (AND BAD) TIMES

'Celebrate every success,' urges physician and philosopher Debasish Mridha, 'but don't forget to enjoy those scars of failure.'

Ah, the scars of failure. Every great project I managed and sponsored was influenced by the scars I've gained through failure, whether on a personal level, a project level or an organisational level.

I'm not talking about catastrophic career-threatening events, but rather those little things that over the years I have got wrong—and of course as a human being I'm still always learning. The failures will never end, but I can see them for what they are, celebrate the new knowledge I have and move on quickly.

As a profession we carry many scars when it comes to failure, but in many cases we're just not learning the lessons of the past and we continue to make the same mistakes. Too often this happens because the organisation (or individual) doesn't bring the reason for failure out into the open, admit what's happened and why, and set about creating the kind of environment where those mistakes aren't repeated. Instead, excuses are made, fingers are pointed then it's all swept under the carpet.

Failure is an opportunity for learning and should be embraced and celebrated in the same way that success is. At one organisation I worked for we even held morning teas for the projects we killed early. We did this for three reasons:

1. to acknowledge and show our gratitude for the efforts of the team in getting us to that point

2. to demonstrate that we took our role as senior leaders seriously, and terminating projects that no longer met our business objectives was one way of showing that

3. to share the learnings with others so those mistakes weren't repeated.

By gaming the failure process in this way, it became memorable for all involved. Organisations that choose merely to fill in a report to signify early project termination—if they do even this!—miss a huge communication opportunity. People remember morning teas much better than they remember the words in a report.

In his TED talk 'The unexpected benefit of celebrating failure', Astro Teller argues that, while getting people to work on risky projects is a challenge and will make people feel uncomfortable, the only way to make them feel comfortable is to make it 'safe' to fail. They are then rewarded for it. They even get promoted for it! Rewards can take many forms. Being publicly complimented for discovering a flaw is just one of them.

Success is not only about completing a task; it's a behaviour shown, a service provided, a habit changed, a fear overcome, a milestone reached. These successes are individual and collective and should be celebrated accordingly.

This is particularly true when it comes to changing something in the way you work. These habits and behaviours (mistakenly referred to as soft skills) are the hardest things to change, so every time someone makes the effort to get feedback on the way they work and chooses to take action, that effort should be celebrated. Charles Duhigg, author of *The Power of Habit*, believes that adding a little celebratory reward after engaging in a change habit acts as a powerful reinforcer.

When I started out as a project manager we could draw on a special budget for celebrating success. I could shout morning teas, lunches, personal experiences, individual gifts and group outings. It was all approved by my various project sponsors, accounted for accordingly, and very clearly demonstrated that we took achievement seriously.

In our rush to bring greater discipline to our projects and budget management, we've lost sight of this, and that's a shame when you consider the benefits celebrating success offers:

- It builds loyalty.
- It's a reminder of what the goal was and how it was achieved.
- It unifies the team around what they've achieved.
- It motivates the team to keep delivering.
- It's a reminder that they're working on a winning project that gets the job done.
- It focuses on the positives.
- It builds momentum.
- It breaks the day-to-day focus on tasks.
- It brings the wider team together.
- It allows for reward and recognition.
- It improves morale inside and outside the project team.

Sponsors who value the importance of celebrating success should ensure that this budget line is included and protected. Work with the project manager on its discretionary use and create the right kind of environment where the team receives very visible credit for its work.

When I work with teams to help them develop their cultures, we do a specific exercise around building a social calendar. One activity per month that brings the team together so they can collectively celebrate what they've achieved over the previous month and can create some shared stories to take them into the next month. These events are suitable for both introverts and extroverts, because both personality types understand they have to step out of their comfort zone a little to build team unity. Activities may range from treasure hunts to bake-offs to simple team lunches.

I've never been a fan of throwing a lavish party at the end of the project. I prefer to see money spent across the life of the project—little and often—to ensure you actually make it to the end, and in a way that everyone appreciates and enjoys. In the absence of this budget, dip your hand into your own pocket and fund it yourself.

Sports scientist Dr Gert Jan Pepping believes, 'The more convincingly someone celebrates success with their teammates, the greater the chances that the team will win'. In project terms, winning means delivering to the customer's expectations, or failing a project when you realise it's no longer going to do so. In the UK we used to say, 'The team that drinks together stays together'. Our cultures have changed (thankfully, for my liver and health) and success is no longer recognised by alcoholic excess. The sentiment remains, though.

The team that celebrates together stays together, and it's your job as sponsor to lead this activity but not take credit for a single thing.

ACTIONS

DO: Ensure you take the time to celebrate successes and failures.

WATCH: Astro Teller's TED talk 'The unexpected benefit of celebrating failure'.

POST: We celebrate success and failure in equal measure. #ProjectBook

CHAPTER 74

OUTCOMES DON'T ACHIEVE THEMSELVES

The Project Management Institute (PMI) found that only 9 per cent of organisations 'do benefit identification extremely well' and that '35 per cent of project benefits are often overly optimistic'. According to a KPMG study, 'Only 21 per cent of organisations consistently deliver on their benefits'. A recent McKinsey report discovered that '17 per cent of IT projects go so badly that they threaten the very existence of a company'. More than a quarter of the organisations surveyed by KPMG New Zealand 'do not undertake any form of strategic review to track the benefits realised by the business'.

I'm deliberately labouring this point—stay with me...

ABC News announced, 'The government approved a $1.5 billion payment to the Victorian state government for the East–West Road Link project, without any form of cost–benefit analysis'. The Auditor General's report into the road project commented, 'The likely net benefits of the project were not sufficiently demonstrated'.

The PMI has calculated that '83 per cent of organisations lack maturity in benefit realisation and waste $122 million for every $1 billion spent'. Turning to the *NZ Gateway Review paper into Government projects:* 'Concerns continue around the application of core project and programme management disciplines and processes, with a startling proportion of recommendations showing a lack of maturity in benefits realisation'.

It's depressing, isn't it? I'm almost in tears just writing it. And every year, we wheel out the excuses, when in reality there are only three reasons for not getting the benefits we expected:

1. We were overly optimistic in the business case (or exaggerated the potential) in order to get the funding in the first place.

2. Market conditions changed during the course of the project, reducing the benefits we could expect. We decided it was worth pursuing anyway.

3. We don't care enough as leaders to do the hard work to get the benefits once the project has finished.

As the project sponsor, you are responsible for ensuring that the project provides the benefits promised. It's not the project manager's job. They are responsible for ensuring that the asset gets built.

So there's no confusion, when I say benefits I mean outcomes, essentially the 'rewards' you get as an organisation once you complete the project. And that's why it's not the project manager's job to ensure you get them. Their job ends once the asset has been built and handed over to operations; yours doesn't. At that point you revert to the role of benefits owner and make sure the organisation does everything it said it would in order to save money, earn money or change the way it operates.

Sadly for most, the project ends but the malady lingers on for one of the three reasons just listed. Here's how to avoid them and be the sponsor and organisation that delivers on its promises every time.

OPTIMISM/EXAGGERATION

When you want something there's a temptation to overstate what you can achieve once you have it. If you've ever bought fitness equipment for your home you'll know exactly what I mean. Not only will you be saving money on that gym membership you never use, but you'll be able to keep fit every day of the week without any excuses. Result? Three months later, the equipment is gathering dust in the garage and you're three kilos heavier.

Avoid the temptation to do this — to overstate benefits I mean, not to exercise. You should definitely exercise.

When doing your analysis in the early stages of deciding whether or not to undertake a project, always err on the side of caution and go with the lowest possible expectations. It's always better to underpromise and overdeliver.

This means ensuring the planning process is comprehensive so you understand what you're in for from the start. I've seen too many projects deliver a negative ROI because not enough work was done to establish the 'true costs'.

If, once planning is completed, the project numbers don't stack up, then stop, straight away. Continuing because you've already spent money on planning (sunk costs) is just about the worst thing you can do. Another is trying to get a different answer to the same question. It doesn't stack up. Period. So stop it.

MARKET CONDITION CHANGES

One organisation I worked with produced a strong business case to introduce Blackberrys across the senior management team, back when the Blackberry was still a thing. It was going to cost around $100 000, but the tangible benefits for fieldwork and their disparate office locations meant it was a relatively easy decision to make. They also wanted to demonstrate to their customers that they were early adopters when it came to technology.

Then the rumours of an Apple phone started to circulate. They were quite wild to begin with, but essentially it was going to do everything a Blackberry could do, but with greater flexibility, increased security and less cost. At that stage the project should have been stopped and deferred until a time when more was known about alternatives, but they ploughed ahead. The money was spent, the handsets were distributed and the training undertaken.

Then the iPhone was released—and no one wanted a Blackberry anymore. Instead they wanted something that gave them the opportunity to use (hitherto unknown) applications to increase productivity further. The Blackberrys were replaced six months later.

In this ever-changing world of ours, there's a good chance that something new will come along once you're in the middle of your project, and ignoring it or pretending it hasn't happened isn't a viable option.

If market conditions change, such that you're unable to get what you expected, then you need to stop and re-evaluate the project before it's too late. An excuse I hear all the time is that organisations simply didn't know they wouldn't be able to get the benefits they expected. In reality they couldn't be bothered to put in the work to find out, or else they took their eye off the ball completely during the project.

What you don't do at this stage is put the project on hold. There's nothing more confusing to the team than when senior managers do this. It creates widespread confusion over whether or not the project is still a priority. What you do is pause the implementation in order to re-evaluate the plan.

If you're using an agile approach, this is much easier to do and is even expected by the team. If you're taking a waterfall approach, though, you may need to commission some people to investigate the potential 'new' option and do some analysis on how it would impact your current time and cost estimates.

Only once you've gathered all the information, and understood its impact on the outcomes, can you make the decision to restart, replan or stop altogether.

NO ONE CARES

Perhaps the biggest reason for not getting the benefits is the fact that senior leaders just don't care enough to follow through. It's too hard. There's not enough time. I didn't believe we could do it in the first place. It's not my job. Excuses, excuses, excuses.

Having committed to the project in the first place, it *is* your job to see it through. Go back to the business case or justification for doing the project and make the changes you promised you would. Show how much you care and help the organisation achieve its strategic goals.

If it's an organisation-wide problem, then suggest that when people declare financial benefits in business cases, they also declare the budget line to be reduced or the sales targets to be increased the following year. Nothing makes benefits real better than taking money from people or increasing their targets.

This was an approach I used successfully in my roles heading up project departments. Where senior managers declared cost savings or revenue increases, then these numbers were immediately baked into the following year's budgets to provide solid accountability for achieving them.

In one organisation, this approach reduced the amount of new business cases by half, which meant we delivered on our business plan promises and weren't distracted by new pet projects. We recognised there were some senior managers who wanted to buy things and cared little about achieving the benefits they themselves had outlined in order to get a project approved. Don't be one of these people.

As sponsor, you're going to ensure that the products the project manager builds will give you the mechanisms to get the benefits you promised. You will follow this up with them every month.

Apathy towards results has no place in leadership roles. Don't become another statistic when it comes to realising the project benefits. After all, they are the reason we do projects in the first place.

ACTIONS

DO: Clearly articulate what outcomes you expect from the project.

DO: Stop the project if it's no longer viable.

POST: Getting the value we expect from our projects is critically important. #ProjectBook

CHAPTER 75

SPOT WHEN IT'S GOING WRONG

At some stage your project will hit the skids, as we used to say in Liverpool. I'd love to be able to tell you this won't happen to you and everything will go swimmingly well, but that's not the nature of projects, I'm afraid. By their nature, they are evolving entities that often generate uncertainty. Your job is to see that this uncertainty is well managed and to course-correct when you spot things are going wrong.

Here I'll give you a few insights from my experience into how to spot when your project is going wrong, in case it's not obvious to you.

1. NO ONE UNDERSTANDS WHY YOU'RE DOING THE PROJECT

For the project to really matter and for the people who are working on it to really care, it's got to align with what your company said they would address at the start of the year—in other words, your strategy. The second you deviate from that, you lose people and the kitchen conversations start: 'I have no idea why we're doing this' or 'This doesn't line up with what we said we'd do' or 'We're only doing this because the HR Manager went to [*insert name of competitor*] and saw what they'd done', and so on. The project *has* to fit your strategy, not the other way around, and as the sponsor you have to ensure the value is clear at the start and it has ongoing viability.

The moment it deviates from what was originally planned, doubt and suspicion arise and you have to reassure everyone that it will still deliver the expected outcomes. Constantly reiterating the 'why' is vital to maintaining interest and engagement.

2. WATERMELON PROJECTS

Ah, my favourite! The name derives from the 'traffic lights' we often use in our organisations to signify how we're progressing towards the key elements of our projects, usually time, cost and quality.

There are some projects we know are in trouble. The project manager will tell us of issues we're dealing with, or if risks are going unmanaged. In winter, projects often lose people to sickness. Still there remains a blind confidence that everything can still be achieved, so the project is reported as 'green'. All the traffic lights are set this way, yet the narrative on the project report doesn't reflect it.

They're called watermelon projects because they are green on the outside, but as soon as you cut them open by starting to ask questions, you find they're actually red on the inside, with bits of black here and there!

What you require at all times from your project manager is honest reporting. Otherwise you won't be able to make the decisions required to keep it moving towards achieving its objectives.

3. INCREASE IN EMAILS

In the first part of this book I talked at length about the project manager's role in relation to communication and relationship building. They walk, they talk and they constantly have their finger on the pulse of the project. Every now and then, though, they'll resort to writing. Emails that

0

confirm conversations are fine and to be expected (although you should never be copied into these). Then there are the passive-aggressive emails, often sent late at night, that speak to different problems.

These are a sign that a project manager has stopped talking and has resorted to an 'audit trail' of information instead. This is counterproductive for their role and what the project is trying to achieve. At this stage you'll show empathy and ask the project manager what the issue is in order to help them overcome it.

4. MISSED DEADLINES

If you haven't taken the time to plan properly, then you're going to miss deadlines. It's your responsibility to make sure this doesn't happen.

If you have taken the time to plan properly, then you're halfway to success and it's now the project manager's responsibility to ensure that it's actioned accordingly. It's their job to inspire and motivate the team, to set expectations, to help them manage their priorities and drive them to deliver. This is what project managers are paid to do.

When the first deadline is missed, it's a cause for concern, because in my experience there is often a domino effect. You can't afford to let this happen.

If there's no consequence for a project manager who misses a deadline, then they will continue to excuse them away. You have to hold them to the promises they make and be tough on them when they don't deliver. Remember that for any project to be successful you have to push each other to succeed. There really is no other way.

5. DOCUMENTS AREN'T UPDATED

As the sponsor you should regularly ask to see documents such as the schedule, risk register and issue register. If the project is being delivered in an agile way, these will still all exist, though they're more likely to be visual or talked about during the daily stand-up, where you'll be present. What these documents provide is another level of confidence that the person managing their project is doing their job properly, not skipping the important bits.

I would never allow my project managers to present anything to me that was more than a week out of date. Things change so quickly in projects that if you're not on top of the detail, then milestone delivery can get away from you.

A project manager should be spending a minimum of a day a week updating their documents or visuals to ensure that the information presented is up to date. If it's 'all in their head' (and extroverted project managers are a nightmare for this), you have to remind them that it needs to be documented too.

6. INCREASED SICK LEAVE

Projects can be stressful. Very stressful. If they're not handled in the right way it can lead to increased levels of sick leave, and that's bad for everyone.

In my experience, increases in sick and mental health leave are usually linked to one or more of the following factors:

a. **Project manager.** The role of the PM is to inspire and motivate, which means they have to show empathy and emotional intelligence. They have to understand the emotions and personalities of the team and manage them judiciously. That means no shouting, screaming or unreasonable demands. It means not talking behind their backs or embarrassing them in any way. And it means ensuring they have everything they need (including clarity) to be able to deliver as needed. Any deficiencies here often lead to stress and/or anxiety, and may result in people taking time away from their work.

b. **Workload**. Organisations often take on more work than they have staff for. This inevitably means people have to juggle multiple projects at the same time as doing their day job. It pushes people into putting in long hours without giving them any time (other than their holidays) to rest and recuperate, while it demands the same undiminished level of performance from them. This is simply not sustainable. As a sponsor you have a responsibility to be reasonable in your requests and to ensure that priorities are clear so people always know what's most important. Where workload is an issue, you need to work with your peers either to reduce low-value work or to bring more people in to help.

c. **Culture**. The environment in which you expect your people to work can often be counterproductive. From poor behaviours and performance going unchecked to unclear roles and responsibilities to a lack of daylight, there are many contributing cultural factors that may impact productivity on a project. In recent years the increasing numbers of emails and meetings has definitely become a problem. This is a cultural issue that can be dealt with, although in my experience, often the will to do so isn't strong enough at a senior management level. If your people department runs a culture survey, this will be the best place to look for potential cultural issues. If you don't deal to them and redefine the way you do things, then expect sick leave to increase.

d. **Competence**. Finally, it's possible the person being asked to complete the tasks is not up to it. Sure, they may be well meaning, enthusiastic and up for the challenge, but if they don't have the right skills, the project will only place extra pressure on them to perform. It's the project manager's job to ensure they're suitably skilled, then to regularly check in on them to ensure they have everything they need to be able to deliver. Should they consistently not meet expectation, however, they're likely to feel the pressure even more, leading to time away from the office. We should never put people in this situation. If we're not able to provide them with adequate training or give them extra time to complete a task, then bringing in someone externally may be the short-term answer.

7. FORECAST SPEND = BUDGET

Once the plan has been approved, it's time to spend the money. Every activity undertaken will cost something. During the planning process estimates will have been provided for the financial value of this work, and those estimates will likely be wrong because, well, they're estimates.

But that's fine. Any project manager worth their salt will understand this and make sure the financial estimates are greater than what's required, so towards the end of the project they'll have some money left either to give back or to use to address scope items that weren't anticipated at the start.

All of which means that if at any stage of the project the forecasted spend matches the budget exactly, then the project manager isn't doing their job. In my 20 years, no project ever came in exactly on budget. Ever. There will often be considerable flex, week to week or month to month, and in collaboration with the project manager you have to decide whether or not this is acceptable.

If you're ahead on the plan, then you may bring some work forward, causing an overspend against forecast; if you're running behind, then it's likely that you will underspend. But the forecasted spend never matches the budget. If you find it does, then you may have a problem.

ACTIONS

DO: Keep your eyes and ears open at all times for the things that aren't being said

DO: Continue to refresh your own skillset

POST: I'm keeping my eyes and ears open to potential project failure #ProjectBook

PROJECT SPONSORSHIP
SUMMARY

So there we go. As I said in the introduction for this section, it starts with you. Don't look to the project manager or the team to take the lead or set the example. Show them how it's done.

For a successful project, you must build the team, build the plan, then deliver the project. Always in that order, with each stage given the time it needs to get the job done to the satisfaction of the stakeholders. Got a year to complete a project? That means at least two to three months' planning. Going agile? You'll need to make sure everyone has the right mindset and understands the level of involvement required *before* you start, not during the project.

Successful project sponsors aren't lucky. They put time and effort into stewardship, make timely decisions and in any number of ways ensure that the expected results are achieved. They value project management as a discipline and performance manage project managers who can't get the job done.

Before you join their ranks, you will probably need to change a few habits — to:

- choose to be different
- choose to build relationships
- choose to role model behaviours
- choose to get involved
- choose empathy

- choose fun
- choose continual feedback
- choose flexibility
- choose to prioritise
- choose to celebrate
- choose to hit deadlines
- choose to continually measure outcomes
- choose to succeed.

Others do it well—you can too.

FREQUENTLY ASKED QUESTIONS

Every time I give a speech or run a training session on sponsorship with senior managers I'm consistently asked the same six questions, so I thought I'd end by including some answers to them.

1. SHOULD WE SET UP A PROJECT MANAGEMENT OFFICE (PMO)?

The PMO is a product of the early 2000s. They were designed to 'enforce' methods to provide consistency of delivery and to ensure that senior managers were given the right information at the right time to make the decisions necessary to deliver against business strategy.

Except, in most cases, that didn't happen. Worldwide project delivery rates stagnated, and researchers found no proof whatsoever that this approach added even 1 per cent to outcome delivery. Indeed, KPMG in New Zealand found that only 25 per cent of PMOs were effective in supporting change.

The PMO has become a honeypot of framework diagrams, process flows, templates, email reminders and self-important people demanding a 'seat at the table'. Yet, with the right person leading it, the PMO can add value to the way an organisation gets its projects delivered. The person needs to be an experienced project manager who understands what it takes to support the business of getting things done by placing emphasis on:

- helping people across the organisation build a new mindset and (real) skill set that fosters agility of delivery *and* thinking

- building talent profiles to facilitate the swift mobilisation of teams

- creating visual spaces where strategic progress can be charted, and great ideas or failures can be shared

- being the hub for cultural evolution initiatives

- leading design-thinking (or similar) workshops

- providing measurable data that gives senior managers insights and highlights potential risks.

Forward-thinking organisations do not need a central group to tell their people how to get the job done or to produce endless, pointless reports that no one reads. They need people who role model what a growth mindset looks like, who know how to communicate, who value swift delivery and who create an environment where teams are allowed the time to concentrate on what's important.

The PMO's emphasis should be on support, sustain and role model, not command, control and report. If you must set up a PMO, it needs to model the former behaviours, not the latter.

2. SHOULD WE GO AGILE?

I cover agile extensively in chapter 43, where I stress the importance of understanding the method in detail. Whether you should 'go agile' is a different question and is often constrained by the fact that the organisation doesn't have people who are flexible enough to respond to change or else have no conceivable way of ridding themselves of the red tape they believe is holding them back.

Many organisations, however, are making the same mistakes with agile as they did when they implemented PRINCE2. Indeed, lots of organisations are actually rolling agile out in a waterfall way, which goes against everything that agile is. Nowadays even original Agile Manifesto signatories are calling for software developers to abandon it! In mid 2018, Ron Jeffries, one signatory of the 2001 manifesto, called for software developers to abandon agile. He argued, 'Too commonly, the "Agile" approach a team uses has been imposed. Larger-scale "Agile" methods appear actually to recommend imposition of process. These "so-called" methods are pitched to the enterprise, and the enterprise is expected to "install" them, or "roll them out"'.

My view is this. If you have people with a growth mindset who understand that the culture (and therefore its ways of delivering) need to continually evolve to meet the expectations of your culture, then you don't need to go agile. You already are. You may like to send them on a training course to equip them with different skills, but make no mistake that what will make an organisation and its people agile is their mindset, not the methods.

If you don't have people with a growth mindset, then delivering in a more agile and flexible way will require a change in culture, not in methods. It will require emotional intelligence training and that you performance manage out those who don't want to be part of the new culture. Training people with a fixed mindset on a new method in an existing poor culture is going to make things worse, not better. You'll end up blaming the method, when it's people who are the problem.

3. WHAT DO I DO IF I DON'T HAVE TIME TO SPONSOR THE PROJECT?

As you've now realised, sponsoring a project is not to be taken lightly. It's a pretty big job and assuming that someone can do it based merely on their place in the hierarchy is a mistake.

When I headed up project departments we used to say that project managers can manage only three projects effectively at any one time — one in planning, one in delivery and one closing out. The same is true of project sponsors given the demands of your business-as-usual role. So if you're asked to sponsor a fourth and you simply don't have the time to do everything I've set out in this book, then you need to find someone who does.

There are usually enough senior managers in a business to share the accountability, but to be clear, if you're passing the accountability on to others, then that's what you do. You can't have them checking in with you so you can approve their decisions. They should also have full delegated financial authority on the project; otherwise it shows a lack of trust, and that's not how you want to start any project.

Often people will tell me this isn't possible in their organisation, to which my reply is, 'Don't let your culture stand in the way of getting things done'.

4. WHAT DO I DO IF I DON'T BELIEVE IN THE PROJECT?

As I mentioned in chapter 68, every initiative you undertake should link to the organisation's strategy. It should line up with the vision and provide tangible value for the organisation. Where a project doesn't do this and you're asked to sponsor it, you need to speak up. This is what it means to be ethical and to have integrity.

Your role, as a member of the senior management team, is to ensure that the organisation spends public or shareholder money wisely and that every dollar spent provides a return or improves the lives of those who use the outputs.

Ignoring these things is not an option. You have to speak up.

There will be times when you don't like a particular project—for one reason or another—but have been asked to sponsor it nonetheless. If the justification is sound and the ROI can be achieved, then you'll have to suck it up and do the job to the best of your ability.

For the duration of the project and during the achievement of the outcomes, you have to be present and positive at all times, and never talk about the project as something you don't believe in. I've seen this happen and it serves only to undermine the senior management team.

Sometimes in life you have to do things you don't want to, but doing so will make you stronger and more resilient and help you grow as a person.

5. MY PROJECT MANAGER IS NOT DOING THEIR JOB – WHAT SHOULD I DO?

Poor project management (along with poor project sponsorship) is a key reason for project failure. Left unchecked, with project team members alienated, projects can drift and the outcomes never realised.

In chapter 75, I outlined some of the key things to look for with regard to poor project management. As soon as you see it in any form, you need to deal with it.

If you've taken the time to do things in the right way and have built the team first, then the project manager will know exactly what's expected of them. If you haven't, then there's a very good chance that things will go off the rails.

Where poor project management performance is an issue, then a conversation is required and the first subject is support. You may say something like this:

> 'Your performance isn't up to the standard we agreed to. I'd like to know what I can do to help...Do you have everything you need to be successful?...Are there any decisions you need from me to help keep things moving?'

At the end of this conversation, you need to be really clear about your expectations moving forward and that you don't want to have a second conversation around performance. In some instances where you feel like the project manager may be struggling, you may consider a mentor. Someone the project manager can turn to for guidance and technical support.

If there's a second conversation, it will need to be a little sterner (though still delivered in a high-EQ way). At this stage the project manager will know their performance is under scrutiny and should be looking to provide persuasive reassurance that they will improve.

A third conversation will likely have someone from HR in the room. All conversations after this will need to follow the internal process around performance and behaviour.

Given the statistics around project performance outlined in this book, it seems that many organisations around the world aren't doing enough to push their project managers to deliver. We all do our best work on the edge of uncomfortable. Project managers are no different.

If you accept poor performance as the norm, then don't expect your project to deliver. Oh and if you're hiring external project managers, they should be able to hit the ground running, because that's what you're paying for. If they don't, then they don't get three chances. Move them on and find someone who can.

6. WHY DON'T YOU BELIEVE THAT TIME AND COST ARE GOOD MEASURES OF PROJECT MANAGEMENT?

Projects and project management are different things. We often measure the success of projects by time, cost, scope and quality. However, given the uncertain nature of projects, these will most likely change, so they are not a reliable means to measure project managers.

As I outlined in Part I of this book, great project management is built on three elements:

1. **Leadership** — how emotionally intelligent the person is, how they motivate and inspire people and their personal discipline

2. **Culture** — how they build an ever-evolving culture in which good people are able to do great work in line with the project's objectives

3. **Methods** — the technical toolkit to capture the detail required to keep the project on track and to avoid failure.

To this end, I used to measure my project managers on the service they provided to their stakeholders, which included their project team. I took a Net Promoter Score (NPS)–style approach to make it easy for the stakeholders to respond, and I set the project managers a KPI score of between 50 and 75.

This meant the project managers not only had to know their technical stuff, but also had to do the people stuff really well. By conducting the surveys monthly I was also able to spot some early warning signs that wouldn't have been evident in project reports.

In the past, organisations have put measurement of the emotional intelligence of project managers in the 'too hard' basket, relying instead on cumbersome annual reviews that provide feedback way too late for the recipient to change anything.

Don't fall into the trap of measuring the performance of project managers by the things that can change; instead, focus your efforts on measuring the things that shouldn't.

REFERENCES

Preface

The Standish Group 2018 Chaos Report: Decision Latency Theory.

A Gaskell, 'The slow pace of digital transformation', Forbes, 8 June 2018.

H Nash, KPMG CIO Survey, 2018.

KPMG NZ, 'Driving business performance', Project Management Survey, 2017.

PMI Pulse of the Profession 2016.

New Zealand Government, Report of the ministerial inquiry into the Novopay project, 2013.

'Crossrail: What's really delaying the £15.4bn mega-project', Construction News, 1 October 2018.

J Corrigan, 'VA Wasted $11 billion on failed IT projects in 6 years', Nextgov, 8 December 2017.

Project Managers

PART I: Leadership

'The rise of AI makes emotional intelligence more important', *Harvard Business Review*, 15 February 2017.

'The business case for EQ', *Six Seconds*.

M Abrahams, 'Those who can't, don't know it', *Harvard Business Review*, December 2005.

D Dunning & J Kruger, 'Unskilled and unaware of it: How difficulties in recognizing one's own incompetence lead to inflated self-assessments', *Journal of Personality and Social Psychology*, 1999, 77(6), 1121–34.

J Zenger & J Folkman, 'The skills leaders need at every level', *Harvard Business Review*, 30 July 2014.

'A few minutes could change your whole day', meditation app, Headspace.

'Rewarding work: The vital role of line managers', Studylib, 2018.

M Bevilacqua et al., 'Relation of project managers' personality and project performance: An approach based on value stream mapping', *Journal of Industrial Energy Management*, 2014, 7(4), 857–90.

JR Turner & R Müller, 'The project manager's leadership style as a success factor on projects: A literature review', PMI, 36(1), 49–61.

M Toossi, 'A new look at long-term labor force projections to 2050', *Monthly Labor Review*, November 2006.

The Standish Group 2014 *Chaos Report*.

Gallup, *State of the American Workplace* report, 2017.

'The Resilient Leader', *Educational Leadership*, ASDC, Dec. 2011 – Jan. 2012, 69(4), 79–82.

'US Telecommuting Forecast, 2009 to 2016', *Forrester*, 11 March 2009.

'Cisco says telecommuting saves money, and the world', *FastCompany*, 26 October 2006.

R McBrearty & B Sukow, 'The economics of collaboration at CISCO', CISCO IBSG, 2009.

E Griffith, 'Why startups fail, according to their founders', *Fortune*, 25 September 2014.

LB Comer & T Drollinger, 'Active empathetic listening and selling success: A conceptual framework', Taylor & Francis Online, 24 October 2013.

D Sivers, TED talk 2010, 'How to start a movement'.

Deloitte 2015 Millennial Survey, 'Mind the Gaps'.

'Retributive justice, restorative justice and forgiveness', Hope College Digital Commons.

'38 Reasons: The Difficult Conversations Survey', Globis Mediation Group, 2016.

'What's keeping project managers from the C-suite?', Project Management Hacks.

CEB, Leadership, Culture, Governance, Australia Key Imperatives, 20 July 2015.

MJ Gelfand et al., *The Handbook of Negotiation and Culture*, Stanford Business Book, SUP, 2004.

'Good storytelling is more science than art', Virgin.com.

PART II: Culture

SE Barker, 'Cuddle hormone: research links oxytocin and socio-sexual behaviors'.

AJ Oswald et al., 'Happiness and productivity', WRAP, University of Warwick, 2015.

'Leadership skills and emotional intelligence', Center for Creative Leadership, 2003.

L Entis, 'Your employees just aren't that into you', *Inc.*, 14 January 2013.

Deloitte 2015 Millennial Survey, 'Mind the Gaps'.

Comscore, The 2015 US Mobile App Report, 22 September 2015.

McKinsey Global Institute, 'The social economy: Unlocking value and productivity through social technologies', July 2012.

'Debenhams halves email storage with archive tool', ComputerWeekly.com, 13 September 2012.

'Artificial intelligence and the future of humans', Pew Research Centre, 10 December 2018.

G James, 'It's official: Open-plan offices are now the dumbest management fad of all time', *Inc.*, 16 July 2018.

Cushman & Wakefield, 'Introverts vs extroverts: D office environments support both?', 2013.

T Townsend, 'The first question Stewart Butterfield asks in an interview', *Inc.*, 23 February 2016.

L Weber & E Dwoskin, 'Are workplace personality tests fair?', *Wall Street Journal*, 29 September 2014.

Allied HR, Allied Workforce Mobility Survey 2012.

TN Bauer, 'Onboarding new employees: Maximizing success', SHRM Foundation, 2010.

J Sloboda & SA O'Neill, 'Emotions in everyday listening to music', ResearchGate, January 2001.

A Haake, 'How can music boost your performance? The science behind the benefits of music in the workplace', *Totaljobs*, 21 November 2016.

T Lesiuk, 'The effect of music listening on work performance', Sage Journals, 1 April 2005.

WF Thompson et al., 'Fast and loud background music disrupts reading comprehension', Sage Journals, 2011.

R Oliver, *Satisfaction: A behavioral perspective on the consumer*, Taylor & Francis, 2010.

T Ahola, 'Measuring customer satisfaction in the context of a project-based organization'.

B Gallagher, 'Solving the gossip dilemma in the workplace', Teamworks.

Deloitte Insights, Global Human Capital Trends 2015.

P Riordan, 'DFAT attempts day without acronyms in the name of charity', *The Canberra Times*, 27 November 2014.

Bright HR, 'It pays to play'.

M Rau-Foster, 'Humor and fun in the workplace', Workplace Issues.

S Dockweiler, 'How much time do we spend in meetings? (Hint: it's scary)', *The Muse*.

PART III: Methods

Manifesto for Agile Software Development.

'Working better together: A study of collaboration and innovation.'

DA Powner, US GAO. 'OMB and agencies need to improve planning, management, and oversight of projects totaling billions of dollars', 31 July 2008.

KPMG, 'Driving business performance', Project Management Survey 2017.

Z Chaudhry et al., 'Measuring benefits realisation should be integral to any healthcare system', Gartner, 1 April 2013.

S Moore, 'IT projects need less complexity, not more governance', Gartner, 17 July 2015.

'Valuing working software over comprehensive documentation', Oracle blog, 23 February 2013.

PwC, 'Insights and trends: current portfolio, programme, and project management practices'. The third global survey on the current state of project management.

The State of Project Management Annual Survey 2016, Wellingstone Project Management, APM.

M Bloch et al., 'Delivering large-scale IT projects on time, on budget, and on value', *McKinsey Quarterly*, October 2012.

AP Snow et al., 'The effect of optimistic and pessimistic biasing on software project status reporting', ResearchGate, March 2007.

Victorian Ombudsman, 'The Victorian Ombudsman's investigation into ICT-enabled projects', VGSO Seminar Program, 26 April 2012.

Project Sponsors

PART IV: Stewardship

The Standish Group *Chaos Report* 2018.

'$1 million wasted every 20 seconds by organizations around the world', *BusinessWire*, 15 February 2018.

The Standish Group *Chaos Report* 2016: Outline.

New Zealand Government, *Report of the ministerial inquiry into the Novopay project*, 2013.

S Shah, 'CIOs are losing confidence in Agile development methodologies', *V3*, 8 May 2017.

PMAlliance, '2015 PM industry survey released by PMAlliance', 18 May 2018.

P Gurdjian et al., 'Why leadership-development programs fail', *McKinsey Quarterly*, January 2014.

'Leading at the speed of now', *Ketchum Leadership Communication Monitor*, 2015.

LexisNexis, 'Governance: Can you have too much of a good thing?', Governance Institute, 2016.

P Riordan, 'Malcolm Turnbull blames IBM for census failure', *AFR*, 28 October 2016.

P Shergold, 'Learning from Failure: Why large government policy initiatives have gone so badly wrong in the past and how the chances of success can be improved', Commonwealth of Australia, 2015.

PMI *Pulse of the Profession* 2016, 'The strategic impact of projects: Identify benefits to drive business results'.

Victorian Ombudsman, 'The Victorian Ombudsman's investigation into ICT-enabled projects', VGSO Seminar Program, 26 April 2012.

US GAO, Report to Congressional Committees, 'Financial management systems: HUD needs to address management and governance weaknesses that jeopardize its modernization efforts', July 2016.

'Habit 3: Put first things first', FranklinCovey.

P Burek, 'Moving from strategic planning to prioritized project initiatives', PMI, 26 October 2014.

PMI, 'Talent management: Powering strategic initiatives in the PMO', Thought Leadership Series Report, November 2014.

P Achterstraat, 'Why large public sector projects sometimes fail', Audit Office of NSW, September 2013.

Atlassian, 'Welcome your newest teammate…AI'.

PWC, 21st CEO Survey, 'The anxious optimist in the corner office', 2018.

Deloitte, Global Human Capital Trends 2015, 'Leading in the new world of work', Deloitte University Press.

M Meeker, 'Internet Trends 2016—Code Conference', Kleiner Perkins, KPCP, 1 June.

Nielsen Insights, 'Distracted by technology at mealtimes—it's not who you may think', 24 November 2015.

LB Comer and T Drollinger, 'Active empathetic listening and selling success: A conceptual framework', Taylor & Francis Online, 24 October 2013.

Julian Treasure, TED talk '5 ways to listen better', July 2011.

PART V: Decisions

D Goleman, 'What makes a leader', *Harvard Business Review*, January 2004.

LexisNexis, 'Governance: Can you have too much of a good thing?', Governance Institute, 2016.

Victorian Ombudsman, 'The Victorian Ombudsman's investigation into ICT-enabled projects', VGSO Seminar Program, 26 April 2012.

State of the CIO Survey 2016, 'Tools for marketers', IDG, 15 January 2016.

KPMG, 'Driving business performance', Project Management Survey 2017.

M Bloch et al., 'Delivering large-scale IT projects on time, on budget, and on value', *McKinsey Quarterly*, October 2012.

New Zealand Government, *Report of the ministerial inquiry into the Novopay project*, 2013.

R Hogan & RB Kaiser, 'What we know about leadership', *Review of General Psychology*, 2005, 9(2), 169–80.

'Are you happy at work?: The high cost of disengaged employees', *The Passionate Pen*, 3 April 2010.

The Great Project Management Survey 2015, 'Industry trends', P2 Consulting, January 2015.

Ethics Index, Governance Institute, July 2016.

PMI, 'Ethical Decision-Making Framework', 2012.

Deloitte, The 2016 Deloitte Millennial Survey, 'Winning over the next generation of leaders'.

VH Vroom, 'Leadership and the decision-making process', *Organizational Dynamics*, 2000, 28(4), 82–94.

H Mintzberg, The *Nature of Managerial Work*, Harper & Row, New York, 1973.

Manifesto for Agile Software Development.

PMI *Pulse of the Profession* 2016.

Astro Teller, TED talk, 'The unexpected benefit of celebrating failure', February 2016.

PART VI: Results

KPMG NZ, 'Driving business performance', Project Management Survey, 2017.

IBM Making Change Work Study, IBM Global Business Services, 2008.

Victorian Ombudsman, 'The Victorian Ombudsman's investigation into ICT-enabled projects', VGSO Seminar Program, 26 April 2012.

P Gurdjian et al., 'Why leadership-development programs fail', *McKinsey Quarterly*, January 2014.

DA Powner, US GAO, 'OMB and agencies need to improve planning, management, and oversight of projects totaling billions of dollars', 31 July 2008.

National Audit Office (UK), 'E-borders and successor programmes', 7 December 2015.

KPMG, Global Construction Survey 2016, 'Who's on the edge of innovation?'

A Herrin, 'Watch: Mastering the five skills of disruptive innovators', *Harvard Business Review*, 20 October 2014.

S Dutta et al., The Global Innovation Index 2016, 'Winning with global innovation', WIPO, Johnson Cornell University.

PMI *Pulse of the Profession* 2018, 'Success in disruptive times'.

P Shergold, 'Learning from Failure: Why large government policy initiatives have gone so badly wrong in the past and how the chances of success can be improved', Commonwealth of Australia, 2015.

Astro Teller, TED talk, 'The unexpected benefit of celebrating failure', February 2016.

E Barker, 'This is the best way to improve every part of your life', 3 May 2016.

PMI *Pulse of the Profession* 2016, 'The strategic impact of projects: Identify benefits to drive business results'.

KPMG, Project Management Survey 2017, 'Driving business performance'.

M Bloch et al., 'Delivering large-scale IT projects on time, on budget, and on value', McKinsey, October 2012.

KPMG New Zealand Project Management Survey, 2010.

Victorian Auditor-General's Report, East West Link Project, VAGO, December 2015.

NZ Treasury, Gateway Reviews 101–150 (March 2013 – September 2014), 1 July 2015.

Frequently asked questions

Ron Jeffries, 'Developers should abandon Agile', 10 May 2018.

'What is Net Promoter?', NICE Satmetrix, 2017.

READING LIST

Many books have inspired and informed my thinking and writing during this project (some are old favourites I've returned to!). Here's a list of books I refer to and some others I think might interest you.

Chimamanda Ngozi Adichie, *We Should All Be Feminists*

Lailah Gifty Akita, *Think Great, Be Great*

Alain de Botton, *The Pleasures and Sorrows of Work*

Travis Bradberry & Jean Greaves, *Emotional Intelligence 2.0*

Marcus Buckingham and Curt Coffman, *First, Break All the Rules*

Susan Cain, *Quiet: The Power of Introverts in a World That Can't Stop Talking*

James P Carse, *Finite and Infinite Games*

Ed Catmull, *Creativity Inc.*

Matt Church, *Amplifiers: The Power of Motivational Leadership to Inspire and Influence*

Matt Church, Peter Cook & Scott Stein, *Sell Your Thoughts*

Peter Cook, *The New Rules of Management*

Stephen R. Covey, *First Things First*

Stephen R. Covey, *The 8th Habit*

Dermot Crowley, *Smart Work*

Simon Dowling, *Work with Me: How to Get People to Buy into Your Ideas*

Charles Duhigg, *The Power of Habit*

Carol Dweck, *Mindset: The New Psychology of Success*

Roger Fisher & William L. Ury, *Getting to Yes: Negotiating Agreement Without Giving In*

Dr Jason Fox, *The Game Changer*

Jason Fried & David Heinemeier Hansson, *Remote: Office Not Required*

Jason Fried & David Heinemeier Hansson, *ReWork*

Janine Garner, *From Me to We*

Michelle Gielan, *Broadcasting Happiness: The Science of Igniting and Sustaining Positive Change*

Malcolm Gladwell, *Outliers*

Jules Goddard and Troy Eccles, *Uncommon Sense, Common Nonsense*

Seth Godin, *Tribes*

Marshall Goldsmith, *What Got You Here Won't Get You There*

Daniel Goleman, *Emotional Intelligence: Why It Matters More Than IQ*

Jim Highsmith, *Agile Project Management*

Arianna Huffington, *The Sleep Revolution*

Dr Amantha Imber, *The Creativity Formula*

Guy Kawasaki, *The Art of the Start*

Larry Keeley, *Ten Types of Innovation: The Discipline of Building Breakthroughs*

Richard Koch & Greg Lockwood, *Simplify: How the Best Businesses in the World Succeed*

Nick Leeson, *Rogue Trader*

Patrick Lencioni, *The Five Dysfunctions of a Team*

Victor Lipman, *The Type B Manager: Leading Successfully in a Type A World*

L. David Marquet, *Turn the Ship Around! A True Story of Turning Followers into Leaders*

John C. Maxwell, *Failing Forward: Turning Mistakes into Stepping Stones for Success*

Christian Moore, *The Resilience Breakthrough: 27 Tools for Turning Adversity into Action*

Amy Morin, *13 Things Mentally Strong People Don't Do*

Georgia Murch, *Fixing Feedback*

Mark Murphy, *Hundred Percenters: Challenge Your Employees to Give You Their All*

Martyn L. Newman, *Emotional Capitalists: The New Leaders*

Jamie Notter & Maddie Grant, *When Millennials Take Over*

Tom Peters, *The Brand You 50 (Reinventing Work): Fifty Ways to Transform Yourself from an Employee into a Brand*

Tom Peters, *The Project 50 (Reinventing Work): Fifty Ways to Transform Every Task into a Project That Matters!*

Dan Pink, *Drive: The Surprising Truth About What Motivates Us*

Steven Pressfield, *The War of Art*

Eric Ries, *The Lean Startup*

Richard Sheridan, *Joy Inc.: How to Build a Workplace People Love*

Simon Sinek, *Start with Why*

Raj Sisodia & John Mackey, *Conscious Capitalism: Liberating the Heroic Spirit of Business*

Paul Smith, *Lead with a Story*

Emrah Yayici, *Design Thinking Methodology*

Benjamin Zander & Rosamund Stone Zander, *The Art of Possibility*

Time-Life Books, *Time 100: Heroes and Inspirations*

The following resources, referred to in various parts of the book (note particularly the introduction to Part II), provide essential standards, guidelines and good practice methodologies to PM professionals.

- Project Management Institute, *The Project Management Body of Knowledge* (6th edition)
- Project Management Institute, *Governance of Portfolios, Programs and Projects: A Practice Guide*
- Axelos, *PRINCE2* (2009)
- Axelos, *Directing Successful Projects with PRINCE2*

SOUNDTRACKS

I love my music. It's been a constant presence in my life and work, and whenever I can I have it playing as I write (I'm not one for silence). I write best in spaces where there are lots of people — cafés, co-working spaces, parks, libraries, even swimming pools. I love the energy of being around other people.

Most of this book was written between 2015 and 2017. I listened to a lot of different music in those years (and my musical choices reflect that time). So here (in no particular order) is my *Project Book* writing playlist. Looking back at it now, it's a real mixed bag, yet each of these albums gave me a much-needed lift while I was putting the words together.

Leah Senior, *Summer's on the Ground*

Oasis, *Definitely Maybe*

The Stone Roses, *The Stone Roses*

Holst, *The Planets*

Tchaikovsky, *Ballet Suites*

Edgar 'Jones' Jones, *Soothing Music for Stray Dogs*

The Smiths, every album!

Chet Baker, *The Best of Chet Baker*

Depeche Mode, *Violator*

The Tea Street Band, *The Tea Street Band*

Kraftwerk, *Trans-Europe Express*

Circa Waves, *Young Chasers*

The Wombats, *Glitterbug*

City Calm Down, *In a Restless House*

Nick Cave and the Bad Seeds, *The Boatman's Call*

Brian Eno, Ambient 1: *Music for Airports*

Real Estate, *Atlas*

Daft Punk, *Random Access Memories*

London Grammar, *If You Wait*

John Williams, *Star Wars Episode IV: A New Hope OST*

The Open, *The Silent Hours*

Air, *Moon Safari*

Richard Hawley, *Coles Corner*

Brian Eno, *Apollo: Atmospheres and Soundtracks*

Vivaldi, *The Four Seasons*

Birds of Tokyo, *Anchor EP*

Django Django, *Born Under Saturn*

Black, *Wonderful Life*

David Bowie, *Hunky Dory*

David Bowie, *The Best of David Bowie 1980/1987*

Ducktails, *The Flower Lane*

Electronic, *Electronic*

Todd Terje, *It's Album Time*

Maurice Jarre, *Dead Poets Society OST*

The Loungs, *Short Cuts*

Tears for Fears, *The Hurting*

Holy Holy, *When the Storms Would Come*

The Rubens, *Hoops*

The Cure, *Kiss Me, Kiss Me, Kiss Me*

The Courteeners, *Concrete Love*

Morrissey, *Vauxhall and I*

Various, *50s Jazz Lounge*

Various, *La La Land OST*

Frank Sinatra, *Nothing But the Best*

Real Estate, *Days*

The Smiths, *Strangeways, Here We Come*

Sufjan Stevens, *Come On! Feel the Illinoise!*

I Know Leopard, *Another Life E.P.*

DMA's, *Hills End*

New Order, *Substance 1987*

Elbow, *Little Fictions*

Queen, *Greatest Hits*

The Libertines, *The Libertines*

The The, *Dusk*

Holy Holy, *Paint*

The The, *Infected*

Johnny Marr, *The Messenger*

Kraftwerk, *The Man-Machine*

The Beatles, *Rubber Soul*

Circa Waves, *Different Creatures*

Real Estate, *In Mind*

Methyl Ethel, *Everything Is Forgotten*

Kraftwerk, *Autobahn*

CONTACT DETAILS

I talk regularly at conferences around the world on how to deliver consistently great projects. I also run a tailored program for those organisations who are interested in injecting energy, motivation and inspiration into their teams.

If you'd like to know more about either, you can head to my website **www.colindellis.com** for more information, or drop me an email at **hello@colindellis.com**.

If you're interested in checking out more of my writing about project management, leadership or culture please sign up for my fortnightly newsletter by visiting **www.colindellis. com/boom**.

You can also follow me on:

LinkedIn: **www.linkedin.com/in/colindellis**
Facebook: **www.facebook.com/colindellis**
YouTube: **www.youtube.com/+colindellis1**
Twitter: **www.twitter.com/colindellis**
Instagram: **www.instagram.com/colindellis**
Medium: **https://medium.com/@colindellis**

INDEX

negativity 262–263
—cost of 263
negotiation, effective 91–93
—four stage process of
92–93
Netflix culture 84–85, 130,
301, 203, 309
neuro-linguistic
programming (NLP)
261–262
Nightingale, Florence 22

objectives, achieving
306–307
open-plan offices 125–126
opportunities vs challenges
261–262
optimism 58, 324
organisational capacities 46
outcomes, achieving
322–327; *see also* failure;
results; success
ownership 71, 107, 200,
218, 224

Pankhurst, Emmeline 21–22
Parks, Rosa 22
people, importance of 4–5,
7; *see also* communication;
culture; hiring; project
managers; leaders; role
model; staff; team
performance, managing poor
82–85

Permitted Bootlegging
121–122
personality *see also*
extroversion vs
introversion
—influence of 38–39
—measurement 39–40
—types and project
management 39–40
pet projects 199
phones and technology
240–241
plain English 144–146
planning
—business case 145, 163,
170–171, 173, 205, 206,
209, 217, 225, 255, 293,
297, 299, 305–306, 323,
324–325, 326–327
—collaboration 167–169
—examples of poor
305–306
—failure of 330
—need for 166–169, 174,
202–203
—phase 293–294
—preparing 305–308, 333
—project implementers
168–169
—schedule 293–294
—sponsor 222–223,
305–308
—sponsor and manager
306–307
—updating 308

CPSIA information can be obtained
at www.ICGtesting.com
Printed in the USA
BVHW042359210619
551690BV00001B/1/P